THE EQUUS MEN

Rhodesia's Mounted Infantry:
The Grey's Scouts 1896–1980

Alexandre Binda

Helion & Company

G G Books UK

Helion & Company Limited
26 Willow Road
Solihull
West Midlands
B91 1UE
England
Tel. 0121 705 3393
Fax 0121 711 4075
email: info@helion.co.uk
website: www.helion.co.uk
Twitter: @helionbooks
Visit our blog http://blog.helion.co.uk

and

GG Books UK
Rugby
Warwickshire
Tel. 07921 709307
Website: www.30degreessouth.co.uk

Co-published by Helion & Company and GG Books 2015
Designed and typeset by Farr out Publications, Wokingham, Berkshire
Cover designed by Euan Carter, Leicester (www.euancarter.com)
Printed by Gutenberg Press Limited, Tarxien, Malta

Text © Alexandre Binda 2015
Photographs © as individually credited
Maps open source unless otherwise credited
Cover photographs © Alan Collier

ISBN 978-1-910294-04-8

British Library Cataloguing-in-Publication Data
A catalogue record for this book is available from the British Library

For details of other military history titles published by Helion & Company Limited contact the above address, or visit our website: http://www.helion.co.uk

We always welcome receiving book proposals from prospective authors working in military history.

Dedication
To the Grey's who rode out of history for Rhodesia

Whispers of the Past

In a far away land we once called home, the battle cry was made,
A call to serve our country, to fight to save our land.
Some of us were called up, some signed up and some even drafted in,
We answered the call there was no doubt, to keep safe our kith and kin.
Black and white, young and old, we'll keep our country free
We'll make it safe for everyone – not just for you and me.
Men and women, we fought the fight, our hearts beat bravely
We are The Grey's Scouts Regiment, Squadrons, A, B and C.

Year after year the war rages on
Lives lost, loved ones now gone
We kept on fighting, you must understand
We had to fight, to save our land.

In 1980 the War came to an end,
What happens now, to us, to me and you dear friend?
There was no glory and there was no fame,
Our beloved country – no longer the same.

Scattered across this great wide world, wondering just how we'll get along,
Being called when-we's, foreigners and told 'you don't belong'.
New battles lay before us, a different war in a different place
The scars of what we went through begin to mark our face.
Somehow we had to make it, somehow we had to survive
Despite the toils and troubles we still kept the flame alive.
Though we are older now and many years have passed
When we reminisce through yesteryears, those memories come back fast.
Of a time, a place and a war in which we all played a part,
A time lost forever, forever in our heart.

Thirty years later again we hear a call
To pay tribute to our comrades – comrades one and all.
Men and women – one voice, one family,
We are The Grey's Scouts Regiment, Squadrons, A,B and C.

By Kathy Weidemann. 13 November 2010.

The late Major Alexander ('Beaver') Fraser-Kirk whose vision led to the re-birth of the Grey's Scouts Regiment. It is a matter of sad regret that he did not live to see the publication of his regiment's history. Beaver was born in Umtali (Mutare) on 31.03.1928 and passed away in Bulawayo on 21.02.2014. (© Kathy Kew)

Contents

List of maps

Glossary

1. Appointment titles: Rhodesian Security Forces

Appointment	Title
Army	Crusader
Airforce	Cyclone
BSAP (Police)	Bailiff
Internal Affairs	Lighthouse
Support Unit	Mantle
PRAW (Police Reserve Air Wing)	Copper
Tracker	Sparrow
Commander	Sunray
Admin Staff	Manhole
Armour	Ironside
Artillery	Shelldrake
Engineers	Holdfast
G Ops/ Adjutant	Seagull
Liaison Officer	Gloworm
Infantry	Foxhound
Intelligence	Acorn
Medical	Starlight
Ordinance	Rickshaw
Provost	Watchdog
Quartermaster	Nutshell
Workshops/Armourer	Bluebell
Signals	Pronto
Military transport	Playtime
Training rep	Woodpecker
Paymaster	Goldfinger

Grey's Scouts Internal Titles:

Vet Rep	Nitestar
Farrier Rep	Horseshoe
Equitation Rep	Equis
Stable Manager	Pitch Fork
Dog Rep	Goofy

2. General Glossary of terms:

Acorn:	Appointments title for Intelligence personnel
AD:	Accidental firearm discharge
AFA:	African female adult
AFJ:	African female juvenile

Alpha Bomb:	Small circular bomb containing within a mini grenade. Between both some 250 rubber balls were squeezed causing it to bounce on ground impact. It exploded after impact.
AMA:	African male adult
AMJ:	African male juvenile
APA:	African Purchase Area (Rhodesia Land Tenure Act)
APC:	armoured personnel carrier
APL:	African Purchase Land (Rhodesia Land Tenure Act)
AS:	African Soldier/African Staff
AWOL:	Absence without leave
Bailiff:	Appointments title for British South Africa Police
BCR:	Bronze Cross of Rhodesia
Blue Job:	airman (Rhodesian Army slang)
Bombshell:	to scatter or flee in all directions (insurgent dispersal tactic on contact)
Brown Job:	soldier (Rhodesian Army slang)
BSAP:	British South Africa Police (The Rhodesian police force)
c/s:	call sign
Cadre:	insurgent rank and file
Casevac:	casualty evacuation
Charlie Tango or CT:	Communist Terrorist in radio speak
Chimurenga:	Shona appellation for bush war as used by ZANLA (aka 'Liberation Struggle')
Chopper:	helicopter
CIO:	Rhodesian Central Intelligence Organisation
CO:	Commanding Officer
COIN:	Counter-Insurgency
ComOps:	Ministry of Combined Operations
Cordon sanitaire:	border minefield between Rhodesia and Mozambique
CQMS:	Company Quartermaster Sergeant
Crusader:	Appointments title for Army
CT:	Communist Terrorist (derived from the Malayan experience)
Cyclone:	Appointments title for Rhodesian Air Force
Dagga (Afrikaans):	cannabis (maijuana)
DMI:	Director of Military Intelligence
DMM:	Defence Force Medal for Meritorious Service
Donga (Sindebele):	ditch/gully/ravine.
Doppie:	expended cartridge case
Dwala or Diwala:	large rock formation/outcrop
DZ:	Drop Zone
ENS:	Extended National Service

ERE:	Extra Regimentally Employed (applies to members serving with other units)
ES:	European Staff, also European Soldier
FAF:	Forward Airfield
FFA:	Fireforce action
Fireforce:	airborne assault group
Floppy:	RhodArmy slang for a terrorist/insurgent. (Their tendency to 'flop' down when shot).
FLOT:	Front Line of Own Troops
FPLM:	Frente para a Liberacao de Mocambique (Frelimo's Military Wing)
Frag:	fragmentation grenade
Frantan:	Rhodesian euphemism for napalm (lit: frangible tank)
Frelimo or Freds (RLI slang):	Mozambique government troops
G-car:	Gunship. From troop-ferrying helicopter, normally an Alluette III, armed with twin .303 Brownings or 7.62 MAGs
Gomo(Shona):	hill or kopje
Gook (American slang):	insurgent
Graze (RhodArmy slang):	to eat, food,
Gwasha (Shona):	thick jesse/thicket vegetation and trees in the folds of a hill or kopje.
HCV:	Horse Carrying Vehicle
HDF:	High Density Force (usually a large Fireforce)
HE:	high explosive
HMG:	heavy machine gun
Hondo (Shona):	war or conflict
Hooters:	RhodArmy term for the School of Infantry in Gwelo
IANS:	Internal Affairs National Servicemen
Intaf:	Ministry of Internal Affairs
intrep:	intelligence report
IO:	Intelligence Officer
jesse:	thick tangled bush and thorn scrub
JOC:	Joint Operations Centre (also Joint Operational Command)
JPS:	Joint Planning Staff
Kcar:	('K'= Killer) Helicopter command gunship armed with 20mm cannon
KIA:	killed in action
kopje(Afrikaans – pronounced as copy):	hill

kraal:	African village (South African corruption of the Portuguese *curral* meaning a cattle pen
leapfrogging:	helicopter tracking tactic designed to speed up enemy pursuit.
lemon:	Rhodesian Army term for an abortive or failed call-out
LMG:	light machine gun
Loc:	location
Locstat:	map positional co-ordinates
LUP:	lying up place
LZ:	landing zone
MAG (*Matireurs a gas*):	section belt-fed machine gun
MAP/MAAP/MAPP	Mine and Ambush Protected Vehicle
Mealies (or Mielies):	maize/corn cobs
MFC:	Military Forces Commendation
MIU:	Mounted Infantry Unit.
MLM:	Member of the Legion of Merit
MMG:	Medium Machine Gun
MNR:	Mozambique National Resistance (*Movimento Nacional de Resistencia*)
MT:	Motor Transport
MTO:	Motor Transport Officer
Mujiba:	Young insurgent supporter/collaborator (eyes & ears of the insurgents)
Nganga:	Shona word for traditional herbalist aka (incorrectly) witch doctor.
Nyama:	Shona word for meat.
OAU:	Organisation for African Unity.
OCC:	Operations Co-Ordinating Committee
OLM:	Officer of the Legion of Merit
OP:	Observation Post
Ops:	Operations
PATU:	Police Anti-Terrorist Unit
PF:	Patriotic Front (ZAPU& ZANU alliance of convenience formed in 1979)
Pig:	Lightly armoured mine protected Troop Carrying Vehicle
Pookie:	Mine Detection Vehicle (a Rhodesian invention)
POU:	Psychological Operations Unit
Povo:	Portuguese word for people. Used by Central African Insurgents to describe the masses.
PRAW:	Police Reserve Air Wing
PRONTO:	Appointments title for Signals operative.
Psyac:	Psychological action

PV:	Protected Village
RAR:	Rhodesian African Rifles
R&R:	Rest& Recreation (also Rest&Retraining)
RBC:	Rhodesian Broadcasting Corporation
RDU:	Rhodesia Defence Unit
Renamo:	Mozambique National Resistance movement (see MNR above)
RF:	Rhodesian Front
RHU:	Reinforcement Holding Unit (aka 'Dad's Army)
RhA:	Rhodesian Artillery
RhaCR:	Rhodesia Armoured Car Regiment
RhAF(Rhodaf):	Rhodesian Air Force
RhASC:	Rhodesia Army Services Corps
RhE:	Rhodesia Army Corps of Engineers
RhSigs:	Rhodesia Army Corps of Signals
RIC:	Rhodesia Army Intelligence Corps
RLI:	Rhodesian Light Infantry
RR:	Rhodesia Regiment (Territorial Army)
RSM:	Regimental Sergeant Major
SADF:	South African Defence Force
SAP:	South African Police
SAS:	Special Air Service
SB:	Special Branch
SFA:	Security Force Auxiliaries (formed from Muzorewa and Sithole supporters)
SCR:	Silver Cross of Rhodesia
Sellout (*Vatengesi*):	Insurgent term for any African suspected of supporting the Security Forces.
SF:	Security Forces
Sitrep:	situation report
SNEB:	Rocket fired from a fixed wing aircraft in a air-to-ground attack
Sparrow:	Appointments title for tracker
Stick:	(usually) a four man security force group (an Allouette helicopter load)
Sunray:	Appointments title for commander at any level
TCV:	Troop Carrying Vehicle
Ter or Terr:	Terrorist
TTL:	Tribal Trust Land
UANC:	United African National Council
UDI:	Unilateral Declaration of Independence
Vlei (Afrikaans - pronounced as flay):	swampy open grassland
ZANLA:	Zimbabwe African National Liberation Army

ZANU:	Zimbabwe African National Union
ZAPU:	Zimbabwe African Peoples Union
ZIPRA:	Zimbabwe Peoples Revolutionary Army
ZNA:	Zimbabwe National Army

Acknowledgements

In late February 2012, Steve Crump phoned to commission me to write a history of the Grey's Scouts. It was to be a joint commission from Steve's GG Books and Duncan Rogers' Helion Publications. The call was unexpected but, aware of the great privilege, I accepted the offer eagerly. Lieutenant Colonel Chris Pearce, BCR, last CO of the Grey's, contacted me on the same day to voice his immediate support for the project. Shortly afterwards, the enthusiastic Grey's Scout, Al 'Dick' Weidemann, came on board offering to help in any way possible – in fact he was more than true to his word. Throughout this project, at Rhodesian get-togethers and braais, and through Rhodesian contact publications such as *Lion &Tusk* and *Rhodesians Worldwide*, *Rhosarians* etc., Dick has been tireless in rallying former members to come forward with their service accounts and great photos. He has been nothing less than stellar and over fifty percent of the Bush War research items submitted by former Grey's Scouts for this history have been prompted by him.

Lieutenant Colonel Chris Pearce, Major Mike Wilson, 2i/c of Grey's Scouts, Captain Theo Williams, OC 'A' Squadron, Major Cedric Tipping-Woods, OC of 'B' Squadron, and Albert 'Dick' Weidemann, with their combined unrivalled knowledge of the Regiment, have been my 'technical consultants' throughout the writing of this history. I am very appreciative of the advice, help and guidance they have provided.

My very sincere and heartfelt thanks are extended to all those named below who came forward so readily to provide personal contributions, help, advice and guidance throughout the process of writing and preparing this regimental history for publication.

Peter Stiff, Captain Roy Elderkin, former Grey's Scouts Chief Equitation Instructor 1975/78, Neville Croxford, Grey's Scouts webmaster, Major Theo Williams, OC 'A' Sqn Grey's Scouts, Lieutenant Tony Ballinger and Rifleman Kieron Robinson, both of 4 (Indep) Coy RR, Major Bruce Rooken-Smith CO of the Rhodesia Armoured Car Regiment, Captain Peter 'Pip' Erasmus OC 'B' Sqn, Major Mike Wilson 2i/c of Grey's Scouts, Tony Butler, the ever generous Craig Fourie for the very welcome Citations and the fabulous Nominal Roll, Corporal Simon Austin of 1 Troop, 'A' Sqn Grey's Scouts, for his 1978/79/80 diaries and notebooks, Corporal John Coast, SCR, Trooper Adrian Wymer of 3 Troop, 'B' Sqn, Group Captain Peter 'PB' Petter-Bowyer, Rhodesian Air Force, for permission to quote from his autobiography *Winds of Destruction*, RWS Sergeant Rusti Henderson, Grey's Vet Section and Remount Section, WOII Nick van Heerden, Senior Equitation Instructor, Sergeant Mike Wilkinson, BCR, 1 Troop, 'A' Sqn, Corporal Clive Midlane, Sergeant Dave McGillivray, Corporal Mike Bradshaw of 'A'Sqn, Corporal Bruce Hillier of 'A' Sqn, Corporal Neil Johns of 'A' Sqn, Lance Corporal Paul Kirk of 'C' Sqn, Brian Griffiths of 1 RHA, Neill Hales (formerly Halliday) of 'B' Sqn, Major Cedric Tipping-Woods, OC 'B' Sqn, Keith Allan of 'B' Sqn, John Emmerson of PATU (Police Anti-Terrorist Unit), Chas Mosley, HQ Sqn, for the loan of Patrick Ollivier's *Commandos de Brousse*, Lieutenant Geoff Armand, 'A' Sqn, Major Don Price, BCR, OC 1 (Indep) Company The Rhodesia Regiment, Corporal Doug Kriedemann of 1 Troop 'A' Sqn, Trooper Dave Rees of 1 Troop 'A' Sqn, Trooper Alan Collier, 1 Troop, 'A' Sqn, Trooper Graham Longstaff, 2 Troop, 'A' Sqn, Corporal Nigel Ramshaw.

Regarding the Grey's Scouts Regimental and Troop songs, I am indebted to my friend Jimmy Jamieson (Grey's HQ Sqn's SSM) and his wife Julia for providing the complete verses to all the unit's songs.

My thanks to Kathy Weidemann for the Dedication Poem.

Within the narrative I have endeavoured, here and there, to give the odd pronunciation guide for those unfamiliar with Afrikaans/Dutch or Bantu languages. Without, hopefully, being tiresome we can add here that the V in Afrikaans/Dutch is pronounced as F and J is pronounced as Y, thus 'Jansen van Vuuren' would be pronounced as 'Yansen fun Fewrun', the Afrikaans words 'vlei' (swamp or marshy ground) and 'veldt' are pronounced as 'flay' and 'felt' and so on. With Portuguese I have used the more anglicised 'Mozambique' rather than the correct 'Moçambique' (pronounced Moossambique), the Portuguese J is pronounced as the S in sugar and CH is pronounced as SH thus 'Chimoio' is 'Shimoio' ... here endeth the lesson.

My heartfelt thanks to every member of the Regiment for making the writing of his history such a pleasure.

My thanks to Duncan Rogers and Steve Crump for commissioning me to write this history and their faith in my ability to do so. My special thanks to Ann Farr for her professional and technical skill in preparing this history for publication.

Finally, I wish to thank Jane, my lovely wife, for her constant support, love, patience and forebearance during the writing of this history. It can't be easy putting up with someone who, engrossed in recording the exploits and history of a now forgotten, displaced people and their country, appears to be inhabiting a world that has literally and tragically disappeared into the past ...

Alex Binda
Rothbury, Northumberland.

Foreword

I am indeed honoured to be asked to provide a foreword for what will be a definitive record of 'The Grey's' and their role in the Rhodesian Bush War.

The history that follows is told by the people who were themselves engaged in the conflict. The stories bring alive to the reader that sense of pride, camaraderie and commitment which made the Grey's Scouts the outstanding unit it was.

The chapters lead the reader through parts of the Bush War where, for a limited time, the advantages of using man and horse to dominate large areas militarily was achieved very effectively with limited resources. The tactics employed, and specific training that evolved from our willingness and ability to adapt to an ever changing environment, enabled us to achieve the successes we did.

To those who were in, or associated with, the unit this book will resurrect memories funny and sad, good and bad. Some will have been tucked away as being too painful or disturbing to revisit but this is who and what we were and that can never be taken away from us.

This book is not about politics. It is about ordinary men and women who became soldiers for a time. Men and women who fought to protect what they saw as their right to be recognised and treated honourably when their livelihood and that of their friends and families was threatened. Some were professional soldiers and some were conscripts, but the majority were Territorial Army (TA) personnel; part time soldiers who had completed their National Service obligation and were subsequently called up for operational duties. Their lives and occupations were severely disrupted yet they did their duty willingly and with pride, becoming fine soldiers in the process.

The 'Grey's' as we knew it is no more. But the people, black and white, regular, national servicemen or TA soldiers, male or female, were one of a kind. The unit was unique in its ability to punch way above its weight in a war which showed what could be achieved through belief in the common cause and a commitment to each other despite adversity.

Finally, this book would not have been possible if it had not been for the enthusiasm, dedication and hard work of Albert 'Dick' Weidemann. We all owe him a great vote of thanks for making the Grey's 'Ride Again'.

Major Mike Wilson
Former Regimental 2i/c Grey's Scouts.

1

Origins: The Bulawayo Field Force and the Matabele Rebellion of 1896

In 1888, Lobengula, king of the Matabele, was the undisputed feudal overlord of the neighbouring territory of Mashonaland. In October of that year, a clever lawyer, Sir Sydney Shippard, Deputy Commissioner of Bechuanaland, guided by the scout, Johan Colenbrander, visited him with a view to obtaining his signature on a Mashonaland gold mining concession for Cecil John Rhodes' British South Africa Company (BSA Company).[1]

Shippard was successful. On 30 October, in exchange for his X and his bull elephant signature seal on the agreement, the illiterate king was paid in guns and gold (1,000 rifles and £100 a month). Two and a half years later, he put his seal to a further agreement granting the BSA Company land rights in Mashonaland.[2] To this day no one knows if Lobengula knew what he had agreed to.[3] At the time of signing, it had apparently all been explained to him – that he was agreeing to grant the company ' ... the complete and exclusive charge over all metals and minerals contained in my kingdom ... '. The king was intelligent but he may well have understood the concessions to mean something else. In the Africa of his day, minerals and land were not perceived as symbolic of wealth. Wealth was garnered in the form of livestock and looked upon pretty much as Europeans look at their bank balance or the cash in their pockets. Gold was seen as a soft yellow metal unsuitable for the forging of weapons and land was free for all to use. The idea that land could be privately owned by an individual was completely alien to the African tribal mind.

In any case, his *Izikulu* and his *Umpakati* (headmen and advisers) were not fooled. Likewise, his *Induna Yomuzi* (generals) who, additionally, were already having difficulties controlling their *Amatjaha* (young unmarried warriors). These young men considered themselves unbeatable and had come to hate the small groups of independent white prospectors already in the country, and wanted nothing more than to kill them all. These whites were unmolested only because of the strict injunction by Lobengula that no white man be harmed.

In October 1889, the BSA Company was incorporated by Royal Charter with a board of directors that included the Duke of Abercorn and Earl Grey. It was now a British company. The company's shareholders believed that the goldfields in Mashonaland could rival those of the Rand. With Lobengula's concessions, their exploitation by the Company was now possible.

In June 1890, the chartered company had assembled a column composed of prospectors and an armed escort. On 11 July this force, guided by its chief scout, the well-known hunter Frederick Courtney Selous who knew the country, crossed the Shashi River into Matabeleland and erected its first fort at Tuli. From here they set off, cutting a road for Mashonaland. When challenged by a Matabele *impi* (military detachment) under the *induna* Gambo, the district governor of Igaba, Colonel Pennefather, the column's commander, replied that he was a soldier of the Queen and that the column was headed for Mashonaland. The Matabele muttered under their breath but, fully

---

1   The Rudd Concession.
2   The Lippert Concession)
3   Sindebele: *Driven by the Wind*.

cognisant of their king's injunction, they let the column pass but shadowed it until they were satisfied that it did not present a threat to any Matabele settlement area.

In September, the Pioneer Column, as it has become known to history, had reached Chief Harari's kraal (a South African corruption of the Portuguese *curral* meaning a livestock pen or enclosure) where it halted. On 13 September they raised the Union Jack. By the following month Harari's kraal had been named Fort Salisbury. From here the prospectors went out to seek Eldorado.

They quickly found that there was gold – but not much of it (the Company was somehow able to conceal the inadequacy of the Mashonaland goldfields from its shareholders).The incomers noted, however, that the country was mineral-rich, particularly the area now known as The Great Dyke which stretches for 1,000 kilometres from the Umvukwes Hills leading into the Mavuradona Mountains and the Zambesi escarpment in the north to West Nicholson, south of Bulawayo. It is full of serpentine rock which is rich in chrome and nickel.

The die-hards, filled with the unquenchable lust for gold continued prospecting. Others, more pragmatic, began to peg out farms as the land was excellent cattle ranching and farming country, producing two cash crops a year. Selous himself was managing a huge estate in Essexvale, 37 kilometres from Bulawayo, for the chartered company.

In their endeavours, both prospectors and farmers began to employ Mashona labour. The Mashona themselves, observing the influx of whites, now began to view them as being in control and that the rule of their brutal Matabele oppressors was on the wane. Emboldened by this the Mashona chiefs began to withhold their annual tribute. The outraged Matabele decided to reassert their feudal authority by making an example of Chief Lomagundi who had refused to pay his annual tribute which was usually in iron. On 25 November 1891 an *impi* of the Mzinyatini regiment arrived at the chief's kraal, killed him and his family and abducted over eighty women and children.

Incidents began to occur whereby raiding Matabele *impis*, intent on plundering Mashona kraals, now found themselves confronted by armed whites standing between them and their Mashona vassals. The warriors, seething with rage, would turn back – but not always. In one incident an *impi* slaughtered a hapless Mashona at the very feet of his white employer who was warned not to interfere lest he suffer the same fate. The position, for the whites, was becoming unacceptable. For the Matabele the interference by the settlers was intolerable – these interlopers were opposing the traditional rights of the Matabele to do with the Mashona what they liked. By 1893, Matabele raids on the unarmed and helpless Shona had culminated in their *impis* plundering the Shona *kraals* in the Fort Victoria area, even entering the town itself. The young warriors were steadily becoming more and more belligerent and unmanageable.

The company protested to the king who, by now, was losing control over his young hot-headed warriors. These young men had infected the *amadoda* (the senior, older warriors) with their desire for war with the whites. Lobengula, despite being a primitive African monarch, was fully aware that his people were facing a more technically sophisticated race, against whom his declining nation could not prevail. When diplomacy failed in 1893, the company decided on war.

Militarily the Matabele were crushed, with the defeat of their three most powerful *abeZansi* (literally, those from the South, meaning those still retaining a strong Zulu strain) regiments namely the Ihlati, the Insukameni and the Mbizo, at the battles of the Shangani (25 October) and Bembesi (1 November). Armed columns then converged on Lobengula's capital of Bulawayo and captured it on 4 November.[4] The king had already fled in his wagons on hearing of the total defeat of his elite regiments. Broken in spirit he headed north-west to the Gwaai river area to finally die a sad and lonely death in the bush.

The company annexed Matabeleland and now found itself in control of a vast territory covering over 150,000 square miles with a population of some 220,000. It was bordered in the north by the

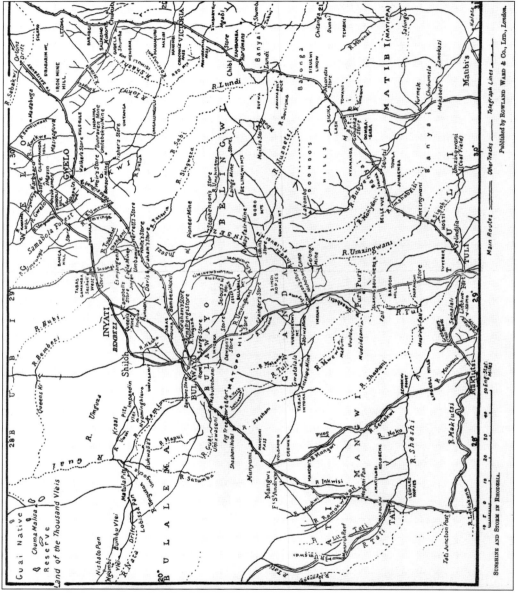

Part of Matabeleland, 1896

Bulawayo in the mid-1890s. Top: 1894, before the township was moved
some three miles to its present site. Centre: Abercorn Street, 1895. Bottom:
the Bank of Africa in Bulawayo. (Rhodesia National Archives)

Bulawayo in the later 1890s, looking south-east. Pictured are the Mines Office, Charter Hotel, the Stock Exchange and the Post Office. (Rhodesia National Archives)

Zambezi River, in the south by the Limpopo, to the west by Bechuanaland (now Botswana) and to the east by Portuguese East Africa (later named Mozambique). They named it 'Rhodesia' after its founder. The native people themselves still lived in an iron age culture which, even by the late 19th century, had not progressed to thinking up the wheel.

Bulawayo itself was declared a town on 1 June 1894. It became well-known for its very broad streets which Rhodes had decreed should be wide enough to turn a full span of oxen without difficulty. In January 1895 the company offered the Zeederburg Coach company the mail contract between Salisbury and Bulawayo, and their American Abbot-Downing stagecoaches became familiar sights in both towns. By the middle of the year hotels, stores and clubs had sprung up as well as a lively stock exchange. The Standard Bank was established in September and in the following year a hospital and a permanent brick post office were built. By this time, Bulawayo had replaced Fort Tuli as the country's port of entry from South Africa.

Despite their defeat and the death of their king the Amandebele were not vanquished. They were still a nation, now ruled by the senior *induna* Umlugulu as regent (Rhodes had sent Lobengula's two sons to school in the Cape). By comparison their former Shona vassals were, despite being more numerous, simply a disunited people made up of five Chi-Shona-speaking clans: the Karanga, Zezuru, Manyika, Ndau and Kore-Kore. These unarmed, pastoral people possessed no military tradition and had been totally and brutally subjugated by the terrible Matabele who, on the run from the Boers and Zulu, had arrived in their midst in 1837.

The Matabele opted to lie low, lick their wounds, recover their strength and plot revenge whilst awaiting a favourable opportunity to exact it. They had weapons and firearms cached up in various locations after their defeat of 1893. In all this they were now spurred on by the priest Mkwati. This individual lived at the sacred Mwari (Mwari: the Karanga supreme deity) shrine at Thabas-zi-ka-Mambo – Mountain of the King – at Manyanga in the Matopos Hills (Matopos European corruption of the Sindebele *Matobo* meaning 'bald heads' which these huge granite boulders resemble) near the ruined fortress of the last *Rozwi Mambo* (Mashona ruler). There is no landscape on Earth that resembles its impressiveness. This majestic rocky outcrop is some 80 kilometres long

The beginnings of Fort Victoria, 1893. (Rhodesia National Archives)

The fort at Fort Victoria, constructed in 1893, forming part of the government
buildings and photographed in 1896. (Rhodesia National Archives)

Lobengula's old five-stamp
battery at Pomposo mine.
(Rhodesia National Archives)

A mine battery at Hartley Hills in the early
1890s. (Rhodesia National Archives)

Market Square, Bulawayo. (Rhodesia National Archives)

A Zeederberg coach. (Rhodesia National Archives)

The hazards of pioneer travel. (Rhodesia National Archives)

and its myriad shapes are incredible. It literally exudes an atmosphere of primeval mysticism which the earlier inhabitants had discerned. Lobengula's father, Mzilikazi, was buried there as, finally, were Cecil Rhodes and Jameson.

From this spiritual abode then, Mkwati had become the deity's spiritual medium and mouthpiece and communicated its wishes to the people, both Matabele and Mashona. The Mwari belief was essentially Karanga, but with time it had made insidious inroads into Matabele custom. Lobengula himself had succumbed to it and would send sacred black oxen to the Karanga rain-makers. From Thabas-zi-ka-Mambo, Mkwati was able to persuade the Matabele that their monarchy would be reborn. He was also playing on the native superstition to which all Africans are endemically susceptible, able to blame the whites for the sudden plague of locusts, unseen for a generation, which darkened the sky and ate the nation's crops. Then, by coincidence, an outbreak of the cattle-killing disease, rinderpest, broke out for which the whites were also blamed. In addition, the Matabele were enduring the hardships common to all beaten peoples – the company had, wrongly and unwisely, taken much of their livestock (70,000 head of cattle). They were paying hut tax and performing forced labour by way of war reparations. Worse, the native police (selected from the Matabele low-grade *Ama-Holi* regiments made up of impressed locals of mixed Matabele and Shona descent) who now enforced the conqueror's law were men from their own nation who had been recruited by the whites. These men, with the traditional Matabele predatory skills, would visit kraals, take what they liked, outrage women and beat up those who had formerly been their betters or against whom they harboured a grudge.

By late 1895 Matabeleland was a powder keg awaiting detonation. The opportunity for this arose when the company's administrator and Rhodes' friend, Doctor Leander Starr Jameson, foolishly believing the country pacified, denuded it of most of the able-bodied whites – over five hundred mounted men – for a raid against the Transvaal. This was in support of the Uitlanders there who were clamouring for political recognition which the Boer leader, Paul Kruger, refused to grant. A successful attack, thought Jameson, would fulfil Rhodes' desire to include the Transvaal into a federation of central and south African states. On 29 December 1895, without any former planning or reconnaissance, Jameson, from his base in Pitsani Potluko in Bechuanaland, led his men across the border into the Transvaal. On 1 January they confronted the awful and deadly Boer marksmen at Krugersdorp where they were quickly and unceremoniously cut down. The remnants surrendered at Dornkop on the following day and were all imprisoned.

The Matabele were rapidly apprised of what had occurred and seized their chance. At dusk on Friday 20 March 1896, eight men of the company's native police and their porters were camped for the night at Umgorslwini Kraal near the Umzingwane river in Essexvale. As they were partaking of their evening meal, a Matabele *impi* led by Umzobo, the *Umlisa go Bulawayo* (Lieutenant of Bulawayo), came out of the gloom and formed up in a line before them. They were all armed with knobkerries. They began to dance and chant tauntingly before the camp. Soon the dancing got heated with the participants performing *jia* (pointing with sticks) as they worked themselves up into a highly excitable state. The policemen, alarmed, stood facing the mob as their sergeant ordered it to disperse. One of the policemen then noticed a man sneaking up on them from the rear. Yelling out a warning, the policeman charged the man who now stood up to reveal himself armed with an assegai which he made ready to throw. The policeman, however, managed to grasp his wrist and, aided by a colleague, disarmed the man and began to handcuff him. As they did so a shot was fired at them but hit the prisoner instead, killing him instantly. The Matabele then melted away into the dark. As the shaken policemen began to regroup by the campfire, they were fired on from the bush and one of the porters was killed. The policemen then beat a hasty retreat and reported the incident to Mr H M Jackson, the Chief Native Commissioner at Makukupen in Essexvale.

The Rebellion had now begun. Beginning at Umzingwane, it spread rapidly to the Insiza, Gwelo,

The Illustrated London News, 26
July 1896. (Neville Croxford)

A patrol at Mangwe Pass with African 'friendlies'
in the background. (Neville Croxford)

Inside Mangwe Fort, Matabeleland. (Neville Croxford)

Mavena, Bembesi and Inyati districts. It involved, actively and passively, about 15,000 Matabele fighting men, 1,000 of whom were armed with the breech-loading rifles that the BSA Company had given to Lobengula as part of the concession deal of 1890. A further 1,000 had firearms of their own, including muzzle-loading blunderbusses (some of these were home-made, others were Tower muskets of 1852 vintage). The rebels cut the telegraph wires, thereby effectively isolating Bulawayo. Many native policemen, anxious to be on the 'winning side', decided to joined in. Forewarned of this, Jackson immediately disarmed his ninety native policemen who were each armed with a Winchester and seventy rounds of ammunition.

Selous, who had earlier moved his wife to Bulawayo after being informed by an employee that 'something was brewing' with the Matabele, heard about the incident at Umgorslwini's kraal from Jackson on Monday 23 March. On that same day, the rebels struck at Edkins' trading store at Filabusi, a sub-station of the Insiza district, some 85 kilometres south-east of Bulawayo. This store, owned by E C Edkins, serviced the mining camps in the vicinity. Apart from Edkins, also present were six whites, two colonial boys and a coolie cook. Taken by complete surprise all were murdered. One of them, Arthur Bentley, was the assistant native commissioner from the Queenstown district who was killed from behind whilst writing at his desk. His writing was headed with the date of 23 March. Another victim was Harry Baragwanath (brother of Orlando Baragwanath who was to discover Northern Rhodesia's fabulous copperbelt) who was grappled from behind and had his neck broken. The only survivor was a servant named Jim who was left for dead by the Matabele. He lived to recover from his horrific injuries and gave evidence later that the attack had been instigated by members of the Matabele royal family, led by the regent Umlugulu and Lobengula's two brothers, Umfaizella and Maschlaschin, along with other members of the king's family.

The Matabele went on the rampage, killing small groups of isolated prospectors and farmers. In very quick sequence they murdered over 140 whites along with their black and coloured staff: eight members of the Cunningham family were murdered at Claremont, Paul and Emal Bertelsen and

The original Grey's Scouts. The four gentlemen with folded arms are, from left to right:
Lieutenant Jack Stuart, Lieutenant F Crewe, Captain George Grey and Lieutenant Hodgson.

The Grey's Scouts 1896. (Neville Croxford)

their four sons on the Shangani, north of the Hartley Hills road, similarly seven whites at Tekwe, and so on. These savage, isolated and uncoordinated attacks were, of course, a tactical error. If the rebels had initially struck at Bulawayo collectively in a massed surprise attack, they could have killed all the whites before they had time to react.

Grey's Scouts and Afrikander Corps in action

The Afrikander Corps

On Wednesday morning, 25 March, a quiet, confident and unassuming Englishman, the Honourable George Grey, in company with his coloured driver, was travelling in his Cape cart from Bulawayo on his way to inspect his mining properties near the Shangani. Grey was the brother of Sir Edward Grey (Foreign Secretary 1905-1911). When Grey got to Pongo Store, twenty kilometres from the Shangani, he found it to be looted. He also saw a large pool of blood in front of the building. He did not, however, see the dead bodies of three white men lying not too far away. Grey knew that something was up. He hurried on to Eagle Mine, seven kilometres further on, and found it abandoned. By now Grey was aware that he was in dangerous country. He turned back to the main road and headed for the Shangani Store. On the way he came across a white man staggering along the road. He was very badly wounded having received two axe wounds, one of which had cut his face open from nose to ear and the other had cut his arm to the bone, severing all the wrist tendons. The man, Mr Scott, said he and two companions had been at work on a nearby farm when they were suddenly set upon by Matabele. They were all wounded but made it back to their hut and the rebels moved away believing the white men now had firearms. They didn't and at nightfall the three set out for Stewart's Store at the Tekwe. The moonlight betrayed them and the awaiting *impi* attacked them. All three scattered into a maize field and became separated.

Grey and his two companions arrived at the Shangani to find seventeen whites in laager (a circle of wagons forming a defensive perimeter). These included the men from Eagle Mine. Making a quick assessment of the situation, Grey decided to return to Bulawayo at once to get help. Alone, and using the post mules along the road, Grey set off. He arrived at Tekwe Store and found it being held by six men and two women. Promising to return with help, he pressed on and reached Bulawayo on Thursday morning, 26 March, having miraculously avoided the marauding rebels throughout.

At Bulawayo, Colonel John Spreckley and the mayor Mr Scott had organised the laager. This consisted of wagons formed around the Market square (where today the Town Hall stands) with a

The Stock Exchange, Bulawayo, used as a hospital during the
rebellion. (National Archives Photographic Collection)

The Charter Hotel, Bulawayo, 1897. (National Archives Photographic Collection)

machine gun at each corner. Barbed wire was placed all around the wagons at a distance of twenty metres. The men slept beneath the wagons. The women and children were housed in the Market Hall itself. Small groups of men picketed various strategic points round the town. Selous recalled that there was a careful count of all whites. These numbered ' ... 632 women and children and 915 men ... '.

A muster was held of all able-bodied, armed men. Some 850 men were assembled and fallen in by George Grey, now designated with the rank of captain. Named the Bulawayo Field Force (BFF), it was commanded by Colonel William Napier and constituted mainly as follows:

a) An Artillery Troop and Engineer Troop of about 100;
b) Rhodesia Horse numbering 170 under Captain Cecil Brand;
c) Grey's Scouts some (initially) 50 men handpicked by Grey himself;
d) Gifford's Horse and Dawson's Scouts totalling 170;
e) Afrikander Corps[5] – three companies numbering 76, 64 and 73 each, raised by Commandants van Rensburg and P H van Niekerk.
f) Johan Colenbrander's Cape Colonial Boys consisting of a mix of 150 reliable and tough Cape Coloureds, Xhosas, Fingos and Zulus.

Between 300 and 400 men would have to remain in the town to defend the women and children.

Selous recorded that there were 77 horses in Government stables in Matabeleland at the outbreak of the Rebellion. A further 117 were in the possession of the BFF and 28 were being used by cattle inspectors. He also noted that, apart from firearms in private ownership, throughout Matabeleland there were 580 rifles in Government armouries. This number was made up of 456 bolt action Mark 1 Lee-Metford rifles with 8-round magazines and 124 Lee-Metford carbines (a cut-down version of the rifle). There were also about 80 old Martini-Henrys 1871 pattern single-shot rifles, most of them unserviceable. Of ammunition, there was a plentiful supply – 1,500,000 rounds. Artillery consisted of two 303 Maxims (more arrived later), a one-pounder Hotchkiss gun, one Gatling, one Gardner and a Nordenfeldt along with a seven-pounder. Additionally there were two 2.5 screw guns but with only 17 rounds of ammunition for both.

The Rescue Patrols

On 24 March, 44 mounted men set off for Nellie's Mine in the Insiza district to investigate the murder by rebels of Mr Thomas Maddocks, the mine manager. The force was made up of 30 Gifford's Horse plus 14 Matabeleland Mounted Police under Inspector Southey; Maurice Gifford was in overall command. Forty kilometres out of Bulawayo they came upon a laden and abandoned donkey wagon in the middle of the road. All sixteen donkeys had been stabbed to death but none of the cargo, consisting of flour, coffee, sugar and whiskey etc. had been touched. None of the Cape Colonial drivers were to be seen but were later found murdered nearby. Continuing on, they came upon three lightly armed Cape Colonial boys running for Bulawayo who told them that there was a general uprising in the Insiza district, and that Dr Langford and his wife and Mr C J Lemon had been killed on the previous day near Rixon's farm: the Blicks and others had all escaped to Cumming's Store.

Taking the three along with them, the patrol arrived at Cummings Store that evening, Thursday 26 March, having marched 100 kilometres. They found 36 men and a pregnant woman besieged therein. The thatch had been removed and the doors and windows sandbagged. Loopholes had also been bored through the walls. At dawn, the renowned Matabele attack time, the rebels launched a fierce and determined assault on the store but were beaten off. But only just! One of them came so close that he was shot leaping through a gap in a window. Another was killed with his hands in a

5   Here I have followed the BSA Company's and Selous spelling of this word rather than the correct and more familiar 'Afrikaner'. We need to note also that, beyond a shadow of doubt, the most experienced and seasoned fighting men in the country were the Afrikanders. These white Africans understood (and continue to do so) the African psyche, thinking and tactics better than any other whites anywhere; this understanding being the natural result of generations of contact, peaceful and otherwise, with their black countrymen. Additionally, their marksmanship was without equal.

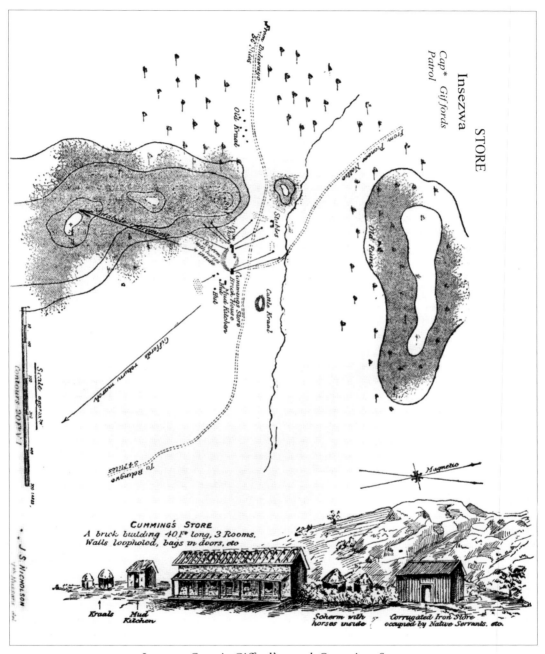

Insezwa: Captain Gifford's patrol, Cummings Store

loophole attempting to pull the sandbags away. Many Matabele made it onto the verandah where three of them were shot down and many others wounded. Unfortunately Sergeant John O'Leary, who was firing from behind a tree in front of the store, was shot dead, his body carried in by Southey. Killed also was an unnamed educated American negro, the servant of Mr Wrey. Corporal Charles Strutt was stabbed by an assegai. Troopers Eustace Hill, Willem Luis and Charles Saunders were also wounded. Later that evening, having been contacted by Colonel Napier, Gifford wrote in reply:

> Dear Napier, Your dispatch duly received. Just a line to let you know that the Kaffirs mean business this time. We were attacked this morning one hour before sunrise by about three hundred natives, who came on in the most fanatical and plucky style – the old Zulu rush. Three natives were shot alongside the wall of our barricade. I mention this to you to put you on your guard, as you must have many new chums with you, and to advise the greatest caution to prevent night surprises. We never thought an attack probable, but fortunately were well prepared. This, in my opinion, will prove a more serious business than the old war, and I'm sure that prompt action is necessary. Yours, M R Gifford

The patrol and refugees got back to Bulawayo at midday on Saturday 29 March.

A day after Gifford set out for Insiza, Colonel John Spreckley with 35 volunteers left for Filabusi. One of them was Orlando Baragwanath. They reached Edkins' Store the following day where Baragwanath was devastated to find the body of his murdered brother amongst the massacred. There was no time for burial and the troop moved on to the Filabusi police camp where every living creature, including the fowls, had been killed. Arriving at Celtic Mine, many of the men were physically sick at the sight of the dead. Spreckley decided to return to Bulawayo.

Selous, with 35 men, left for Essexvale and the area of the Malungwani Hills at 7.30 pm on 25 March. They reached Selous' homestead before dawn. Here they were informed by the company's herdsman that the Matabele had driven off all the cattle. The herder then guided Selous and his men to a nearby kraal where the cattle were found but no inhabitants save the headman's wife. Selous ordered the herder to take the cattle back to his homestead. When he crossed the Tuli road 14 kilometres south-west of Spiro's Store he came up against a large rebel force and, after a brief skirmish during which Troopers A H Stracey and Berthold Muntzberg were wounded, he withdrew.

George Grey had quickly set off for the Tekwe on Friday 27 March with twenty-three of his scouts, arriving there in the afternoon to find that the beleaguered whites were okay. The Matabele had driven off their cattle, however, and left a note to say they would be returning to kill them all that evening. The arrival of Grey and his men gave the rebels pause for thought. The Grey's moved on to Stewart's Store where they made a junction with Colonel Napier's column. The combined force burned down Jingen's kraal which was in an area where the Mlimo was believed to be. They then set off up the Bulawayo-Gwelo road towards Pongo Store on a reconnaissance. Meanwhile the Zeederburg mail stagecoach, which had left Salisbury on 28 March with nine passengers, had passed Gwelo on its way to Bulawayo. The driver, a resourceful Cape Coloured named Peters, had been warned to be on the *qui vive* by the firm's Salisbury manager who had heard rumours of Matabele unrest. Peters kept his mules at a steady ten kilometres an hour to save their strength. At each relay station they heard more and more alarming rumours. At the Shangani Store they found the body of a white man sprawled in front of the building. Peters quickly looked in the stable for remounts but saw only the mutilated bodies of several African staff. He knew they were heading into trouble. Taking charge he immediately ordered four of the passengers onto the roof of the stagecoach and told them to have their rifles at the ready. He then set the mules off at a steady canter for the next relay station, forty kilometres away at Pongo Store. Every few minutes he would slow the animals down to a walk. Everyone was avidly scanning the surrounding bush for any sign of the enemy. Finally the words,

'They are here!' came quietly from his assistant sitting beside him. Peters whipped up the mules and shouted, 'Get ready!' as the Matabele burst out of cover and began to run alongside the stagecoach keeping pace with it and chanting, '*Makiwa ... makiwa ...* (white men ... white men) ... ' and '*Bulala ... bulala ...* (kill ... kill ...)'. The passengers began firing at them knocking over any that came too close. The spectacle from now on was to resemble something out of the American Wild West of two decades earlier. Fortunately not one of the rebels had a firearm with which to shoot the mules and thus stop the coach. Those who tried to attack the animals with their stabbing spears were shot down.

The country had opened up somewhat and Peters was able to walk the mules every two miles or so as they were tiring. At Pongo Store they saw the dead bodies of the whites and the Africans all about. The store had been looted. Still harried by the Matabele they continued on for a short distance before the mules stopped as if by one accord. They were too done in to go on and even the rhino hide whip failed to move them. After a rapid assessment Peters made a decision. Leaping down he ordered everyone off the coach while he and his assistant unhitched the mules which then simply stood about pathetically, heads hanging in tired dejection. One of the passengers pointed out a low small kopje (a little hill) nearby, topped with a rocky outcrop.

'We could hold out up there until dark', he suggested. The passengers began to make a run for it but the cool-thinking Peters stopped them.

'You men' he said pointing out three of the passengers. 'Take your weapons and as much ammunition as you can carry and hold the top until we get there. Now go quickly'.

The three sped away. Peters then said to the others, 'Load up as much food, water and ammunition as you can carry and let's go!'.

The first three men were half way up the hill when the Matabele realised what the plan was. Shrieking, '*Bulala ... bulala!*' they began to scale the far side hoping to reach the top first. But the three whites beat them to it and began to pour fire down on them, checking their advance. Peters and the remaining passengers, now loaded down with everything they could carry, staggered up the slope and joined them. They took up all-round defensive positions and kept up a steady fire on the rebels who began to fall back with howls of angry frustration. Thwarted in their objective the Matabele went to the coach and looted it. They then stabbed the helpless mules to death, the wretched and exhausted creatures being unable to run off. After this the warriors, out of range, squatted around the hill in a circle to await darkness. The clever Peters then suggested, 'They are out of range but if we fire high we might get some of them. That way we might take a few more with us before we are overrun tonight'.

The others concurred and began to fire measured volleys. It was effective because the Matabele were seen to move further back. Not far away, Grey's and Napier's combined patrols on their Bulawayo-Gwelo road recce to Pongo Store heard the firing and spurred their mounts towards it. As they approached, they immediately took in the situation and charged forward firing at the gallop. The Matabele broke away in confusion. Peters and his passengers raced down the hill firing as they ran. There was a very brief pause for an explanation as they mounted up behind the troopers and the combined force turned about and galloped off. Their ordeal had lasted eight hours. Grey and Napier then made for Bulawayo arriving there on 2 April having rescued forty-three people including two women.

On Saturday morning, 28 March, Captain Pittendrigh of the Afrikander Corps set off with 14 men to relieve the people at Jenkins's Store and at Campbell's Store in Inyati. We need to note here that many men volunteered for this patrol but there were no mounts or rifles available for them. In fact the 14 participants supplied their own weapons and horses – one of these was Moodie Thomson, editor of the *Matabele Times*. They rode off, taking a mule wagon with them and reached Jenkins' at dawn of the following day. The store, with the thatch removed, was in laager. There were ten men within, one of whom was Mr Carter the assistant native commissioner. The entire group set off for Campbell's Store and Inyati on the Bembesi forty kilometres away. When they reached the undulating ground of the Lebani Hills they heard a shot from a nearby kopje and saw armed Matabele moving about on the crest, waving their spears and shields tauntingly. They immediately charged up the slope, firing at the gallop, killing a few. But it had been a lure. When they reached the top, they got a shock as the other side was crawling with hundreds of Matabele from the elite *abeZansi* Ingubo Regiment under their induna, Fusi Kanye. These went instantly on the attack, fanning out in classic Zulu horns and chest formation, all roaring '*Usutu* ... *'sutu* ... *'sutu* ... *'sutu* ... ' (the war cry of the Zulu king's faction of yesteryear) as they raced forward. (Note: the sole difference between this Zulu and Matabele main battle tactic was that, with the latter, the chest always lacked a reserve). Most of the Afrikanders had dismounted to fire and began a great execution with their famed accuracy. But they were outnumbered. Here Pittendrigh was kneeling and firing when his horse bolted and ran. He was then set upon by a warrior who attacked him with a stabbing spear and a desperate hand-to-hand fight ensued. Pittendrigh somehow managed to throw the man off and shoot him with his pistol. Carter received a round through the ankle and Sergeant-Major Thomas Haden's bandoleer received a hit exploding three of the rounds, one of them passing through his shoulder and another through his neck and cheek.

The Matabele were thrown off for a few very brief moments which allowed the Afrikanders to fall back onto the road. Here they found, to their dismay, that their wagon drivers had made off taking the spare horses. Leaving the mules and wagon, Pittendrigh formed his men into half sections with the wounded in front and set off at a canter. The Matabele were now coming on at a battle trot rattling their stabbing spears against the shields, mouths agape in a ululating roar. The thirty kilometre ride to Campbell's Store on the Bembesi was desperate but successful. They found Campbell, sitting in his ox wagon, having virtually given himself up for dead and making ready for a final stand. They were quickly put in the picture with the tragic news that the party at Inyati had been massacred. The Afrikanders began to fortify the store. The verandah thatch was cut away and the inner walls knocked down to increase the space, accommodate the horses and allow better communication within. Loopholes were bored through the bricks and bags of maize grain were used to block up the windows. A stock of prospector's dynamite was found and quickly converted into hand grenades and short fused mines; these latter were laid around the store. While these defensive preparations were going on, two volunteers, Fincham and Mostert, agreed to ride to Bulawayo for help. To assist their departure Pittendrigh and a few men created a diversion by pretending to cross the Bembesi and get to the road. The Matabele reacted immediately and raced off to intercept them. As they did so the two men, mounted on the best horses, burst out and galloped off in the opposite direction. Retreating back to the store Pittendrigh and his men, with over 2,000 rounds of ammunition, now prepared for whatever was to come.

The two riders got through to Bulawayo unscathed that evening, 29 March. A relief force was rapidly mustered consisting of 35 men. Twenty were Afrikander Corps under Captain van Niekerk and Commandant van Rensburg, the remaining fifteen were made up of Rhodesia Horse Volunteers under Captain R MacFarlane, formerly of the 9th Lancers. MacFarlane was in nominal command. The force set off at a brisk pace at midnight stopping only at Queen's Mine for a breather. Just before dawn, with troopers Celliers and Henderson in the lead, when less than a kilometre from Campbell's Store, they were ambushed by the Matabele who were deployed on both sides of the track. A running fight ensued with the relief party breaking through the killing ground and racing to the store. On arrival they discovered that, despite having no casualties, their two point men, Celliers and Henderson were both missing. Just before 9am the entire force decided to ride for Bulawayo via Queen's Mine. van Rensburg's men took the right flank and van Niekerk's men the left; the wounded were in Campbell's ox wagon in the centre and Pittendrigh's men made up the rear-guard. They started off cautiously noting the thick enemy spoor all about but no visible sign of life. They reached Queen's Mine at mid-day and decided to press on. At noon, as they approached the Shiloh Hills, the Matabele spearmen attacked from the cover of the thick jesse bush by the roadside while their marksmen fired at the column from the spur of a nearby kopje. Fortunately the firing was typically inaccurate as many of the Matabele, in common with most Africans unused to firearms, tended to aim high, flinch instinctively and jerk the trigger at the same time. They did however manage to kill one of the horses, a fine animal belonging to the Zeederburg Coach company. Those rebels who charged forward on foot waving their stabbing spears were rapidly cut down by the Afrikanders whose withering fire was perfection itself. The Afrikanders, fast and accurate and at the canter, began to run out of targets as the rebels, running alongside, began to use the bush cover. Now any rebel rash enough to venture into the open ended up being bowled over by eight or nine rounds. Making for the Kotki River the column came across a herd of native cattle which they seized. At the river they stopped for an hour to rest the horses and to eat some of the captured beef. Refreshed they mounted up and made the thirty kilometres to Bulawayo without further incident. Moodie Thomson later wrote of the Afrikanders, 'It is useful to testify to their courage, their determination, their skill with the rifle ... the pluck and dash displayed, as well as the good comradeship throughout, are convincing that in a like or even stiffer affray one could neither wish for nor hope to have better men than these'.

Henderson, with a badly wounded Celliers mounted up on his horse, finally walked into Bulawayo on Wednesday morning, 1 April, and gave an account of what had befallen them. When the Matabele had ambushed the relief party by Campbell's Store, Celliers had been shot through the knee from very close range. His mount was hit five times. Both men immediately spurred off the track and into the dense bush. At the gallop they rode out of the immediate killing zone and reined in. Here Henderson saw that Celliers was wounded and in excruciating pain. He led them away a short distance and then Celliers' dying horse collapsed. Henderson leapt off his mount, dragged Celliers free and lifted him onto his horse. Taking the reins he led them away from the battle area. All the while Celliers, in agony and suffering severe blood loss, pleaded with him to leave him and save himself. Henderson ignored the appeal and continued on. At dawn he stopped and attended to his comrade's wound. After a brief rest they continued on, heading for Bulawayo some 55 kilometres away. Without food, for two days and a night Henderson led them through the bush, his faithful horse bearing the wounded Celliers. He picked his way around the numerous Matabele camps and *kraals*. The entire area was crawling with marauding rebels and, on several occasions, they only narrowly escaped detection. The most tense and hair-raising experience was having to weave through the numerous *impis* encircling Bulawayo. Finally, dehydrated and exhausted, they staggered into the town.

Celliers was taken to hospital and his leg was amputated. Sadly however, the loss of blood, shock and pain of the injury proved excessive and he died on 16 May.

Captain MacFarlane, the patrol leader, wrote to the BSA Company Administrator recommending Henderson for the award of the Victoria Cross. The recommendation was approved and the honour was awarded and recorded in the *London Gazette* on 7 May 1897. This was the first Victoria Cross won in Rhodesia.[6]

On Thursday evening, 2 April, Captain Brand with 100 men and a Maxim drawn on a gun carriage left Bulawayo. They were headed for Dawson's Store at Amanzi-inyama (Manzi-Izama), 130 kilometres away on the Tuli road in the Gwanda district to effect the rescue of prospectors and farmers said to be in laager. Fifty of his men were from the Afrikander Corps under the very capable Captain van Niekerk; the rest of the force was composed of 'C' Troop Rhodesia Horse Volunteers. Accompanying the patrol was a Doctor Levy with his ambulance, Zeederberg the post contractor, and a mule wagonette containing provisions and ammunition.

The first rest was at Spargot's Store, ten kilometres from Bulawayo where Jim, the African mutilated at Edkin's Store, was found, having made his way there in painful stages. The patrol next halted at Dawson's Store on the Umzingwani River. The building had been burnt down but the mule

---

6   See VC citation, Appendix II.

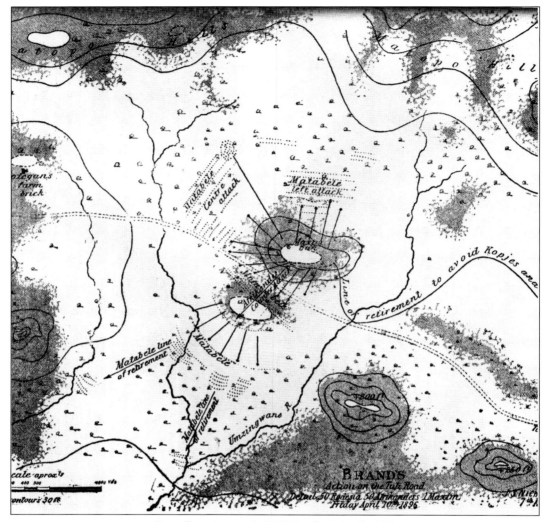

Brand's action on the Tuli Road, 10 April 1896.

stables were still intact and contained a good store of maize for the horses. They put out pickets and then based up for the night, stabling the mounts and sleeping behind their saddles on the rising ground in front of the burnt-out building. The pickets came under fire in the early hours but the Afrikanders drove the enemy off. Shortly afterwards they heard the rebels calling to one another in the hills by the river.

At dawn, the patrol headed for Spiro's Store, sixty kilometres from Bulawayo and found it burnt to the ground. Twenty kilometres further on they came up to Grainger's Store No1 and were surprised to find it still intact. They then saw signs of a hurried departure by the enemy with evidence of preliminary looting everywhere. Maize was again found in the stables and the horses were fed. By evening they had reached Grainger's Store No2 which was also found still standing. They camped for the night and set out for Dawson's Store at dawn. On arrival they found it deserted and looted. From here they moved seven kilometres on to Mr Nicholson's camp believing it to be occupied by the remaining whites in the Gwanda district. On arrival they found it deserted but discovered a good fort atop a nearby kopje and occupied it. Zeederberg and three of the patrol then went down the Tuli road on a recce and to send telegrams to Bulawayo. They came across the people from Dawson's Store travelling in a wagon and headed for Tuli. Two of the patrol then returned while Zeederberg and the other continued on to Tuli.

At the kopje fort it was decided to return to Bulawayo as by now the patrol knew that the enemy were in great numbers all about. The rebels observed the departure preparations and began to make plans to attack it in force on its return trip. Brand and van Niekerk got warning of this from a native scout and, on Sunday 5 April, sent two men on the best horses back to Bulawayo to get a Hotchkiss gun and reinforcements to meet them somewhere along the return route. On Wednesday 8 April, the two men returned to report that no help could be spared for the moment. On the following morning the patrol saddled up and moved out. Arriving at Grainger's Store No2 they found it had now been burnt down but decided to base up there for the night. At dawn the next morning they reached Grainger's Store No1 and it had suffered a like fate. The patrol was now acutely aware of its dangerous and vulnerable position. They moved rapidly on and at mid-morning saw a herd of cattle in the bush at the base of a range of kopjes. The wily Afrikanders immediately and correctly realised this was a lure to entice the patrol off the track and into the bush. They cantered on for a few hundred metres and saw several hundred Matabele hiding in ambush in the thick jesse. They turned the Maxim on to them and the warriors turned tail and fled up a hillside. As the patrol approached the ruins of Spiro's Store, everyone became very tense and an air of foreboding began to be felt. Ten kilometres from Spiro's and parallel with nearby Latijan's farm a column of smoke was seen ahead as the Matabele signalled each other. The track now entered a tight nek amongst the rocky kopjes with many *gwashas* (thickets and dense tangled jesse bush in the folds of the hills) – ideal ambush country.

The patrol moved forward with the Afrikanders in the lead. As the column began to negotiate the nek they came under fire from the left flank from the enemy concealed in the rocks. Fire was returned as they pressed on through the narrow pass. Unfortunately one of Brand's inexperienced 'C' Troop men standing before the provision wagon opened fire right in the face of the mules. The animals reared back in terror and the disselboom broke, rendering the wagon immobile. Roundly cursing the culprit, the men set about repairing the damage which occupied nearly half an hour during which several men and horses were wounded. During this time Trooper Jobson, the Maxim gunner, quickly and coolly brought the weapon into action and kept the rebels at bay. Emerging through the gap van Niekerk rapidly got the disorganised patrol into skirmish order. Lieutenant Webb of the Afrikander Corps estimated that they faced no less than 1,000 Matabele. He recorded:

> They followed us for over five miles at a distance of no less than 200 yards … Our route lay over successive ranges of ridges and valleys and afforded plenty of cover for the enemy, as the grass was about three feet high, and the country thickly studded with bush and trees. They formed a half moon round us and skirmished excellently, taking advantage of every bit of cover. They also fought with ferocious determination, and often showed pluck verging on lunacy. They were kept well in hand by their leaders, who constantly urged them to fire low. Our horses and men were now falling with deadly monotony and we all saw the importance of getting into more open country. Our men were firing steadily and rapidly all this time and the Maxim did good service; but being on the move and owing to the enemy tactics it did not do the execution we saw in the first Matabele war of 1893 … [7]

The running battle went on for over three hours. A halt to rest the mounts became necessary and a very small rocky outcrop on a rise, about five metres high was then seen and chosen. As they made for it, the Matabele tried to outflank them and occupy it first. An exciting race for it was then made

---

7   Selous F W. *Sunshine and Storm in Rhodesia* pp122-123.

by both sides but an Afrikander section got there first and held it until the rest of the patrol arrived. The kopje top was found to be flat rock. They took up defensive positions all round and looked about. What they saw on the plain beyond was the carcasses of horses and the bodies of dead men lying where they had fallen. They very quickly had to look to themselves, however, as the Matabele had crept up to within 40 metres of their position using the rock-strewn terrain and trees as cover. From here, ululating with rage, they fired up at the patrol to such effect that only after three or four spirited charges by the defenders did they begin to fall back. Here the gallant performances by the experienced Afrikander campaigners – old Mr Steyn, Loots, Ferreira and others – steadied the younger men and gave them inspiration.

Brand and van Niekerk took stock of the situation. They reckoned to have killed between two and three hundred rebels for the loss of four dead, all 'C' Troop – Edward Heyland, Christopher Packe, Stuart Greer and J McAinish Forbes – and two more fatally injured. Over twenty others were wounded and they had also lost thirty-three horses. They conferred very briefly and Brand handed over command to the more experienced van Niekerk who decided that prompt action was needed before the Matabele organised for a general attack and overran their position. The dead were to be left behind. van Niekerk ordered eight of the worse wounded into the wagonette. Three others were placed on the Maxim gun carriage and the patrol set off. It was now twilight and they expected to be attacked at any moment but to their total surprise the Matabele had vanished. Travelling in the dark and keeping close together they were met at dawn by the relief force that had been sent for them. It was Saturday, 11 April, and two hours later they halted in front of the Government Buildings in Bulawayo. That afternoon, Lieutenant Webb buried his friend Richard Baker, one of the wounded, who had died on the Maxim gun carriage during the return journey.

The Fighting Patrols

In the early hours of Saturday, 4 April, Lieutenant Colonel Maurice Gifford, in command of 167 men, set off up the Red Bank Road on a mission to the Khami river hopefully to disperse the enemy *impis* believed to be there. From there he was to go on to Fonseca's Farm near which rebels were reported to be massing. After this he was to return to Bulawayo via Campbell's Store having recced the Shiloh and Inyati areas. The force comprised his own Gifford's Horse, thirty-one men of Dawson's Horse, eleven Grey's Scouts under Lieutenant Fred Crewe, forty-nine men of Colenbrander's Cape Colonial Boys under Captain Cecil Bisset who had previous experience of native warfare in Basutoland and Zululand, two ammunition and supply wagons and a Maxim on its gun carriage. Twenty kilometres from Bulawayo they outspanned at M'Kisa's kraal. Here, two Cape boys employed on George Grey's farm and on their way to Bulawayo told Gifford that a Matabele army was encamped on Holm's Farm on the Umgusa river a further twenty miles to the north. Gifford decided to take them on. Laager was inspanned after lunch and the patrol crossed Capsize Drift where they saw a large and recently occupied enemy *scherm* (temporary camp encircled with cut thorn-scrub). By mid-afternoon, as they began to get into open country, the Grey's scouting ahead on the right near a low ridge at the base of some kopjes, came under fire and were nearly cut off. An *impi*, two to three hundred strong, came over the top of the ridge at a running charge, roaring defiantly. Gifford's 'B' Troop under Captain Fynn shook out to engage them. As the two clashed, Gifford ordered Dawson's Troop and Bisset's Colonial Boys up immediately in support. A very brisk firefight ensued lasting over an hour, after which the Matabele began to retire back into the hills. The column then laagered up for the night on Wessel's farm 600 metres from the Umgusa river. At dawn they set off again and, after two or three kilometres, as they moved along the Umgusa river they saw some Matabele moving about to their front. Gifford's 'A' Troop under Captain Meikle was the advance guard and received a frontal attack. At the same time over three hundred rebels were seen to the right about 500 metres away and on the other side of the Umgusa. These, moving along the bank, began to fire at the column but made no

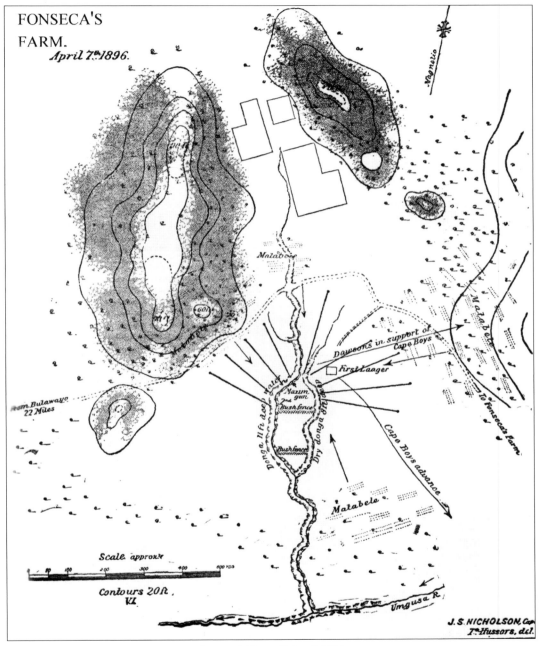

Fonseca's Farm, 7 April 1896.

attempt to wade across and engage in closer combat. Gifford ordered the Maxim to open up on them. At this the Matabele, as if of one mind, immediately all sat down in the grass and then lay down for some moments, after which they began to spread out in a crawling withdrawal until out of range, then stood up and strutted off shouting defiance and gesticulating threateningly.

Meikle's 'A' Troop had, by now, beaten off the initial frontal attack. The Colonial Boys under Bisset had come up on the left flank and fallen upon the defeated rebels, killing over thirty. The column had a brief rest to feed the horses. Each man had a biscuit and some water as they stood to on the *qui vive* as the enemy appeared to be all round them. They moved on towards Fonseca's Farm being shadowed all the way by a large *impi* to their right on the far bank of the Umgusa. They outspanned and laagered behind their saddles in an open *vlei* (swampy grassland) with their backs to a range of nearby kopjes on one of which was the homestead. There was much muttering about having to bed down in a swamp but this choice of site was to prove a salvation. At dawn on the next morning, Easter Monday, 6 April, a clearance patrol under Lieutenant Rorke went out and the Colonial Boys were sent to look for some stray cattle that had been seen by the riverside as there was only tinned bully beef to eat. While they waited the rest of the column began to brew coffee. Rorke and his men in the meantime had ridden to a kraal and stumbled upon a large *impi* who were having an *Indaba* (debating conference). Both sides, fortunately for the patrol, were completely surprised at the encounter. Reacting immediately and reining back, Rorke roared 'Fire' and his small group began an instant withdrawal, firing on the move as the Matabele leapt up and came for them. Rorke's horse unseated him and ran off and he was forced to run for it. Fortunately his men came about to his aid and the Colonial Boys suddenly appeared out of nowhere and gave covering fire. Coffee mugs in hand back at the column the firing was heard and Gifford immediately ordered Dawson and his Troop out. He followed this up with an order to his second-in-command, Captain J W M Lumsden and Captain Fynn to take 'B' Troop out.

The battle now became general. There was very heavy fighting to the left where the Colonial Boys, Fynn's and Dawson's men were fully engaged. Gifford then ordered the two wagons into a *donga* (gully, washed out streambed) with all the troops in position spread out in the *vlei's* streambeds which actually formed a natural laager. Realising that they were outnumbered he sent gallopers out to recall all the troops. During the withdrawal Trooper Kenneth McKenzie of 'B' Troop fell from his horse shot through the head. Trooper Fielding was wounded in the leg and lost his horse. Lumsden's horse was shot from under him but Fynn managed to bring everyone back to the laager in good order, firing as they retreated. Dawson and the Colonial Boys, with the Matabele on their heels, also got back into the laager. The rebels then made a determined charge on the laager from the rising ground to its front and right but the swampy ground slowed them down. Many parties crept up from the left flank and opened fire on the defenders. A few rounds from the Maxim, mounted on its tripod on the wagon, checked both attacks and sent them reeling back.

The battle now became a marksman's duel. Among Gifford's men was Orlando Baragwanath and his mining partner, Frank Lewis. The Matabele lined the bush to the laager's immediate front 200 metres off and also occupied the nearby kopjes, a distance of about 400 metres. Fire from both positions poured down onto the laager. The brave Gifford, completely oblivious to the incoming fire, was standing on the wagon in a totally exposed position so as to direct the Maxim's fire and point out targets to his men. The enemy to the front were proving effective, using rifles as well as blunderbusses which were loaded with stones, nails and anything else. Trooper Ernest Reynolds was mortally wounded, being hit in the arm and chest. Gifford himself was then hit in the arm so badly that later it required amputation. His men saw him hit but he continued on with a shout of: 'I'm all right. Just carry on giving it to them! Give it to them!'. Shock and loss of blood, however, soon took their toll and he was carried down into the *donga*. Lumsden, his 2 i/c, leapt up on to the wagon and took over Gifford's role. Troopers J Walker of Gifford's Horse and Trooper Eatwell of Dawson's

Troop were both wounded. The enemy fire began to slacken off noticeably and Lumsden jumped down from the wagon and consulted with the other officers. Two of Bisset's Colonial Boys were then despatched to Bulawayo to report the situation and to request reinforcements and ammunition which was beginning to run low. As the rebels moved off, the horses were let out to graze while the men began to fortify the *vlei* as best they could by cutting down bushes to make a second fence to the laager front. At sundown, as the horses were placed in the *donga*, the men noted smoke from the Matabele campfires and the enemy sentries silhouetted on the hill crests all around.

The night passed quietly and at stand to every man had a biscuit and water. Some Colonial Boys were sent on a recce to a kopje to see what the Matabele were up to. As they approached the top the Matabele appeared on the crest, seemingly out of nowhere, and began to come down to engage them. The troops turned about sharply and ran for their lives back to the laager. The rebels repeated the previous day's tactics, spreading out all round and firing at the laager. Lumsden, walking about and directing fire, was hit in the leg by a large rusty pot leg from an African cooking cauldron, loaded into and fired by a blunderbuss. The wound inflicted was fearful and Lumsden collapsed in absolute agony. The limb required prompt, on the spot, amputation and his obvious subsequent discomfort affected everyone. Cecil Bisset had by now assumed command and the fight went on for a further two hours, during which two Colonial Boys were killed as well as six horses. Wounded were Lieutenant J H Hulbert (Gifford's Horse), Troopers Fielding, J Walker and W J Eatwell.

Orlando Baragwanath and Lewis, in common with all the others, were duelling with individual enemy marksmen. Baragwanath's first target appeared to be an older warrior who would pop his grey head out of cover, fire a rapid shot and duck back down. Baragwanath focussed his aim on a spot he judged the man would next pop out of and, when he did, Baragwanath shot him through the head. He got a few more in like manner and then got into a long duel with a trickier opponent. This man was in excellent cover between several boulders and refused to budge. They exchanged shots for some time before Baragwanath decided on a ruse. The next time the enemy sniper fired, Baragwanath let out a scream and flopped over as if dead but with his rifle pointing to the sniper's hide. The rebel was very cautious, however, and fired three more rounds at his 'dead' opponent which all fortunately missed. Finally, satisfied, he turned about in the hide to select another target. Baragwanath noted the slight movement and fired at it, only to hear it ricochet off the rocks. He cursed and settled down to wait it out. A few minutes later he realised that his opponent had ceased firing. After the battle Baragwanath went up to the hide to see what had happened. He found the sniper dead, strangled by his own loincloth. Baragwanath's ricochet had struck the man in the thigh, inflicting a fearful wound. Realising the hopelessness of his situation the warrior had stripped off his loincloth knotted one end to a bush and the other around his neck and strangled himself by arching his back.[8]

The enemy fire began to die down at mid-day enabling the Colonial Boys to go out and collect McKenzie's body. Both he and Reynolds were buried in the centre of the laager.

At mid-afternoon Captain MacFarlane arrived with a relief column. The entire force left for Bulawayo the following morning, Wednesday 8 April, and got into Bulawayo late that night. They had expended 3,850 rounds of Martini-Henry ammunition and 2,600 rounds of Lee-Metford.[9] Lumsden, a much respected individual, died in hospital the next day.

Several patrols were going out on a regular basis to conduct reconnaissances and in the hope of finding further isolated whites or to bury those found massacred by the rebels. George Grey and

8   This stoic, fatalistic behaviour by the Matabele was commonplace. At the 1893 Battle of Bembesi, where the Mbizo Regiment had been decimated, Jack Warringham, walking across the battlefield, found a fatally wounded warrior. They exchanged Zulu greetings and Warringham gave the man some snuff. He then asked if he could help. The man looked at him and said, 'Shoot me as I cannot live'. Warringham blanched at the request. The warrior sneered up at him. 'You are a woman. Find me a spear and I will do it myself.' Warringham shot him. See also Bulpin. *Trail of the Copper King* pp128-129.

9   BSA Company Reports 1896-97, pp32.

twenty of his Scouts went out on 5 April to Molyneux Farm, found nothing and returned the same day. On the same day Lieutenant Hodson with twenty men went out to recce the Hope Fountain area. No rebels were seen and the patrol returned that evening.

On the morning of 7 April, Selous with 16 men went on a patrol of the Umgusa North area and returned the following day after an uneventful recce.

On 11 April, Captain Molyneux with 50 men left to build a fortified post at Figtree. This was constructed on a small rocky kopje with a small stream at its base, about 200 metres from the existing telegraph office, hotel and stables. The finished product was dubbed 'Fort Molyneux' and contained a recess large enough to stable twenty horses. Two days later Selous, Lieutenant H H Blocker and Lieutenant Marquand with 57 men and 20 horses left to construct a similar fort at Mabukitwani. Marquand, an architect by profession, designed and superintended the work which, on completion, was named 'Fort Marquand' in his honour.

The Matabele were reported to be gathering in large numbers along the Umgusa river which forms a semi-circle around the northern suburbs of Bulawayo. George Grey and 42 of his Scouts left on Thursday 16 April to conduct a reconnaissance of the area. They quickly found the report to be accurate and had a smart brush with a large number of rebels during which Trooper George Harker was wounded and two horses were killed.

In the early morning of 19 April a riderless horse came galloping into the town. Its saddle was covered in blood. It was quickly ascertained that it belonged to Henry Montgomerie of the Afrikander Corps who, along with two fellow Afrikanders, J Heineman and Wirnand van Zyl, had been detailed for picket duty not far from Government House the previous evening. All three had been surprised and killed by the Matabele at dawn, a favourite Matabele attack tactic and which had earned them the soubriquet of *Madzviti* (the Surprisers).

On Monday morning, April 20, Colonel Napier leading a force of 128 mounted men plus a seven pounder gun and a Maxim made for the Umgusa where the enemy were known to be encamped in large numbers. They certainly were and, after a brisk and inconclusive engagement in which no casualties were incurred, Napier, aware of the Matabele's overwhelming numbers, returned to Bulawayo that afternoon. The enemy encircling the town now presented a very grave threat.

In the pre-dawn of Wednesday 22 April, the Bulawayo laager was roused by the sound of large numbers of the enemy mustering in the low ground between the Umgusa river and the town (where Lobengula Street is today) as well as on the kopjes beyond the river.

Something had to be done pretty urgently to counter the build-up. After a brief conference, Cecil Bissett was placed in command of a force of 120 mounted men (a quarter of the town's white able-bodied men), 60 Cape Colonial Boys armed with Martini-Henry rifles and carbines, with Colenbrander in charge, and 100 'Friendlies' jointly under Selous, Captain G H Cardigan, Lieutenant E C Windley, and H J Taylor, with orders to dislodge the enemy from the area. Bisset's mounted men were made up of 40 Afrikanders under Captain P H van Niekerk, 20 Gifford's Horse under Captain S J H Meikle and 20 Grey's Scouts under George Grey, 20 under Captain Brand and a further 20 unattached individuals. Bisset also had a Hotchkiss one-pounder and a .303 calibre Maxim. The column was provided with a surgeon, Dr A Vigne, and an ambulance cart. Napier and the Acting Administrator of Matabeleland, Mr A J F Duncan, decided to come along as well.

Bisset set off in a westerly direction for about three kilometres then halted on a ridge. Here he received the report that Matabele detachments had reached the Brickfields area, so the force turned northwards to face them. This move by the enemy was a lure to draw Bisset into the thick bush across the river. The disselboom of the Hotchkiss then broke and the weapon itself rendered useless when the breach struck the firing mechanism. There was a 45 minute delay as a tree was cut and fitted as a replacement disselboom. The force continued on with Grey's Scouts in the lead and covering the front, the Afrikanders on the left, Meikle on the right and Brand forming the rear-guard. They went past

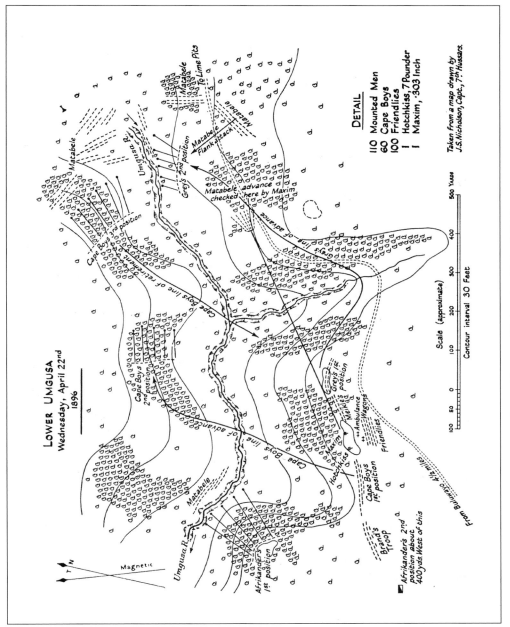

LOWER UMGUSA
Wednesday, April 22nd
1896

DETAIL

110	Mounted Men	
60	Cape Boys	
100	Friendlies	
I	Hotchkiss, 7 Pounder	
I	Maxim, .303 Inch	

Taken from a map drawn by
J.S. Nicholson, Capt., 7th Hussars.

Scale (approximate)

Contour interval 30 Feet

Lower Umgusa, Wednesday 22 April 1896.

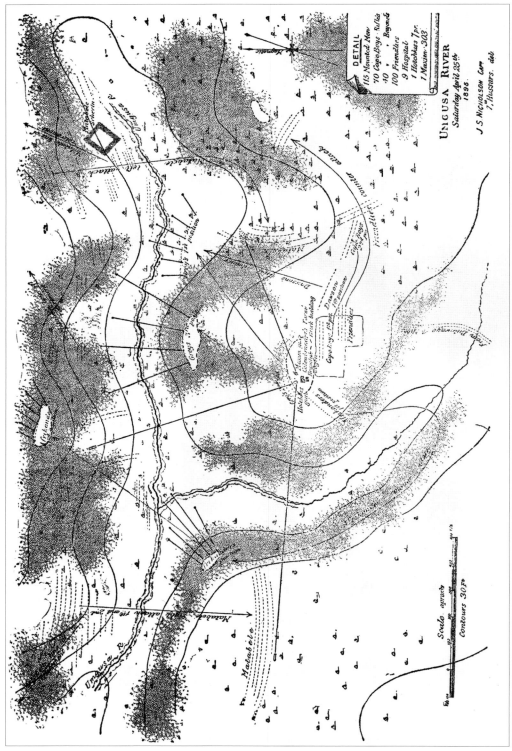

Umgusa River, Saturday 25 April 1896.

Government House and down a slope towards the Umgusa. The small rebel detachments began to fall back before them, enticing the troops on. It was now mid-morning.

When the force reached a ridge near the river bank a dog, belonging to one of the Afrikanders who were covering the left flank, flushed out an enemy warrior lying in ambush in the low scrub along the ridge. This man stood up and fired his blunderbuss at the Afrikanders. Taking their cue, his comrades lying alongside and all along the ridges then stood up as one man and opened fire. The battle had begun. Bisset's column instantly began a three-pronged frontal advance: Grey's Scouts, now on the right of the column, reacting first by returning immediate fire from about 500 metres. van Niekerk's Afrikanders, on the left, galloped forward to the river, dismounted and began to fire at the scores of Matabele in the river's hollow bed. They were soon hotly engaged as the Matabele right flank counter-attacked. The rest of Bisset's force, in the centre, had now reached the ridge's crest line and the highly aggressive Colonial Boys led by Cardigan charged forward to the river bank in support and cleared the enemy out of its bed, killing dozens as the rebels escaped across the stream. Fording the river, the Cape Boys boldly continued on in pursuit of the luring enemy. They negotiated the further slope and moved along it parallel to the river and then found themselves in trouble as enemy fire suddenly erupted from front, left and right. The Colonial Boys, full of battle lust, had probed too far ahead, just as the rebels had intended. The Greys, on Bisset's orders, began a 700 metre gallop along the south bank to give support. They got to within 150 metres of the Matabele and, for three minutes, poured a flanking fire on to the enemy and eased the pressure off the Colonial Boys.

Bisset has been blamed by Selous, and others for failing to send the Brand, Meikle, and the Maxim forward until later. Selous wrote:

> The position was now this: the Matabele had been driven from the banks of the river, and two or three hundred of them, panic-stricken and demoralised, were running in a crowd across some undulating ground, but scantily covered with bush, and had only Captain Meikle and Captain Brand been sent in support of the Colonial Boys and the Scouts, they might have galloped in amongst them and could not have failed to kill a very large number of them. But no; although these officers and their men were chafing and cursing at their enforced inactivity, they were kept idly standing round the Maxim doing nothing, which was all the more inexcusable as Captain van Niekerk with his forty Afrikanders had by this time silenced the enemy's fire on the left flank ... [10]

Hugh Marshall Hole, who prepared the Matabele Rebellion portion of the BSA Company Reports on the Rebellion, wrote:

> Sufficient use does not appear to have been made of the force at command, and if the firing line had been supported by the main body moving parallel with it on the high ground, a great success would undoubtedly have resulted. The friendlies, armed with assegais, were not engaged; this was the first time they had come into action with us, and were not absolutely relied on.[11]

Unlike Bisset, neither Selous nor Hole had any experience or understanding of Zulu/Matabele battle tactics and appeared unaware that the enemy's initial attack was a ploy to bring the column on and into more favourable fighting terrain. With hindsight we can see that Bisset had no idea exactly how many rebels his men faced. Judging from their battle roars and firing he would have correctly deduced that he faced thousands. In addition one of his two major support weapons, the Hotchkiss, was out of action. With his own eyes he could see that his outnumbered forward and flanking

---

10   F C Selous. *Sunshine and Storm in Rhodesia* p159.
11   *The '96 Rebellions*. Schedule E. Action on the Lower Umgusa River p33.

troops were heavily engaged and very hard pressed. Deciding against sending support forward Bisset, correctly, ordered a withdrawal. The Colonial Boys, on foot, began to retire and had to be sharp about it as they were almost completely surrounded. Selous, Windley and a few other mounted officers galloped up to give their retreat what covering fire they could. Selous dismounted, sat in the grass, and began firing. Suddenly he heard Windley's urgent, 'Look out. They're coming from the left!' Selous looked about to see the Matabele coming on at a run. He reached for his pony's bridle to mount up but a stray shot grazed the animal and it reared and ran off. Windley, on a big, powerful horse, galloped after it as the 45-year old Selous began to run for his life. As he had only one round in his rifle and one left in his bandoleer, he didn't give himself much hope. Behind him he could hear the pursuing Matabele pounding up, accompanying their run with a long drawn out and terrifying hissing of ' … *jeee … jeee … jeee …* '. But then Windley was suddenly back, pulling his leg out of the stirrup and urging Selous to mount up behind him. Selous grabbed the pommel but realised there was no time to mount up properly as the enemy were now very close. He grasped the thong around the horse's neck and told Windley to let the animal go. As they sped off, two enemy rounds struck the ground by Selous' foot and a third knocked the heel off Windley's boot, but they got away.

The Grey's who had begun to move back at the same time were almost immediately ambushed from the thick jesse bush to the left of their withdrawal line. Letting his men get on, Grey and a few others began a covering rearguard action, dismounting and firing at the advancing rebels as they moved back. Corporal George Wise was their first casualty, being hit in the back as he was mounting up. His horse galloped off. Seeing this, Trooper Frank Baxter came up, dismounted and put Wise up on his horse and sent him off. Afoot now, Baxter began to run. Grey and Lieutenant Hook, who had both witnessed the incident, galloped up and got Baxter along as best they could as the roaring Matabele, with their deafening battle cry of ' *'Sutu … 'sutu … 'sutu …* ' were virtually upon them. Hook was then shot in the groin and the sciatic nerve was severed. Almost simultaneously, Grey sustained a head wound when a round grazed his forehead leaving him half-stunned. 'Texas' Long, an American and well known member of the Scouts, now came to Baxter's aid. With Baxter hanging on to Long's stirrup leather, they went along until suddenly Baxter was shot in the side and fell to the ground where he was quickly set upon by the Matabele and assegaied to death.

Still moving back, Hook's horse was shot from under him. He got to his feet and hobbled on. Fred Crewe, who was nearby, came over and put Hook up on his horse, sending them galloping back as he himself made a run for it on foot. Seeing him thus, the rebels ran for him and he was forced to retreat backwards, holding them off with his revolver. Troopers Button, Radermeyer and Jack Stuart were helping to cover his retreat with a steady rifle fire as were the Colonial Boys to the right, whose cross-fire was being directed by Captain Fynn and Lieutenant Mullins. Seeing Crewe's plight, Trooper Lester galloped up and gave him his horse. The still groggy Grey also came up and took Lester up behind him. The Maxim now finally opened up from 800 metres and checked the Matabele charge. Crewe's escape was miraculous – the enemy had been so close that a knobkerrie had struck him in the back.

It was now mid-day. The column headed back to Bulawayo unimpeded as the Matabele, who had taken very heavy losses, retired to lick their wounds.

On May 7, 1897, Frank Baxter was recommended for a Victoria Cross. The Honour was awarded eleven years after the event on 15 January 1907. This was the second Victoria Cross awarded in Rhodesia.

On Saturday morning, 25 April, Captain R Macfarlane, commanding a column of 115 mounted men consisting of 35 Grey's Scouts under George Grey, 25 members of the BFF's 'B' Troop under Captain Fynn, 15 men of Dawson's Troop and 35 Afrikanders under Commandant van Rensburg set off up the Salisbury Road for Colenbrander's Farm on the Umgusa. Infantry support was provided by 100 Colonial Boys under Captain Cardigan and 70 Friendlies under Chief Native Commissioner

Taylor. Macfarlane also had a Hotchkiss and a Maxim. Dr Vigne and an ambulance with stretchers were in the centre of the column. Along for the ride came Colonel Spreckley, Captain J S Nicholson of the 7th Hussars (Nicholson drew the Rebellion's battle map sketches illustrated in this chapter) , the Mayor Mr Scott and Captain Wrey.

When the column got past Government House, it left a vedette patrol on the high ground nearby to watch the column's rear. Moving on George Grey's Scouts took the point as usual with the Afrikanders opening out on the left and Dawson's Troop covered the right flank. The Infantry provided the column's centre and rear-guard. Five kilometres from Bulawayo they came up to the ruined remains of the farm buildings, now just four walls, which were sited on rising ground. Between the buildings and the river was a circuit of scrub; beyond the river there was jesse bush through which enemy scherms (thorn-encircled encampments) could be seen as well as smoke from their camp fires. The Grey's were ordered to the river to draw the enemy on while the rest of the column took up the position shown on the sketch map, setting up the Hotchkiss and the Maxim and placing the horses on the reverse slope behind the walls. Grey's Scouts, galloping to their first position (see sketch map), saw the Matabele gathering across the river and opened fire on them. This prompted hundreds more rebels to come pouring down from a large scherm on the right with the intention of outflanking them. The Matabele raced forward yelling challenges. When they came within 200 metres Grey and his men turned about and cantered back to the farmhouse taking up their second position, as shown on the map, facing north-east between the Hotchkiss and the Maxim. The Matabele, still charging forward, burst out of the scrub and made for the Maxim hoping to take it, their riflemen firing rapidly and on the run. Their fire killed one member of the Ambulance Corps, George Whitehouse, and wounded another, Lieutenant M H Lyons, in the head.

When the rebel charge reached within 300 metres of the laager, the Maxim opened up on them with great effect and the enemy frontal chest formation was stopped. Their left horn, however, raced on and Dawson, along with the Colonial Boys, engaged them at short range for a few intense moments after which the rebels began to fall back in twos and threes. During this encounter, Trooper Charles Gordon was killed and Trooper Edward Appleyard of Dawson's Scouts was badly wounded, dying later that day. The Matabele right horn was seen running forward towards the laager. When they got to within 1,200 metres the Hotchkiss opened up and cut big gaps in the enemy's charging front line. But the enemy still came on. Macfarlane then ordered the Afrikanders forward to engage them and this was done so brilliantly, every shot scoring a hit, that all who witnessed it afterwards spoke of it with admiration. Galloping forward, dismounting, firing, mounting up, going forward, dismounting, firing – all with almost calm drill-like precision – the advancing Afrikanders' deadly fire checked the Matabele charge. It faltered and began to move back. Many of the rebels attempted to hide in the hollow ground of the *vlei* by the riverbank but the Afrikanders flushed them out, killing dozens. Many of those that began a running retreat across the river, desperate to escape the Afrikanders' withering fire, were cut down. A later count of the bodies in the *vlei* alone totalled 76. Grey's Scouts, meanwhile, had moved forward in skirmish order to their third position on the map, on the rising ground above the river bank where their fire converged with that of the Afrikanders who had crossed the river in pursuit of the enemy's broken and fleeing right horn. During this skirmish, Trooper Ronald Lovett was very badly wounded.[12] The Friendlies, wearing red capes (to distinguish them from the rebels) and armed with assegais and shields, had launched an effective counter attack on hidden groups of the Matabele left horn, now threatening the Colonial Boys' right flank. They killed several rebels and recovered two enemy rifles.

The action was now virtually over. The troops re-grouped. Three other members of the column were found to be wounded. The column got back to Bulawayo at mid-afternoon to the sad news that the vedette patrol had been cut off by over 500 Matabele and, in the running retreat, Trooper Ben

---

12   Lovatt died on 29 April.

Grey's Scouts memorial gates at Bulawayo Memorial Hospital. (Rhodesia National Archives)

Parsons had been killed.

The actions by Macfarlane's patrol appear to have been very decisive. The Matabele had taken severe casualties particularly during the patrols of 22 and 25 April. They would, from now on, be merely on the defensive. They had suffered huge setbacks but were certainly not defeated. On 3 May the newly arrived Administrator declared that, 'Bulawayo was as safe as London'. Bulawayo had received a re-supply of food and ammunition from 27 Zeederburg wagons. Rhodes, in Gwelo, was determined to get to Bulawayo to attempt to resolve the problem personally. He set off on 20 May in a column consisting of 300 mounted troops and 200 Colonial Boys. Napier set out from Bulawayo to join up with him at Pongo Store. There were over 4,000 Matabele in their scherms by the Umgusa and at Thabas Induna who intended prevent Rhodes linking up with Napier. Thousands more, including their best fighting men, had mustered on the Shangani River to oppose Rhodes but were defeated. Napier's patrol engaged the Thabas Induna rebels on 22 May as they contested his line of march, and inflicted severe casualties. Troopers Arthur Parker and George Rootman were killed during the engagement. Rhodes and Napier met at Pongo Store on May 24. From here the combined columns made for Bulawayo via the rebel kraals in the Insiza district but met no notable opposition. Rhodes and Napier arrived in Bulawayo on 1 June.

The Bulawayo Field Force was disbanded on the arrival of Colonel Plumer's Matabeleland Relief Force on 4 July. They had participated in an intense and eventful 100 days of frontier history. Plumer and Baden-Powell took the fight into the enemy strongholds such as the Matopo Hills and elsewhere. Rhodes accompanied the troops on these forays and was demonstrably and genuinely affected by the suffering of the troops and tribesmen, particularly during the fight at Thabas-zi-ka-Mambo. He said, 'We must put our thinking caps on and see what best is to be done'. He was then seen to spend much time hunched over the campfires in deep thought. Finally, coming to a decision, Rhodes, accompanied by Colenbrander, Dr Sauer, Mr Dent, John Grootboom and John Makunga, all unarmed and at great personal risk, rode ten kilometres into the Matopo Hills on 21 August. From here the Matabele were approached and persuaded to cease hostilities. The courageous Rhodes showed himself at his best throughout the negotiations and incurred the admiration of all with his patience in the face of the suspicious and hostile Matabele. Addressing ten of the principal indunas and 34 headmen, Rhodes, in an *Indaba* lasting over four hours, laid out the terms upon which peace could be made to the satisfaction of both sides. The indunas were asked to lay down their arms, return to their kraals and begin sowing their fields in safety. He also assured them that the Native Police, against whom the Matabele had major complaints, would be disbanded. The Matabele listened intently to Rhodes' carefully considered conciliatory and sympathetic arguments, at the end of which he appeared to have won some of their trust and gained their confidence. The indunas asked leave to consult their people. During this period, Rhodes camped nearby without protection of any sort as he awaited the decision. When it came, the Matabele opting for peace, Rhodes told them that an official great *Indaba* would be then held on 9 September to formalise the agreement. This was conducted successfully and was followed by a final huge *Indaba* on 13 October during which the final peace agreement was concluded.

From the above we can see that the Matabele Rebellion ended in some sort of draw as the rebels were never defeated; instead they had been asked to cease hostilities on somewhat mutually acceptable terms.

We last hear of The Honourable George Grey prospecting for the Tanganyika Concessions Company when he met Baragwanath and Lewis near Victoria Falls while on his way north to the Congo. He became associated with Robert Williams and both became famous for the Katanga and Tanganyika Concessions. Of his ultimate fate, the author has no knowledge despite an arduous search. On pages 36-37 of Cherer-Smith's *Avondale to Zimbabwe* (published by Mardon's, Salisbury, Rhodesia) we read that the mining buildings at Bushtick Mine, 52 kilometres from Bulawayo, were converted into a boys school in 1938. One of its houses was Grey House named, writes Cherer-Smith,

' ... after George Grey, a pioneer who lost his life as a result of an attack by a lion'. If this is our George Grey, then one can only laud the fact that he died a death worthy of any old Africa hand – in the land he loved and by its laws.

As a footnote to this chapter we need to note that, although not forming part of our history, on 15 June the Mashona had risen up in rebellion. This may have been because they were witnessing their two conquerors locked in mortal combat and decided to break with both. In whatever case they were exhorted to revolt by their spirit mediums, Nehanda and Kagubi. Like the Matabele they set about murdering isolated farmers and prospectors. Salisbury went into Laager. Sixty-five Grey's Scouts under Captain Charles White arrived in Salisbury from Bulawayo in July to assist in the relief operations. White with the Grey's, 42 Natal Troop (all volunteers from South Africa) and 40 Zulus of the Native Contingent set off from Salisbury for the beleaguered laager at Harley Hills on 19 July. Support weapons were two Maxims and a seven pounder. Three miles out of Salisbury, the Scouts were fired on from a kopje near Norton's farm. Trooper W Gwillim was killed, as was a Zulu. Three others were wounded. They moved on, crossing the Hunyani River in the afternoon. They came across the skeletons of Dr Edward Carrick the BSA Company's medical officer and several of his companions murdered on 19 July. They outspanned on the Serui river for the night. By 21 July they were 12 miles from Hartley Hills. They set out at first light the next morning and relieved the garrison at 09.45am. They remained there for a day, then White decided to return by the same route. On 26 July the Grey's and the Natal Troop attacked Umfula's kraal and killed over 40 rebels. Here they found property belonging to people murdered by the rebels, recovering 500 head of cattle belonging to the murdered Nortons and Henry Grant of Altona farm in the Charter district. They arrived back in Salisbury on 28 July. (Source: *Rhodesiana*. Publication No 3, 1958. Pub by The Rhodesiana Society)

Honours and Awards granted for the Bulawayo Field Force in the Matabele Rebellion of 1896

Below are the Honours and Awards gained by the BFF during their brief existence (25 March 1896 – 4 July 1896). Strangely, not one member of the Afrikander Corps appears to have been awarded a distinction, despite their gallant conduct throughout. Without them, the situation in the country may well have suffered a different and more tragic outcome.

The Victoria Cross

Trooper Herbert Stephen Henderson was born at Hillhead, Glasgow, on 30 March 1870. The son of an engineer he was educated at Kelvinside Academy in Hillhead and served his apprenticeship with J & J Thompson Engineers. He then moved to Belfast where he worked for Harland & Wolf. In 1892 he left for the Rand Goldmines in South Africa and worked there for two years. In 1894 he moved to Rhodesia and became manager of Queen's Mine. At the outbreak of the Matabele Rebellion he joined the Bulawayo Field Force initially as a scout then as an artillery gunner. His Victoria Cross citation reads as follows:

> *London Gazette*, May 7, 1897: 'H.S. Henderson, Bulawayo Field Force. On the morning of 30 March 1896 just before daylight Captain MacFarlane's party was surprised by natives. Troopers Celliers and Henderson, who formed part of the advance guard, were cut off from the main body and Celliers was shot through the knee. His horse was also badly wounded and eventually died. Henderson then placed Celliers on his own horse and made the best of his way to Bulawayo. The country between Campbell's store, where they were cut off and Bulawayo (a distance of 35 miles) was full of natives fully armed and they had, therefore, to proceed principally at night, hiding in the bush at daytime. Celliers, who was weak from loss of blood and in great agony, asked Henderson to leave him, but he would not, and brought him in, after passing two days and one night in the veld without food.'

Henderson passed away on 10 August 1942. He is buried in Bulawayo cemetery in a grave unmarked but for the number 887.

Trooper Frank William Baxter was born at Croydon, England on 29 December 1869. He arrived in South Africa in 1887 and attested into the British South Africa Company Police on 21 September 1890. He was alocated Service No. 290 and posted to 'A' Company. He went with the Pioneer Column to Rhodesia in that year. In 1891 he took his discharge and went prospecting. He ended up owning Nellie's Reef gold mine eighty kilometres from Bulawayo as well as property in Umtali, Rhodesia's border town with Portuguese East Africa. Additionally he had shares in various syndicates and companies. At the outbreak of the Matabele Rebellion he immediately joined Grey's Scouts.

His posthumous Victoria Cross award was granted eleven years after the event and its Recommendation Memorandum of 1897. His Victoria Cross citation reads as follows:

London Gazette, January 15, 1907: Trooper William Baxter of the Bulawayo Field Force, on account of his gallant conduct in having, on 22 April 1896, dismounted and gave up his horse to a wounded comrade, Corporal Wise, who was being closely pursued by an overwhelming force of the enemy.[1]

John Vollaire in Vol 1 of his *The History of Rhodesian Honours and Awards 1890-1980* noted one of Lynn Lyster's poems from Ballads of the Veld (Pub 1913) and directed at the anti-colonial lobby 'back Home':

On you at home in Britain with friends on Afric's veld,
Should lie a debt of Honour; and obligation felt
To guard your distant kinsmen from slander's coward blows
The cruel fabrications and vaporizing of those
Who prate of what they know not; the burden of whose song
is ... The native wears a halo and the Settler's always wrong.
When you hear them ranting libels will you bid them heed their ways,
And listen to the story of Baxter, late of the Grey's

Baxter is buried in Bulawayo cemetery, grave No 114. There is no mention of the VC on his tombstone. The distinction was, however, added to his name on the Matabeleland War Memorial in Bulawayo. With the advent of black rule in Rhodesia, now Zimbabwe, the ruling ZANU PF government of Robert Mugabe ordered the Memorial removed.

The most distinguished Order of Saint Michael and Saint George.
(From page 149 of '*The '96 Rebellions*'.)

The Queen has been graciously pleased to give directions for the above appointment to:
William Napier, Esq, Colonel of the Matabeleland Field Force. To be Companion of the said Most Distinguished Order.

John Anthony Spreckly, Esq. Colonel of the Matabeleland Field Force.To be Companion of the said Most Distinguished Order.

Recommendations for Conspicuous Gallantry in Action
(The recommendations below have been extracted from *The '96 Rebellions* pp144 – 158.)

Lieutenant E C Windley, BFF, 22nd April 1896, went back to the assistance of Captain Selous who was surrounded by the enemy, his horse having run away. Windley brought Selous out safely, closely pursued the whole time by the Matabele.

Lieutenant F H Crewe, Grey's Scouts, BFF, 22 April 1896, turned back for Trooper Hook who had lost his horse and was wounded, gave up his own horse to Hook, running on foot himself till knocked down by the enemy who were in close pursuit. He was rescued in turn by Trooper Lester.

Trooper Lester, Grey's Scouts, BFF, 22 April 1896, came to the assistance of Crewe, who was dismounted and hotly pursued by the Matabele. Lester gave up his horse to Crewe and escaped

---

1   The original Memorandum of Recommendation of 7 May 1897 has the same text as above but ends with, ' ... would have been recommended for the Victoria Cross had he survived.'

himself, being taken up on his horse by Captain Grey. (Note: Trooper Lester was awarded the medal for distinguished conduct in the field and a gratuity of £5.)

Captain G Grey, BFF, 22 April 1896, assisted Trooper Baxter after this man had lost his horse. Also, although wounded, he took up Trooper Lester on his horse when closely pursued by the Matabele.

Lieutenant Sinclair, BFF, 22 May 1896, picked up Trooper Rothman who had fallen from his horse mortally wounded, and put him on his own horse and carried him out of the action (two miles) under heavy fire.

Sergeant Farley, BFF, 6 June 1896, gave up his horse to Trooper Combrink who had been knocked off his horse and stunned, and would have been killed, as the enemy were within a few yards of him. (Note: Sergeant Farley was awarded the medal for distinguished conduct in the field and a gratuity of £5.)

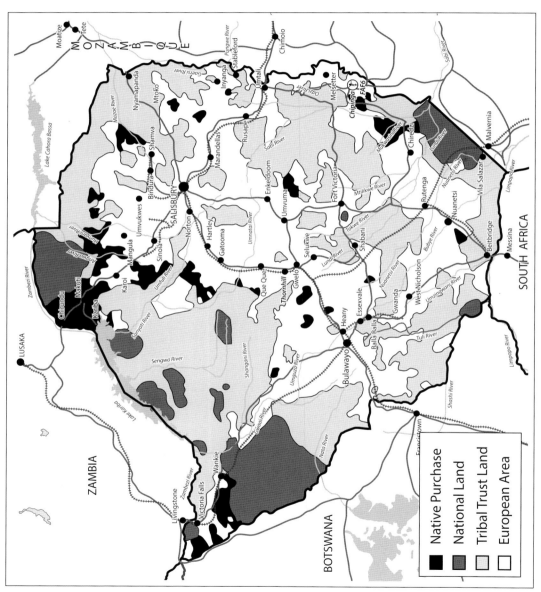

Map showing the Tribal Trust Lands in Rhodesia in the 1970s. (George Anderson)

2

Rhodesia 1975–76

Seventy-nine years after the Matabele Rebellion, Rhodesia once again had her back to the wall. In the intervening years the country and its people had come a long way. They had participated in the two major world wars of the 20th century in support of their mother country and had emerged from both conflicts with an enviable record. The combined talents of the black and white population had built a prosperous and energetic nation. The whites had contributed their technical and administrative skills whilst the blacks had provided their labour. For the most part, there existed a large reservoir of goodwill between them. Both peoples had multiplied, the Africans markedly so, thanks to the European introduction of medicine, peace, agricultural and industrial development. By 1975 the population numbered some 7,000,000 of which, due to the Rhodesian policy of selective immigration, just over 250,000 were whites.

After the Second World War, Britain looked at the map of her global empire and decided it was unsustainable. She reckoned that her future lay with Europe, despite the fact that this meant dealing with people she had never trusted and who had been her traditional enemies. But her political leaders were optimistically self-indulgent and socialist in outlook. They were very keen to embark on their European adventure. This meant they would have to abdicate their imperial responsibilities by getting rid of the empire as quickly as possible. In their post-war euphoria they began to dismember it willy-nilly. Australia, Canada and New Zealand, whose native populations had been virtually wiped out by the British settlers, could not be handed back to the few surviving natives. India, Africa, the West Indies, Malaysia etc. however, presented a different aspect as the natives in these territories constituted majority populations above the settlers. In addition these countries were all now clamouring for independence. Gradually, from the late 1940s onwards, these countries were granted independence whether they were ready for it or not. With the removal of colonial government, most of these countries, particularly the African ones, became one-party states and very rapidly descended into poverty, political instability and mediaeval barbarity. The present state of the African continent is plain for all to see. It is the direct and tragic result of the West's policy of handing power over to peoples who were not ready for it.

Southern Rhodesia had been a self-governing colony since 1923. Her white rulers viewed the changes now taking place on their continent with growing alarm. They repeatedly requested that Britain grant them the independence it had promised. The mother country refused on the grounds that the colony was ruled by a government maintained by the white minority population. The white Rhodesians rebelled and, on 11 November 1965, their elected leader, Ian Smith, defiantly declared the country unilaterally independent. The black nationalists in the country very soon reacted by exhorting the native population to take up arms against the 'illegal and racist' white regime.

The stage was now set for a 15-year bloody conflict.

The black nationalists and their military arms were divided as follows:

- ZANU (Zimbabwe African National Union). A predominantly Mashona party headed by Robert Mugabe and backed by China. Its military arm was ZANLA (Zimbabwe National Liberation Army). Host and harbouring country: Mozambique.

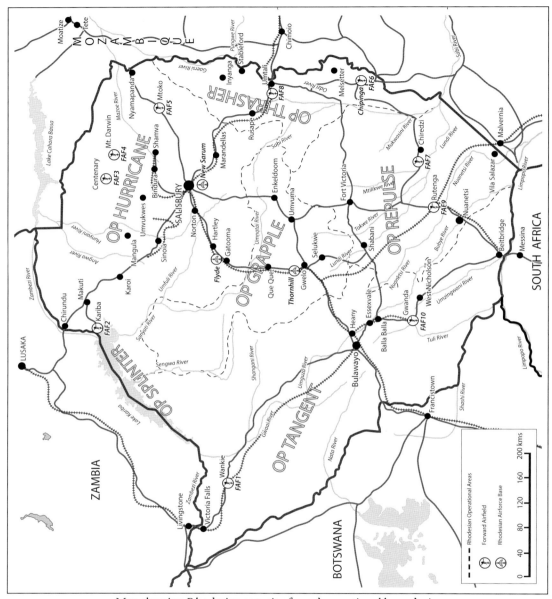

Map showing Rhodesian security forces' operational boundaries.
Operation Hurricane opened in December 1972; Operation Thrasher in February
1976; Operation Repulse in May 1976; Operation Tangent in August 1976; Operation
Grapple in 1978 and Operation Splinter in October 1978. (George Anderson)

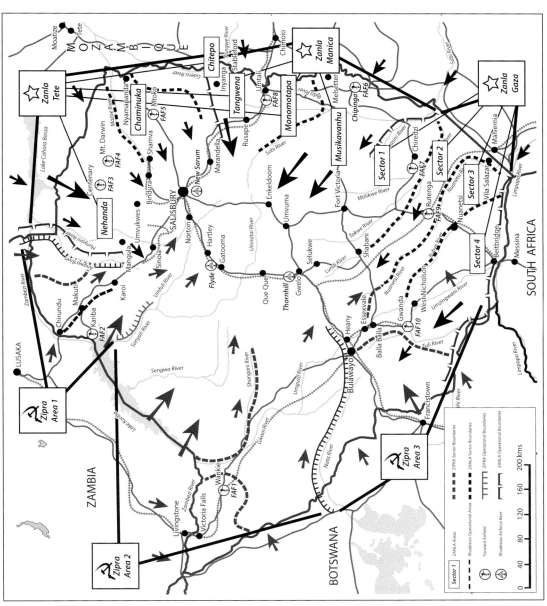

ZANLA/ZIPRA infiltration routes and operational boundaries. (George Anderson)

- ZAPU (Zimbabwe African Peoples Union). Predominantly Ndebele headed by Joshua Nkomo and supported by Russia. Its military arm was ZIPRA (Zimbabwe People's Revolutionary Army). Host and harbouring country: mainly Zambia.

After their military defeats of the 1960s both organisations paused to re-assess their strategies. For ZANU this meant that her strategy had to change from an unsuccessful policy of direct military confrontation with the well-trained Rhodesian security forces. Their Chinese mentors taught that success could only come by first gaining the active and passive support of the population. It was a Maoist strategy and required that the outlying rural population be politicised (brought on sides by subversion) first before the armed struggle could successfully attempt to paralyze the main opposition in the centre. By 1972 ZANU had, through ZANLA, by intimidation, torture and murder, significantly subverted the Shona tribes folk of north-eastern Rhodesia. Then, believing itself ready, it resumed its armed struggle in December 1972 by attacking Altena Farm in the Centenary District of north-east Rhodesia. This was, for them, the beginning of the final stages of 'Chimurenga' – the War of Liberation. To this end they opened up three operational sectors from their Tete operational headquarters – code-named, north to south as: 'Nehanda', 'Chaminuka' and 'Chitepo'.

The Rhodesian security forces were completely taken by surprise. They found that grass-roots intelligence from the locals had suddenly dried up. Land mines became a daily travel hazard and casualties began to mount. The north-eastern border area of the country became an operational zone code-named 'Operation Hurricane', opened up in direct response to ZANLA's Tete offensive. But the Rhodesians were nothing if not fighters. They reacted by changing their tactics. They knew they had to beat the enemy at his own game. To this end they created the Selous Scouts pseudo operations unit. The Scouts, posing as insurgents, were able to mingle with the enemy, find out where he was based and what he was about. Then, at the appropriate moment, they would call in conventional helicopter-borne security forces that would eliminate the enemy group. The Rhodesians also created the Rhodesian Intelligence Corps (RIC) and the Psychological Operations Unit (POU). To deny the insurgents their vital grass-roots support, the tribes people were moved into Protected Villages (PVs) manned by Internal Affairs national servicemen and (later) given extra security by the Guard Force which was formed in 1976.

By far the most innovative, unique and successful combat tactic developed by the Rhodesian Army was the Fireforce concept.

The Rhodesians had, since the operations of the 1960s, established the Joint Operations Command (JOC) system. These were commanded by the senior military officer in the particular operational area. In the early days of Operation Hurricane, this was either at Bindura or Centenary. Here an allocation of infantry troops, usually RLI or RAR, would be based alongside helicopter support. On receiving notification of a terrorist group from the Selous Scouts or an OP, troops would deploy to the area in helicopters and engage the enemy on the ground. Very soon it was discovered that the idea, though excellent, required refining. What eventually evolved was a combat system which, in January 1974, was named Fireforce. It required an optimum of four helicopters crewed by a pilot and an airtech/gunner. One of these aircraft would be the command helicopter armed with a 20mm cannon and known as the Kcar (K=Killer). The remaining three were troop-carrying gunships known as Gcars (G=Gunship); each armed, initially with a single mounted 7.62 calibre MAG (later two were mounted in parallel and finally quads, all 7.62 MAGs). These each ferried a stick of four infantrymen for deployment into the contact area. One of soldiers was armed with an MAG to give the stick greater firepower on the ground.

On call-out to a terrorist sighting, the Fireforce commander in the Kcar, usually (but not always) a major, would initiate the contact by marking the insurgent position with smoke or cannon fire. The Gcars would drop the four-man sticks around the area as stop groups or sweeps. These would engage the enemy and eliminate them. The process was known as vertical envelopment and it proved, 90% of the time, to be absolutely lethal.

If a large enemy group was engaged the Gcars would ferry in further troops. Additionally the troops at base would move by vehicle to the contact area as reinforcements and resupply. In a later development a Dakota could bring in a further 16 paratroops. A Lynx (Cessna) could be called in to attack the insurgent position using Sneb rockets.

Fireforces operated, mainly, from what were known as Forward Airfields. There were, eventually, ten of these:

- FAF1 – Wankie
- FAF2 – Kariba
- FAF3 – Centenary
- FAF4 – Mount Darwin
- FAF5 – Mtoko
- FAF6 – Chipinga
- FAF7 – Chiredzi
- FAF8 – Grand Reef
- FAF9 – Mabalauta
- FAF10 – Gwanda

By mid-1975 the Rhodesians' new tactics had been so successful that fewer than 300 insurgents remained in the country – most of them on the run. But politics, as usual, was to turn success into failure. The Portuguese *coup d'état* of 1974 resulted in the new socialist Portuguese government handing over Mozambique to an unelected Frelimo government headed by Samora Machel who was only too ready to help and harbour ZANLA. Additionally, John Vorster, South Africa's Prime Minister, had decided at the end of 1974 to engage in *détente* with the leaders of the so-called frontline black states of Zambia, Tanzania, Mozambique, Botswana and Angola in a bid to end the Rhodesian problem. What he proposed was this: if the Rhodesian Nationalists united under the moderate Bishop Abel Muzorewa, a political settlement with the whites would come about. When this happened they (the Frontline States) in turn would officially recognize South Africa's Government. To enable this to come about, Smith was co-erced by Vorster (i.e., if you don't we will cut off your petrol and ammunition) to release all the detained nationalists and the Rhodesian security forces would observe a cease-fire.

The now free Mugabe and Nkomo refused to contemplate anything of the sort, and the security forces' enforced inactivity gave their guerrillas the opportunity to re-establish themselves amongst the tribal population by pointing out that this meant that they had won the war. Vorster's plan had failed but the miscalculation had signalled the beginning of his ditching of Rhodesia in this bid to buy time for his own country.

After this the Americans entered the 'Rhodesian Settlement' arena. Henry Kissinger met Smith and laid down the minimum terms demanded by the world. Basically what he told Smith was that, unless he accepted the principle of majority rule, the West would stand by if the Soviet Bloc decided to intervene with major military force in Rhodesia. As a result of this Smith, in September 1976, informed his people that his government had accepted the establishment of majority rule within two years.

A Unit re-born

In Rhodesia, after ten years of internationally imposed economic sanctions, fuel had become a rationed commodity. For the army, furthermore, the insurgent landmine offensive was taking a severe toll on

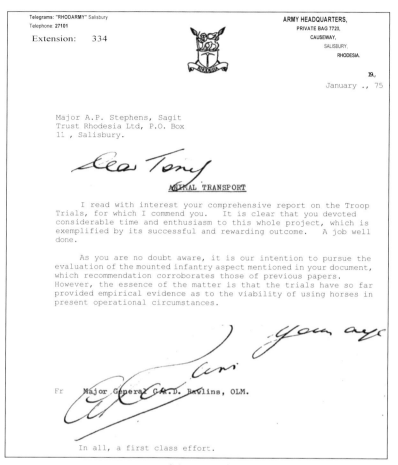

Formation of the ATU. (Alex Binda)

its soft-skinned vehicles, resulting in increasing troop casualties in an irreplaceable and incredibly thin front line. Rhodesian talent for improvisation was operating at full speed – and on overtime – devising, designing and constructing mine-proofed vehicles and evolving mine-detecting techniques. Border control patrolling was still conducted mostly on foot assisted by limited aerial reconnaissance. The need to include any other swifter and practical method of bush mobility in a technically advanced age was needed, no matter how archaic it appeared.

Sometime in the early 1970s Captain Bruce Rooken-Smith, then G3 (Ops&SD) at Rhodesian Army Headquarters was instructed by Colonel John Shaw (Col G) to 'knock up a paper' about a mounted infantry unit. Rooken-Smith assumed he was chosen for this task because, like Shaw, he was ex-British cavalry (Shaw had been Horse Guards and Rooken-Smith had served with the 17/21st Lancers).

Rooken-Smith, after much scratching around, unearthed a Portuguese newspaper cutting about mounted infantry operations in Angola. Armed with this he visited the BSAP HQ seeking further information on the subject. He extracted as much as he could and wrote the paper which he then put forward. The concept was then shelved until in 1974 Captain Alexander 'Beaver' Fraser-Kirk, a Services Corps officer, with the blessing of Army HQ, re-activated it under the provisional title of 'Animal Tranport Unit' (ATU). Fraser-Kirk, in truth, may be said to have originated the re-birth of the Grey's Scouts Regiment.

The unit was to be based near the Corps Training Depot (formerly Inkomo Garrison) 50 kilometres north-west of Salisbury. This location was ideal as Inkomo was on the line of rail, a necessary requirement for horse troop transportation. Additionally, troop pay administration could be effected from the CTD Pay Office. The ATU was allocated a fine 2,000 fenced and watered acres belonging to Mr. D C 'Boss' Lilford.[1] As an aside we can note here that, also nearby and to the east of the CTD, the newly-formed Selous Scouts were busy building their own barracks. The author, at this time, was serving as their 'Goldfinger' (paymaster). The Selous Scouts' camp was eventually named Andre Rabie Barracks. The ATU camp would later be named Umgusa Barracks after the battle area in which George Grey and his Scouts had fought so bravely in 1896.

Major Tony Stephens, a former RLI officer and, prior to that, a National Service officer with the Irish Guards, was appointed the new unit's first OC.

Fraser-Kirk and Stephens conducted a tentative trial in late 1974 with the embryo unit being provisionally titled 'Animal Transport Unit'. Greatly encouraged by the results and the unit's long-term possibilities, they reported their findings to Army Headquarters. On 25 January 1975 Stephens and Fraser-Kirk were pleased to receive a reply in the form of an approving official notification from 'Q' Branch's Major General G A D Rawlins.

Army Headquarters in Salisbury then followed this up with a signal to all Rhodesian Army units to the effect that volunteers were being sought for the formation of a mounted unit. One of the units notified was 4 (Independent) Company, The Rhodesia Regiment, consisting of national servicemen of Intake 140, based in Victoria Falls.[2] Intake 140 had recently completed their basic training at Llewellin Barracks in Bulawayo and at Gwelo's School of Infantry. From their base at Victoria Falls they would be deployed, initially, on six weeks border control operations. This involved patrolling the Rhodesian-Zambian border area along the Zambezi from the top end of Lake Kariba in the east to Kazungula to the west. The Company CSM (Company Sergeant Major), an RLI Warrant Officer, fell the Company in and barked out: 'Who wants to shovel donkey shit?'

He then proceeded to tell them that volunteers were being sought for a 'mounted mortar platoon'. Standing in the ranks was a young Keith Allan. He listened to this proclamation with interest. This was mainly because his national service commitment was due to end in July. This new unit was based near Salisbury. Allan knew how to ride so reckoned to himself that, if he could wangle a posting to this new unit, he could enjoy his weekends in Salisbury where his girlfriend lived. He approached the CSM about wanting to join the new unit and was promptly told: 'Fuck off. We need section commanders here to do real soldiering.'

At this rebuff Allan resigned himself to serving the rest of his commitment at Victoria Falls. Some weeks later, however, whilst deployed on patrolling along the Zambezi, he was recalled back to base where he found out that he was being posted to Inkomo to join the 'mounted mortar platoon'. The CSM had a soul somewhere …

When he arrived at Inkomo all he found was what appeared to be an abandoned farm. There was a small wooden shed and a number of large paddocks containing a range of motley-looking horses. There was tented sleeping and mess accommodation in a paddock sited alongside the dirt access road. He joined five other volunteers – all RLI. He also met Captain Beaver Fraser-Kirk and a TA riding instructor from Lewisham Riding School. He was told that he was joining a mounted infantry unit not a mounted mortar platoon.

The TA instructor initially attempted to teach them the niceties of horsemanship, i.e., riding school style – heels down, hands held just so, etc. Fraser-Kirk saw very quickly that this method would take a lot longer than the allotted six weeks and had a word with the instructor. The upshot

---

1   Lilford was a major behind-the-scenes power figure of Ian Smith's Rhodesian Front Party.

2   At this stage National Service was only 12 months. One infantry company was raised from each intake.

was that a handful of essentials would be taught at this stage: turning the horse right, left, stop and go at variable speeds. During this training the riders had to somehow stay in the saddle. It was during this period that the term 'buying a plot' came into use. The phrase was used when a rider had an involuntary dismount and ended up lying face down on the dusty ground whilst his mount trotted off with stirrups bouncing and reins trailing in the dirt. Very soon afterwards they were taught how to steer the horse with one hand (neck reining) as the other was required to carry a rifle. Along with this they learnt how to saddle up, groom and clean hooves. Allan remembers that the horses had come up from South Africa. Many were found to be unsuitable and a few died as a result of poor health.

Sometime in April about 30 TA soldiers arrived for a six week mounted infantry trial. To the twenty-year-old Allan they were 'older' guys many of them in their late twenties. Most were Rhodesian Afrikaners who farmed in the country's eastern districts. It was soon apparent that they were expert horsemen. Allan recalls:

> I don't remember any of them being the 'jolly old hockey sticks' or 'gin and pinkers' types such as our recent TA instructor. These guys were mostly polo crosse players and polo players. A lot of them brought along their own horses. One of them had a beautiful thoroughbred former racehorse called Fireship. What these men brought with them was tremendous enthusiasm. They were very determined to make the experiment work. They had both the skills and the aggression to make the goal achievable. They were certainly keen to kill terrs!

During this tentative five week trial period they discovered and dealt with the following issues:

1. When tying up a horse for the night it had to be kept on a short rope. If this was longer than the length of the animal it would inevitably get caught up in its legs during a panic and cause rope burns.
2. Rifle scabbards were tried out and discarded virtually immediately. This was because, in the event of a contact, if the rider 'bought a plot' the horse would disappear with his weapon. The universal Grey's Scout mounted armed stance henceforth depicted a rider with his rifle held by the stock and the butt resting between hip and groin.
3. Tracking from horseback was quicker than on foot.
4. The animals panicked when live firing was attempted. This was partly resolved by firing off rounds during feeding time. The animals then began to associate firing with food and the problem lessened.
5. Transportation of the horses was initially envisaged as problematical. The solution finally arrived at was to heighten the sides of the standard army Bedford RL 3-tonner. Longer tail boards were added to be used as ramps. The animals were then loaded on to stand side by side and nose to tail. It was, however, essential that the vehicle was fully loaded or the horses would fall over. Allan writes that, after this innovation, actually loading the beasts on to the vehicle was not easy. Some of the animals could be really stubborn and would baulk at the steep ramp. With time, however, they adapted.
6. Nose bags were brought in and discarded. Different numnahs (saddle blankets) were trialled, including the standard army issue soldier's blanket – the blanket was used on the horse during the day and for the rider to sleep under at night.

After this the TA members left and the few men at the unit marked time. Everyone was waiting for Army HQ's official approval for the formation of their MIU (Mounted Infantry Unit). Allan remembers:

We didn't do guard duty or have muster parades at this early stage while Army HQ slowly processed the paperwork. We spent every night in Salisbury. In camp our brief, for the time being, was to keep the horses fit. To this end we would saddle up our favourite horses and herd those remaining around the paddocks at Inkomo. This was usually done at the full gallop. We got so blasé about this that we took to riding bareback. In a very short while we became completely comfortable with this. This actually made me realise that balance was far more important than holding on with your legs when it came to staying on the horse.

Keith Allan had enjoyed a peaceful national service which ended in July. This time of relative ease, for the Rhodesia Army, was also ending – the enemy were about to launch the next phase of 'Chimurenga' (Liberation War) ...

On a day in early June 1975, Roy Elderkin, a former bombardier in the British Army and now an employee of Lilford's, was ordered to go and remove some fencing on the land. When he arrived he was surprised to see a score of horses grazing nearby. He then saw Fraser-Kirk who immediately informed him that no f – – – fences were to be removed. The curious Elderkin then inquired as to the presence of the horses. Fraser-Kirk told him that the plan was to establish a MIU. He then asked Elderkin if he knew about horses. The 34 year-old Elderkin replied that he had once been a driver rider in the King's Royal Horse Artillery (RHA) and had some training experience. Fraser-Kirk must have noted the comment because a few days later Elderkin was approached by the unit's OC, Major Tony Stephens, and asked to join the army as an equitation instructor. The upshot of the approach was that on 16 June Elderkin attested into the regular army as a staff corps sergeant.

Elderkin then discovered that this embryo unit already contained a handful of regulars – SAS Sergeant Nick Jooste who was the only professional senior NCO in the unit at that time and very involved in developing tactics, Corporal, The Right Honourable Mark Wrottesley, 'Sharkey' Dwinger, both RLI,(Rhodesian Light Infantry) and Tubby Clarke.

The unit had been given a limited amount of set-up money and some help with equipment, tentage and messing facilities. The only building was the wooden shed already mentioned in which horse feed was kept.

In September the designation of Animal Transport Unit (ATU) fell away and the unit was re-named the Mounted Infantry Unit (MIU). Stephens and Fraser-Kirk along with their small group of volunteers now had the task of transforming the MIU into a formal teeth arms formation of the Rhodesia Army.

A beginning was made. During the second half of 1975 stable blocks, messes and an HQ Block were erected. This meant they could move out of the tents. Some African civilian staff were also employed to help with cooking and feeding the horses. While this was happening, the first batch of horses arrived from South Africa. They came via Eric Stock of Bulawayo and had been purchased with funds donated by the South African branch of the Friends of Rhodesia Society. The animals were Boerperdes[3] and came from the Colesburg and Newcastle districts. There would be more to follow. Boerperdes are incredibly hardy animals. They descend from the Arab and Barbary horses imported into South Africa during the 17th century by the Dutch East India Company. These animals mingled with other horse breeds over the years (they even mixed with some of the Australian Walers that were brought over during the Boer War). All this crossbreeding had resulted in an uncosseted animal which, by the end of the 19th century, was totally acclimatised to the arid and inhospitable landscape of central South Africa. It is one of the toughest and bravest horses in the world and can carry a full-grown man for over 100 kilometres a day. It has a strong shoulder and is amazingly sure-footed. Its maximum height is 15.8 hands; Elderkin says that anything bigger would not have been suitable. In character the Boerperde is known to be fearless and extremely self-reliant.

---

3   Boer horses.

As far as the MIU were concerned, the horses had to be 'salted' (i.e., not susceptible to African horse sickness). To this end blood samples were collected before the animals came into Rhodesia. The horses had to be tested for durin (a social disease in horses) before a vet certificate could be issued. Elderkin recollects that the documentation of all the horses followed the same recording system as used by the South African Defense Force.

On the inside page we gave the description of the horse, markings, socks, blazes, scars, tattoos etc. The animal was described with the height and colour recorded. Every horse has a whorl on its forehead. It is particular to the individual animal and no two horses have the same whorl. This is akin to a fingerprint on a human and is used in horseracing as an identification aid. Each was then allocated a number, this being branded on the foot (freeze branding was later introduced to avoid the numbers growing out). Here Tony Stephens apparently used George Grey's numbering nominal roll and continued it on from the last number of 1896! Dr Richard Smith, a local vet, became the unit's first Veterinary Officer and inoculated all the animals for horse sickness and tetanus. He was later commissioned as a Territorial Army (TA) Major and was the unit's senior Vet Officer. "Every animal was given a full physical examination by Major 'Doc' Smith and me. Every horse was inoculated for tetanus and horse sickness, after which a medical certificate was issued" says Elderkin 'It really was one of the most comprehensive and detailed recordings ever undertaken by anyone.'

Tony Stephens added:

With the aid of modern veterinary science it was possible to keep disease to a minimum. This enabled horses to operate in areas where, in the past, they could not have survived. Willing veterinary officers, mainly Territorial Army officers and members of the unit, launched into a massive research programme designed to improve the health and use of the horse in the field. This research included blood chemistry which provides for a blood cell monitoring system prior to a horse being deployed on operations. A blood sample is taken from each horse and the haemoglobin level of the blood determines that the animal is not only visibly fit, but is also clinically sound and not suffering from internal parasites such as worms which could detract from its operational efficiency. Once the programme was started the "breakdown" rate on operations became negligible.

Farriers too play a vital role in the unit, making sure that patrols can be switched from soft going to hard rough country at a moment's notice without going lame. To ensure that this is the case all the unit's horses are shod. Hot shoeing is the order of the day, even in bush base camps, with each horse being re-shod on an average of once a month.

Stephens noted additionally:

The British South Africa Police, who gave up mounted patrols in the early 1960s in favour of motor-cycle and Land Rover patrols, are now following in the "hoofprints" of the Grey's and now have a mounted Support Section. This welcome addition to the 'Equine Strike Force' has been mainly engaged on anti-cattle rustling operations – a major source of food supply to the terrorist ...

All members joining the unit were volunteers. Initially there was no farrier or quartermaster and the unit was composed of a small force of regulars (TA members would come later). All had to be combat-trained and able to ride as, at this stage, there was no time to teach anyone the basics. 'All this' writes Elderkin, 'Saved a lot of time and these regulars became troop leaders. As they were all volunteers we were able to put together a well-formed troop ... '

Initial unit trials would be conducted in Chipinga which is in the mountainous eastern border region of south-eastern Rhodesia, and not far from a now very hostile Mozambique. Before this, however, various items of equipment were looked into. Firstly, the flat-soled SAS boot replaced the DMS boot which was not suitable for quick release from stirrup irons. Canvas saddle bags were introduced and placed over the saddle's rear arch, plus a canvas bucket which could be used as a water bucket then turned inside out for use as a feed bucket.

The troops themselves were to use the buddy-buddy SAS system when basing up (i.e., 'don't eat where you sleep, and don't eat where you slept'). Sleeping bags were tied behind the saddle. Taking a page from the Boer War book, the weight carried by the rider would not exceed forty pounds which included weapons and saddlery. Each man carried two water bottles and had a change of clothes. Ammunition consisted of one hundred rounds of 7.62 ball for the rider's FN contained in five magazines.

The initial trial ran from 17 February to 10 March 1975. The unit was to proceed to Chipinga in the newly opened (February 1976) Operation Thrasher area and tasked with patrolling Rhodesia's south-eastern border with Mozambique. The Operation Thrasher operational area had been created to counter ZANLA's opening of three insurgent operational sectors from their Manica Headquarters named, north to south, 'Tangwena', 'Monomotapa' and 'Musikavanhu'. Operation Thrasher, with JOC (Joint Operational Command) Headquarters in Umtali, extended from the Salisbury-Nyamapanda road in the north to the Sabi-Turgwi Rivers in the south. In the short notice granted, Corporal Willie Venter, a farrier, attempted to shoe as many mounts as he could before the departure date. Also shortly before leaving, the unit received its first batch of saddles and bridles from the Friends of Rhodesia organisation. These saddles were to prove unsuitable and were a poor make of the SU (Soldier's Universal) saddle. The main fault was that the felt pads tended to roll off the swivel trees.

The horses were entrained into cattle trucks at Inkomo Siding – ten horses and two men per truck. From here they would leave for Umtali, Rhodesia's picturesque eastern border town. The wheeled transport, carrying the unit's usual requirements plus horse rations and hay, was made up of two Bedford five-tonners and a couple of Land-Rovers – not enough for what was required. Beaver Fraser-Kirk came up with a welcome horse box and a TA member, Rifleman Julian Sholtz, helped out with further transport.

At Umtali the unit camped at the Show Grounds. They then headed for Chipinga by road. There was a feeling of some apprehension amongst the men as both they and the animals were untried at this. Additionally several of the mounts were still unshod and many others were unfit.

The move was begun. The first stop was at the Melsetter turn-off. The following night they camped at Skyline which is at the Melsetter-Chipinga junction. The third night's stop was at Moodie's Farm and grave site. From here the unit would eventually base up at Chipinga and begin patrolling.

The Chipinga trials proved to be a success. Apart from border patrolling, one of the duties they performed was to provide security and resupply to the signals unit based up in a disused mining camp. This unit was setting up a radio listening station in the Sabi catchment area. The initial obvious advantage of mounted patrolling was speed. A mounted man could track a lot faster than conventional trackers. Vision was heightened as the rider could now see over the tall grass and scrub. Additionally, spoor could be seen better from the additional height and the horse's natural movement enabled troops to get closer to the enemy without detection. A bonus was that the animal's natural sound and scent attributes also let the rider, if he was in tune with his mount, know if 'something was up' close by. A great asset was a horse's almost 360 degree vision and an ability to pick up detail from over a kilometre away. These attributes could be an early warning to the rider who was 'as one' with his mount. On detecting the enemy, the mounted infantryman's immediate and speedy reaction into contact would have a psychological intimidating effect on the insurgents thus engaged. The sweep and follow-up after contact would be at the gallop for a short distance (trotting proved totally impractical). For the enemy, the sight of a mounted rifleman crashing through the jesse towards him was terrifying to say the least.

On the subject of tracking, we can note here Colonel DH Grainger's observations on the subject:

Tracking represents the ultimate in bush craft skills ... The first principles are:

1. Identification of the spoor and establishment of a definite starting point.
2. Flexibility and anticipation.
3. Sign interpretation before speed.
4. Preservation of the spoor.

Trackers work best in pairs, leapfrogging when the trail is faint, the man on the tracks keeping it until the spoor is lost or he is tired – and tracking is a tiring business – the man behind watching for tracks breaking to left or right. Should both lose the spoor, they will search the obvious spots for sign and, if unsuccessful, work in a complete circle (termed 'doing a 360') for a fresh lead in case the quarry has doubled back.

Things the tracker will look for are:

1. Footprints and impressions of footwear; the rhythm of the spoor or length of stride of the quarry, as a guide to where the next footprint can be found.
2. Trampled grass.
3. Disturbed stones, sticks or soil and cracks in the soil where indirect pressure may have left no impression.
4. Leaves turned, crushed, kicked or pulled off trees; branches and twigs bent or broken; vegetation pushed aside and the reflection of light from broken vegetation; scratched or chipped bark.
5. Discarded wrappings and masticated vegetation.
6. Cobwebs broken or obviously wiped off on the nearest tree or bush.
7. Urine and excrement, frequently indicated by houseflies, mopane flies, bees and yellow butterflies, and by dung beetles during the rains.
8. Snares and traps, robbed bees' nests and smoke.
9. Signs at fruit-bearing trees and observation points.
10. The state of dew on a trail.
11. Mud displacement from streams; mud or scratches on stones and logs.
12. Moss scraped from trees.
13. Disturbed game or birds; the spoor of running animals not disturbed by the tracker is often a good indication that other humans have been in the locality.[4]

On returning to Inkomo everyone was delighted to see that, during their absence, Army HQ had sent builders in to roof the stables. Colour Sergeant Bill Lewis, a farrier, had also arrived. Lewis, ordered to construct his own farrier shop, was allocated a tarpaulin, an anvil and a hand-turned forge. This last was changed to a proper brick-built forge complete with an electric fan which Elderkin purloined from his wife's washing machine. Colour Sergeant Bill Smudge Smith had joined the unit as Stable Manager. Smudge was a former member of the BSAP who, ironically, had previously taught

---

4   Colonel DH Grainger. *Don't die in the Bundu* pp73–75. Pub. Howard Timmins Cape Town, 1967. Grainger was a Rhodesian Army Officer. The book was prescribed reading for Rhodesian Army NCO promotion exams.

Elderkin to ride.

Since passing out as a national serviceman in the previous year, Keith Allan had been called up to the MIU several times as an 'A' Reserve Territorial Army member. He was a qualified land surveyor by profession. Taking advantage of this skill on one call up, the unit tasked him with setting up a polo crosse field! He doubts if it was ever used much as the military situation in the country was changing rapidly and dramatically. During 1976, most of the TA members of the unit spent their call ups (six weeks in, six weeks out) at Twiza which was on the line of rail from Gona-re-Zhou to Mozambique in the Operation Repulse area.

Training staff had also arrived headed by Colour Sergeant Don Kenny who had served in the British SAS, the Parachute Regiment and the Foreign Legion. Kenny was a quiet, tough and completely dedicated soldier. As a training instructor he set and demanded an extremely high standard. He became the unit's legendary disciplinarian and began the training of 'A' Squadron. Along with him came Colour Sergeant Aubrey Brookes, Bruno Rabie (brother of the late legendary Selous Scout, Andre Rabie), the SAS's Hennie Pretorius and, from New Zealand, Corporal Tony Jackson.

Another new arrival was the unit's first TA vet, Lieutenant Bill McGuire. His start at MIU was not the most auspicious – he went out on a ride and was scalped as he went under a tree branch. WO11 van Tonder, the medic, stitched him up after which McGuire was seen examining the result with a hand-held mirror. When van Tonder asked what the problem was McGuire replied 'I'm looking to check if you've stitched it up properly!'

The Chipinga trials showed that further items required altering and adjusting. These related to feed, saddles, webbing and shoeing. The first was resolved when Major Smith, Smudge, Elderkin and the rep from a major livestock feed company sat down and put together what became known as the MIU cube. When looking for a replacement for the unsuitable SU saddle, the unit managed to find an American cavalry saddle – the McClelland – which had a wooden tree. Gordon Johnson, a local saddler, looked at the McClelland and affirmed that the tree could be made from fibre glass. This solution proved to be the correct one as they now had a lighter, more hard-wearing saddle which was also easier to repair. The practical and imaginative Don Kenny resolved the webbing issue by introducing the one-piece vest/waistcoat Chinese-style chest webbing.

At this time the Rhodesian military engineers were establishing a *cordon sanitaire* – a wide minefield eventually running to 1400 kilometres – the full length of the border between Rhodesia and Mozambique. This has been described by Richard Wood, Rhodesia's premier political historian, as the greatest military obstacle outside of the Great Wall of China. The unit was approached by the engineers to help with the transportation of fence posts and barbed wire rolls over the rugged terrain. Roy Elderkin designed a way of carrying the items using Basutu ponies donated by farmers in the Orange Free State with pack saddles obtained from the BSAP.

Between late 1975 and mid 1976 the persistent Tony Stephens was in constant contact with the South African Friends of Rhodesia, trying to raise funds for the setting up of an indoor riding school for the unit. He was eventually successful and construction went ahead. The floor was made of a mixture of sand and rubber shavings, these last being donated by local tyre manufacturers from the tons of residue they had. The resulting surface proved ideal.

Lilford donated a block of pre-fabricated stables which were then sited behind the main block. Colour Sergeant Lewis, the unit's farrier, had somehow managed to find a stamping mill which meant the unit could now make its own shoes. Lewis had been joined by Corporal Willie Venter and, a little later, by Sergeant 'Rusty' Leggit.

The Rhodesian flag was set up in an anthill between the stable block and the HQ block. The anthill had initially been dug into. Colour Sergeant Nick Jooste poured some contaminated aviation fuel into the hole and set it alight. The resulting eruption resembled Vesuvius but it did bake the hill hard dry. The flagpole was the highest in Rhodesia until it was moved later to the new HQ block.

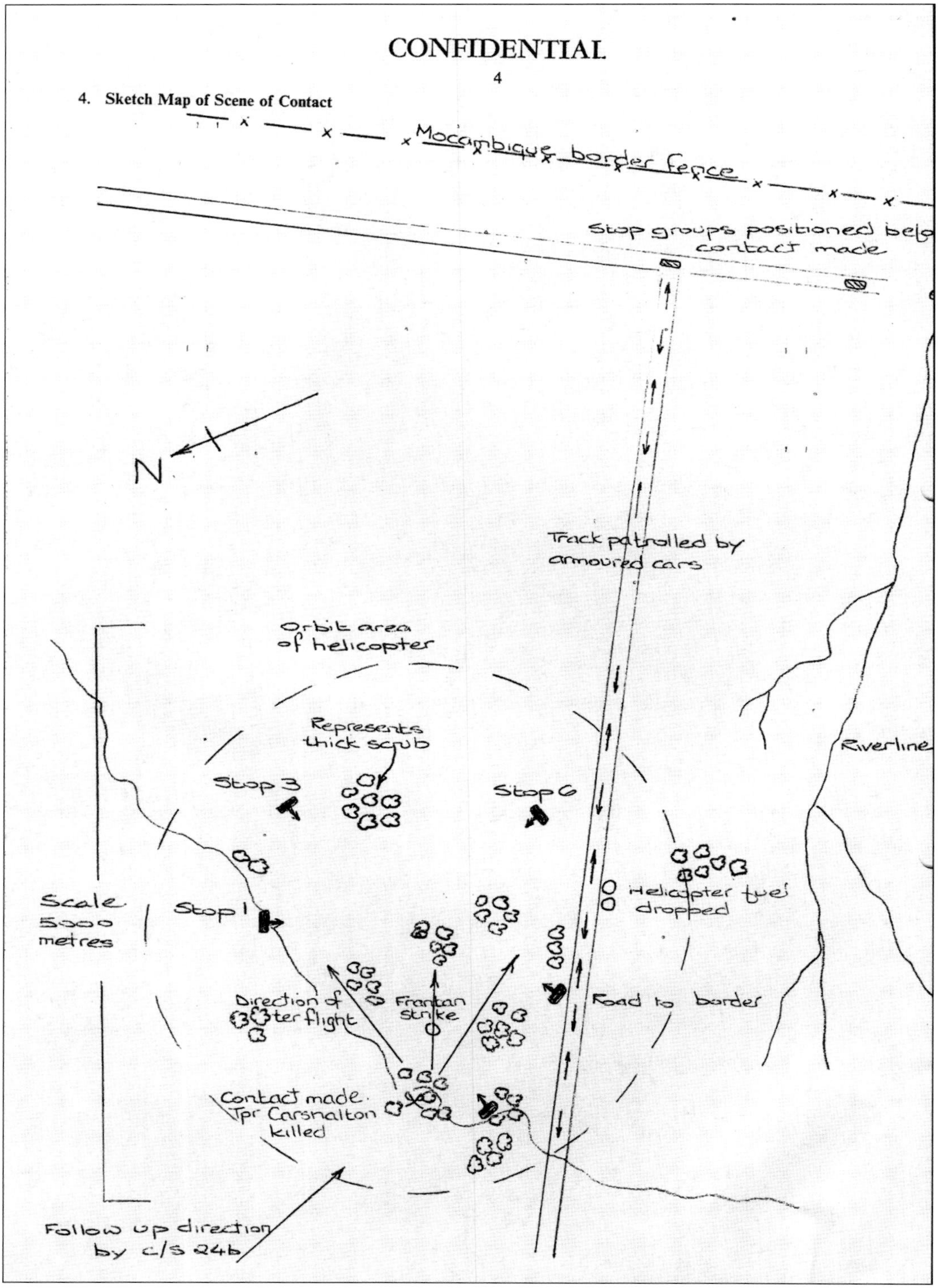

CONFIDENTIAL
4

4. **Sketch Map of Scene of Contact**

Moçambique border fence

Stop groups positioned before
contact made

N

Track patrolled by
armoured cars

Orbit area
of helicopter

Riverline

Represents
thick scrub

Stop 3   Stop 6

Helicopter fuel
dropped

Scale
5000
metres

Stop 1

Direction of
counter flight   Frantan
strike

Road to border

Contact made.
Tpr Carsnalton
killed

Follow up direction
by c/s 24b

Contact of 27 August 1976, Grey's Scouts. Lt R J A Passaportis's sketch.

A Unit Reformed

On 1 July 1976 the unit was officially renamed the Grey's Scouts and became part of the Rhodesian Army order of battle.

The unit's headdress was a grey beret with a cap badge depicting a horse bust within a light infantry horn beneath which were the words 'GREY'S SCOUTS'. This was issued only when recruits successfully completed training. A slouch hat was worn with the ceremonial 'greens' dress.

In Formation Order No 5 of the Rhodesian Corps of Infantry, the role of the Grey's Scouts was defined as:

1. Long range patrolling and reconnaissance of rural areas.
2. Tracking and follow-up on horseback.
3. Deep penetration in support of armoured cars.
4. To be prepared to act as dismounted infantry when required.

The unit was, initially and officially, made up of one squadron, i.e., 'A' Squadron (though there was also an unofficial 'B' Squadron in existence). Later, during 1977, it was able to field two squadrons, i.e., 'A' Squadron composed of regulars, with Don Kenny and 'B' Squadron which was composed of TA members.

From 1977 onwards, 'A' Sqn was made up of regulars, both officers and non-commissioned officers and national servicemen (conscripts). It comprised 1, 2 and 3 Troops. Each Troop numbered 24 men split into three 8-man 'sticks'. Each stick member was armed with the 7.62mm FN, the Rhodesia Army standard infantry weapon (later supplemented with G3s of identical calibre). 'B' Squadron members were territorials who were called up to serve a yearly commitment. By late 1977, early 1978, this commitment was six weeks in, six weeks out, making these men effectively into regulars in everything but name. From this we can see that each squadron had, theoretically, between 70 to 80 fighting men with a further 30 serving as farriers, vets, drivers, and signalers. Most of the drivers were black as were the trackers most of whom were Shangaan. The base staff at Umgusa Barracks at Inkomo had a further 40 or so personnel, not all of them men, who served as HQ staff, signalers, vets, farriers, horse handlers and training staff.

Section 2 of Chapter 4 of the Rhodesia Army COIN (Counter Insurgency) manual states that infantry

... will invariably be the dominant arm during ATOPS (Anti-Terrorist Operations) because:

1. The inherent characteristics of infantry make them ideally suited for employment on any unconventional task, under any circumstances, with or without the support of other arms.
2. The nature of operations, terrain, climate and the characteristics and tactics of an irregular enemy will often make the employment of these other arms tactically impracticable and uneconomical.

Section 4, however, devoted to the role of cavalry (and obviously referring to mounted infantry), declares:

1   **Characteristics**. Experience has taught us that cavalry can be effectively used in fairly open country to reach inaccessible and remote areas. The characteristics of cavalry are:

a.   **Radius of action**. An increased radius of action for patrols, especially where units have large areas of responsibility.

b.   **Speed**. Mounted patrols have greater speed than normal foot patrols.

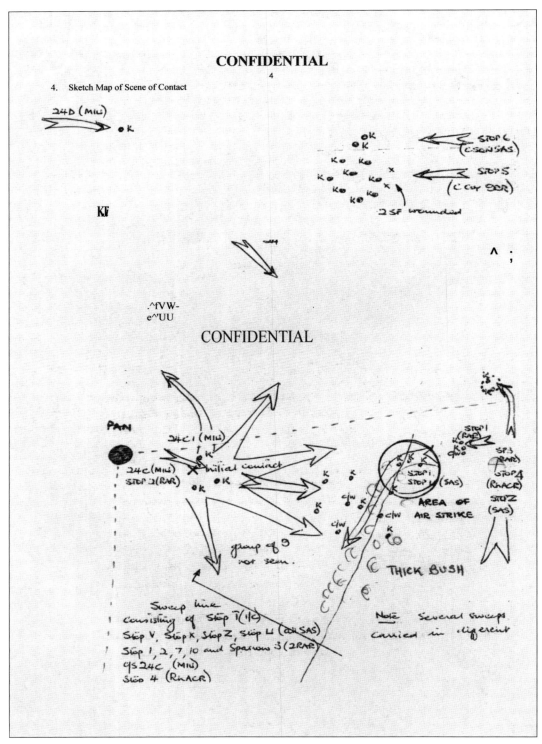

Contact of 30 September, Grey's Scouts. Major N G C Fawcett's sketch.

c. **Surprise**. The speed at which mounted patrols can move may lead to the achievement of surprise.

d. **Shock effect**. Speed of movement and surprise may have a shock effect on the enemy. This will result in a psychological effect on the enemy, especially if the mounted men are able to engage the enemy with fire while on the move.

e. **Ability to follow up**. Because of greater speed, mobility and endurance, mounted patrols have a better follow-up capability than troops on foot.

f. **Endurance**. Mounted patrols, with the addition of pack animals, can be self-supporting for periods of up to ten days. It must be borne in mind, however, that the addition of pack animals will reduce the speed and mobility of the mounted troops.

g. **Psychological effect** on local population. It is a generally accepted fact that a mounted man has a psychological advantage over a dismounted man.

h. **Dual role**. Depending on terrain and local conditions and the tactical requirement, cavalry units can be employed in the dismounted role. For example, the mounted unit can reach an area inaccessible to vehicles, etc., dismount and then carry out operations as a dismounted force.

i. **Adaptability to terrain**. The movement of mounted patrols need not necessarily be confined to roads, tracts, etc. They have the capability of moving rapidly over open terrain and with ease over most other types of terrain.

j. **Ability to sense danger**. The horses' instinct will often provide the rider with early warning of anything unusual.

k. **Carrying capabilities**. The horse is capable of carrying loads that are not usually carried by a man.

2. **Capabilities**. The capabilities of mounted patrols are as follows:

a. Mounted patrols can operate at distances of 150 to 250 kilometres with relative ease in most types of terrain.

b. These patrols can move at an average speed of six to seven kilometres per hour in most types of terrain.

c. Mounted patrols can be on the move for six to eight hours daily, giving a daily operational radius of approximately 30 to 50 kilometres. For maximum performance they should rest one day in four.

d. They can be self-supporting for periods of up to five days. This period can be increased up to ten days by making use of pack animals.

e. They are useful in capturing and/or rounding up scattered elements of the enemy or population.

3. **Limitations**. These are as follows:

a. Difficulty in moving through dense bush.

b. Difficulty in moving through marshy areas, swamps or muddy areas.

c. Slowness in crossing major water obstacles e.g. large rivers.

d. Increased logistical support of cavalry units because of quantities of fodder and water that have to be carried to provide for the horses.

e. Difficulty in maintaining silence. Natural horse noises, such as blowing through their nostrils and the jingle of equipment, make silent approach difficult.

f. Certain geographical areas may be denied to horse-mounted patrols because of certain animal diseases or sicknesses, e.g. areas of tsetse fly infestation.

Lynn Massyn – Miss South Africa 1976 & Grey's Scouts

Operational Log

In May 1976 the Rhodesians opened up a new operational area. This was Operation Repulse with JOC Headquarters in Fort Victoria. It was created to counter ZANLA's new front based in Mozambique's Gaza Province. ZANLA had numbered it simply, from north to south, as Sectors 1, 2, 3 and 4.

In August the Rhodesians opened up a further operational area code-named 'Operation Tangent'. A huge operational area extending from Panda-ma-tenga (a settlement some 45 kilometres from Matetsi on the Botswana-Rhodesia border) to Beit Bridge on the Limpopo River (the entry point into Rhodesia from South Africa). This was because the erstwhile comatose ZAPU were given an ultimatum by the OAU (Organisation for African Union) states to the effect that their funding would cease if ZAPU did not resume active participation in the Zimbabwe liberation struggle. Accordingly, ZIPRA, ZAPU's military wing, declared the area between Feira and Kariba as their 'ZIPRA Area 1', the vast Zambia-Botswana border area between Kariba and the Nata River as 'ZIPRA Area 2' and, from the Nata River to Beit Bridge (entry point into Rhodesia from South Africa), as 'ZIPRA Area 3'.

Grey's Scouts in Operation Hurricane

Towards the middle of 1976, both Squadrons of Grey's Scouts were operating in the Operation Hurricane area on a rotational basis.

At first light on 2 June, a stick of seven men from 'B' Squadron's 3 Troop left their base in the Kandeya TTL. Their brief was to patrol the TTL on a 'showing the flag' basis; for them it was the last day of this particular bush call-up after which they would return to base and hand over to the incoming Squadron. A young brown and white pointer, Gus, belonging to the sergeant, was along for the outing.

An hour later, as they moved through a *vlei*, Trooper Adrian Wymer spotted what looked to him to be a possible enemy camp in a nearby tree-covered anthill. He nudged his grey, Talley Ho, away from the stick for a closer look. When he was about ten metres from the anthill he was fired at from above. He immediately leapt out of the saddle, snapping his watch strap in the process. The remainder of the stick had also leaped off their startled mounts and had split into two sections returning fire as they moved forward. Wymer, at this stage, was more concerned about recovering his Seiko wristwatch than anything else. He put down his rifle, retrieved the watch and put it into his combat jacket which he carefully buttoned up. Talley Ho was standing before him and, fortunately for Wymer, was blocking him from enemy view. Recovering his presence of mind, Wymer reached up and took a white phosphorus grenade from the saddle bag. Before he could use it the enemy fired towards him again. Wymer saw, incredibly, a round actually pierce the horse's rein. Talley Ho, who had been standing patiently still up till then, suddenly turned about and made off. An RPD was now chattering away, churning up leaves and undergrowth in its search for the troops. Wymer saw one of the horses, the mare Shaleena, also begin to run off, moving awkwardly as she had been shot in the rump, the round going straight through. Aware of his exposed position Wymer jumped up, fired a quick five-round burst in the direction of the enemy camp, and then turned and ran for cover. As he sprinted he actually felt the shock wave from the enemy's RPD rounds hit his back. He made it to where his stick mate Dave Short was kneeling returning fire. The firefight went on for a while before the order to cease fire was given. Under covering fire from two flanks, one half-section began to move forward to assault the enemy position. When they had advanced a few metres they were fired at again. The troop sergeant and two troopers returned fire and were rewarded with a shrill scream from the enemy position. After a few moments, as everything had gone deadly silent, the stick charged the position and found it empty. The enemy had 'gapped it' (fled). The troops did a 360 degree sweep and found tracks which Wymer followed. He recalls ' … I continued to follow the spoor which led down to a *donga*.This was densely bushed with jesse but I found a very fresh half-eaten melon which must have been in the process of being consumed just as we arrived! I also found the boots that had made the tracks – made in Zagreb!'

The stick had been ambushed by a few insurgents, apparently a rear-guard for a larger group that had fled before the contact. The body of a dead insurgent was later recovered. It was the unit's first kill.

The wounded mare, with Gus trailing it, found its way to an Internal Affairs Keep about two kilometres away. 'The mare' says Wymer, 'made a full recovery and eventually produced a foal.'

Grey's Scouts in Operation Repulse

On the morning of 27 August 1976, in the thick *mopani* (pronounced as moparnie) woodland veldt of the Matibi No2 TTL (Tribal Trust Land), Grey's Scouts c/s (call-sign) 24B led by Sergeant David Scott located tracks for 30 insurgents and began following them for a considerable distance. The tracks were reckoned to be three hours old. The c/s passed the sitrep on to Fireforce and began to follow up. Fireforce, consisting of one Kcar and three Gcars and one Cyclone 4 known as Lynx (in fact a Cessna light aircraft) were prepositioned at Chiredzi. The excellent Lieutenant Richard Passaportis, BCR (Bronze Cross of Rhodesia), was the Fireforce commander i/c a company of 2 RAR (2nd Battalion, Rhodesian African Rifles). Just after mid-day the Grey's c/s radioed in to report the spoor as now being less than one hour old and that the insurgents had crossed into the Gona-re-Zhou[5] National Park area. Acting on this, Passaportis decided to reposition Fireforce closer to the area to cut down enemy reaction time. The tracks were now heading for the border. Passaportis dropped his 2RAR stops 2, 3 and 4 along the game fence which ran parallel to the border fence. The Gcars then turned to Boli airfield to refuel and collect more troops. The Kcar, with Passaportis aboard, accompanied by the Lynx, then overflew the area in an attempt to locate the enemy and slow them down. A second Kcar was sent to the area and kept on the ground with the remaining Fireforce.

At 14.30 Scott and his Grey's clashed with a large group of insurgents. At the same time, the Kcar, now overhead, engaged the enemy who were running. Many were seen to fall. Others took cover. Scott led his section on swiftly and with admirable command and control. The second Kcar was called up. The action is described in Passaportis' own words:

> Immediately contact was made, the second Kcar and Fireforce were called to proceed to the contact area. Until the Fireforce arrived, both the Kcar and the Lynx engaged a number of groups of running terrorists. Call sign 24b at this time were also involved and accounted for a number of the enemy and the loss of one trooper killed.[6]

---

5   'The secret place of the elephants.'
6   Grey's Scout Trooper David Carshalton.

As soon as Fire Force arrived overhead, the contact area stop groups were positioned to the South East, and the West of the contact in the direction of the terrorist's flight path.

The first Kcar then had to leave the area to refuel and the second Kcar took over. There then followed a number of skirmishes between the stop groups and running groups of the enemy which lasted for approximately three hours. During this time both Kcars also fired at a number of fleeing enemy groups.

Because of the large group of terrorists/recruits contacted and their subsequent splintering into smaller groups, the overall contact developed into a running sweep/skirmish with the Kcar directing ground forces onto the areas of thick cover where the enemy were hiding. At last light, the air effort had to return to Buffalo Range and the stop groups in the contact area were instructed to lay ambushes on likely paths and game trails in the area. The stop groups positioned on the fence line were also instructed to maintain their ambush positions. During the night Stop 1 called two terrorist recruits to their position by pretending to be terrorists and subsequently captured them.

The following morning a large sweep of the contact area was conducted and the bodies of one armed terrorist, three unarmed terrorists and thirty six recruits were located over an area of approximately 2,000 metres by 1,500 metres. A total of thirteen recruits, some of them wounded, were captured during the contact on the afternoon of 27 August, during the night and also during the first light sweep of the following morning.

The Grey's had seemingly tracked a group of seven armed insurgents and their ninety recruits. Of these 40 were killed and 13 captured. Half of the 44 escapees appeared to have been wounded. Intelligence reports subsequently revealed that some of the fugitives fled into Mozambique and made their way to Malvernia (the former Portuguese border post opposite Rhodesia's Vila Salazar – also a former border post. Malvernia was now a Frelimo base). Others returned to their kraals – this was confirmed by a Fireforce deployment two days later in which two recruits were captured by a stop group in a kraal in the Matibi No2 TTL. Only one weapon, an SKS, was recovered which meant that the outstanding six weapons had been taken by the remaining three escaping insurgents. A stick grenade and four packs were also recovered. The weapon and the packs were handed into SB Chiredzi.

Under Observations/Recommendations (Part V of the Contact Report) Passaportis recorded:

The success of this contact was due to the aggressive manner in which the call sign from the Grey's Scouts conducted the follow up and the use of both the Kcar and the Lynx flying overhead and the terrorist line of flight, thus slowing them down and enabling the follow up to catch up.

The comment from the Unit Commander (2RAR) Lt Colonel PJ Hosking reads:

A speedy follow up by Grey's Scouts and repositioning of Fireforce resulted in a good contact with terrs and recruits.

The Brigade Commander, Brigadier H Barnard commented: 'Well done, Grey's Scouts'
Sergeant David Scott was awarded a Military Forces Commendation (Operational) for his conduct in this engagement.[7]

At 0700 on the morning of 30 September, c/s 24C, an eight man stick of Grey's Scouts, located fresh tracks for 30 to 35 insurgents in the featureless *mopani* woodland of the Gona-re Zhou National Park. The c/s contacted Fireforce and began an immediate follow up. Fireforce was being provided by 'C' Coy 2RAR with Major Nick Fawcett, BCR, as Fireforce commander. Fawcett recorded:

---

7   See Honours and Awards section of this history. See also the author's description of this contact in *Masodja*, pp291-292.

Spoor was fresh and follow-up progressed at great speed. Fireforce, consisting of one Kcar and two Gcars were positioned at 24Z (the Grey's Forward Base at grid ref.UM759133).

C/s 24c advised the spoor lost, then almost immediately reported that they had eight to nine terrs visual.

Fireforce deployed to the sighting and c/s 24c directed the Kcar overhead. Despite repeated efforts to locate them, the terrs could not be seen.

C/s 24c was instructed to advance to contact. It almost immediately came under fire. The Kcar was then also subjected to heavy fire emanating from a large area of ground cover.

On turning into its orbit the Kcar observed a large number of terrs running in an eastwards direction.

The terrs were engaged over a very wide area until all the Kcar's Matra MG151 cannon's 20mm ammo was expended. The enemy were then engaged with hand held FNs. Thirty minutes after the initial contact the Lynx and an additional Gcar arrived. The Lynx put in four strikes (37mm Snebs) on a group of terrs hiding in the riverine on the eastern edge of the contact area. The Lynx was subjected to very heavy ground fire on each strike.

Stop 1 in the east, Stop 2 in the west and 'C' Coy Sparrows (trackers) as well as c/s 24C began sweeping forward and made contact with several terrs, resulting in ten terrs being killed and three captured wounded.

After re-arming, Kcar returned to the area and further contacts ensued with twelve terrs five kilometres north of the original contact area and ten terrs were killed. During this firefight two members of Stop 5, Rifleman van Vuuren and Rifleman Ellerman were wounded and casevaced by Cyclone 7 (helicopter) to Chiredzi.

Stops were ferried in almost continually throughout the day. These reinforcements consisted of:

1. Stop 4 made up of elements from the Rhodesia Armoured Car Regiment.

2. 'C' Coy 2RAR Stops 7 and 8.

3. Stop 5 consisting of a four man stick from 'C' Coy 9RR (9th Battalion Rhodesia Regiment).

4. Grey's Scouts call signs 24B, 24D, 24A, and 24E (8 men each).

5. Six stop groups – Stops 6, T,U,V,W and X of 4-man SAS sticks were ferried in as additional sweep troops. Five hours after initial contact a further twenty-two men from C Squadron SAS were para-dropped by Dakota into stop positions to the east. L/Cpl Pyke was injured in the para-drop.

Skirmishing continued for the rest of the day with call signs making contact right up to last light.

During the night elements of 'B' Sqn of the RHACR(Rhodesia Armoured Car Regiment) clashed with a group of four terrs 10 kilometres south of the main contact area and killed one.

The remaining terrs were killed and captured in repeated sweeps on the following morning. The total number accounted for (including the terr killed by the armoured cars) was 28 plus 4 captured wounded. Sixty eight escaped of which 10 to 15 would have been wounded.

We recovered 4 AKMs, 23 AKs, 3 SKS, 3RPGs, 2 x 60mm mortar tubes, 2 RPDs, 8 anti-tank mines, 4 TMH46 mines along with a large quantity of ammunition, grenades, detonators, gelignite sticks, boosters, mortar bombs and rockets.[8]

In the Comments//Observations section of the Contact Report Fawcett wrote:

Had more helicopters, particularly a 2nd Kcar, been available at the start of the contact the result

---

would have been very different. Notwithstanding this, it was a successful combined operation with the many units involved acquitting themselves with credit. The majority of terrs contacted had already been wounded by the Kcar's cannon – once more demonstrating that weapon's indispensability. Despite a most courageous performance by the Lynx, this aircraft, without front guns, cannot withstand the volume of fire which can emanate from large groups of terrs.[9] Once again Grey's Scouts has demonstrated its capabilities. That unit's capacity for covering ground and for fast follow ups makes it ideal for the type of terrain in which it is deployed.

If contact with large terr groups numbering 100 or more becomes the norm the following must be considered:

a. Each aircraft must be fitted with a second radio to allow for an intercom channel and a battle channel.
b. Provision must be made for a joint command helicopter divorced from the gunship effort.
c. Airborne forces (SAS) must be given the capability in terms of available Dakotas to carry out airborne envelopment of the contact area at short notice.
d. Vast effort was expended in recovery of dead bodies. Camera-equipped teams drawn from Army/SB must be on stand-by at sub JOCS to carry out identification and disposal of corpses in situ.

Lt Colonel Hoskings, CO of 2RAR, concurring with all the above, commented:

A well-coordinated combined operation with excellent results. Subsequent reports from Military Intelligence indicates that of 20 terrs who returned to Mozambique, 17 were wounded four of whom died. The Company Commander's recommendations are agreed. Sub-para d will be actioned by this sub JOC in future.

The Brigade Commander, Brigadier Barnard added:

Good contact. Use of Grey's Scouts and airborne troops in the JOC area essential. Difficult contact to control. Major Fawcett's command was first class. His recommendations will be studied further.

As a footnote to this contact Rusti Henderson, a Grey's remount rider, adds;

Dave Carshalton was nearly engaged to my sister at the time of his tragic death. His mare was a farm horse and was blind in one eye. Despite this he rode her thus on operations. She was an amazing animal and later went on to show jump with Dave's sister Debbie.

Roy Elderkin writes:

Grey's Scouts were formally introduced to the public at a medals parade in RLI Barracks. We were ordered to send a detachment there so I had to teach them mounted rifle drills. They responded to the same orders as if they were dismounted troops. The RLI RSM was concerned that different orders would be needed for the mounted detachment. I reassured him that he would not need

---

9   This vulnerability had already been noted by the Air Force. The Lynx was subsequently fitted with twin .303 calibre guns enabling it to fire right down to the point of rocket or Frantan (napalm) release.

to change anything as we would respond to the same orders. The Grey's detachment was led by Lieutenant Graham, son of Lord Graham, who was doing his national service with us. The entire ceremony went off very well and the standard of riding was every bit what it should have been for such an important parade.

In late 1976 the unit detailed three of its members to the South African Defense Force Equitation Centre. The candidates were Sergeant C Greyling, Sergeant B Greyling and Sergeant Rob Early. Elderkin says this was because

... we wanted to know if our training methods were on a par with theirs and if we could learn anything new. The resulting answer surprised and pleased us: they couldn't teach us anything new. In fact we were far more advanced than they were!

3

Rhodesia 1977

In January the leaders of the so-called Frontline States – Mozambique, Angola, Zambia, Botswana and Tanzania – met in the Angolan capital, Luanda, to declare their backing for Robert Mugabe and Joshua Nkomo's Patriotic Front alliance.

By the end of January the Kissinger proposals had fallen away. There was a new power in the White House whose foreign policy towards the last white regimes in Africa was ultimately to lead to the tragedy that is present day Zimbabwe. In the meanwhile they were set to reject anything Ian Smith proposed or did as progress. They wanted rid of Smith and what they termed his illegal and racist regime. To Rhodesians this was difficult to accept as they, black and white, were now fighting and dying side by side. In their dictionary, the word 'racist' was defined as 'an Englishman who has lived in Africa for three months'.

In Smith, unfortunately, the leaders of western democracy had come across that extremely rare politician – a man both honest and shrewd who could not be easily fooled. Additionally, he believed in duty, loyalty and patriotism. This was confounding to the British and American politicos. Against him they sent all their finest, seasoned in 'statesmanship' and highly skilled in debate (duplicity and deception). He outlasted them all.

In March Smith, in the face of opposition within his own Rhodesian Front party, opened land purchase to all races (the Land Tenure Amendment Bill). His government now also finally admitted that the insurgency had developed into a major revolutionary war. This led to the formation of the Combined Operations Headquarters (COMOPS). From now on the JOC commanders would assume leadership and direction of COIN operations in their own particular areas.

By the middle of 1977 ZANU had over 3,000 of its ZANLA insurgents operating in Rhodesia, two thirds of whom were active in the Operation Thrasher area. These 3,000 had infiltrated through (initially) Mozambique's Tete province. The more comatose ZAPU had roughly 300 of its conventionally trained ZIPRA fighters in the country using the Zambia/Botswana infiltration route. An attempt to unite both these armies was made this year by ZAPU's Jason Ziyapaya Moyo in order to give credence to the claims of ZAPU and ZANU's Patriotic Front Alliance. Moyo, as chairman of the ANC (Nkomo) external mission had been given full powers to deal with 'military affairs'. He was, however, blown up by a parcel bomb in Lusaka on 22 January 1977 a few hours after returning from Maputo. Both insurgent armies subsequently continued to go their own separate ways. From late 1977 onwards, there were violent clashes between detachments of both sides wherever their operational boundaries overlapped. This was mainly because ZANLA knew and resented the fact that it was doing most of the Liberation War's spadework while ZIPRA stood by and watched. ZIPRA, in truth, now had an army of over 6,000 conventionally trained troops 'standing by' in both Zambia and Angola, biding their time whilst ZANLA, totally committed to the war effort, took the brunt of Rhodesian security forces' fearsome and devastating attacks/assaults internally and externally.

In the previous year the Rhodesians had taken the gloves off. In August of that year the Rhodesian Selous Scout Regiment initiated the tactic of large-scale raids into neighbouring Mozambique. The Scouts, dressed as Frelimo, and in a complete surprise attack, drove right into the ZANLA camp at Nyadzonya and killed over 300 of the many cheering and welcoming insurgents assembled on the

Chief Equitation Officer, WOII Nick van Heerden, 1977. (Nick van Heerden)

parade ground. The strategy had proved itself. In May 1977 the Zambian leader, President Kaunda, placed his country on a war footing after being informed that Rhodesian security forces would attack ZIPRA bases in his country which were known to be deploying insurgents into Rhodesia. In late 1977 a very big raid on ZANLA's main camp at Chimoio (pronounced Shimoio) resulted in huge enemy casualties and again confirmed the tactic to be correct.[1] A factor not understood by many non-Rhodesian analysts and students of the Bush War was that the Rhodesians had a complete and utter understanding of the enemy – a vital asset in warfare.

But the precedent was by now well established. What many Rhodesian soldiers in other units did not realise was that the Grey's Scouts were also conducting cross-border recces and operations. These, on a smaller and less spectacular scale, nevertheless constituted very dangerous and difficult work.

In April conscription had extended to include the 38 to 50 age group. Those under 38 were now performing 190 days a year in six week call ups. The over-50s were volunteering for police and 'home guard' type duties.

Regimental and Training

With the increasing intake of regular and TA soldiers, the Grey's Scouts now found itself very deficient in riding instructors. In early 1977 the unit detailed three of its members, namely Corporal Phanuel Ndokanga, popularly known as Corporal Fanwell, Corporal RGB Baker and Corporal I Veldsman, to attend the Horsemasters' Course (Potomac USA). This course was rated as the most advanced of its type at the time. It was run at the Ascot Equitation Centre, Borrowdale, and was very extensive. The candidates were required to learn animal and stable management, hipology, as well as advanced riding and instructional techniques. Elderkin, who taught the same course to civilians, knew how

---

1   This was Operation Dingo, 23–25 November 1977 (the attacks of Chimoio and Tembué). See Alexandre Binda, *The Saints*, pp 255–273. Dingo is now regarded as the greatest special forces raid in history.

GREY'S SCOUTS — RECRUITS COURSE
16 JULY 77 TO 26 AUGUST 77

Back row from left to right: Tpr Burden A. A. Tpr Wheeler T. G. Tpr Huck I. R. Tpr Watt-Pringle J. D. L/Cpl Greeff J. Sgt Ford B.B
Tpr Silva N. A. Tpr Warth G. Cpl Brown D. G. J. Cpl Olds D. C. Tpr Van Geems C.

Second row from left to right: Tpr Wilkinson A. Tpr Grimwood C. A. Tpr Harcourt J. Tpr Sletcher C. Tpr Van Schalkwyk J. Tpr Barker
C. Tpr Olds M. Tpr Muncaster P. Tpr Britts L. L. L/Cpl Mellett J. (Instr). Tpr Godfrey B. K.

Sitting from left to right: Cpl McGillivray D. (Instr). C/Sgt Elderkin R. (Instr). C/Sgt Brooks A. F. V. (Instr). WO2 Jamieson J. A. (SSM).
Maj Stephens A. P. (OC). Sgt Botha R. A. (Best recruit). Lt Allen P. W. (Adjt). WO2 Van Heerden N. B. (Instr). Tpr Greeff B. Tpr.
Pienaar C. Cpl Baker R. G. B. (Instr). Cpl Veldsman I. (Instr).

Grey's Scouts Course 1977. (Dick Weidemann)

tough it was and recalls how proud he felt to see all three Grey's Scouts pass the course, particularly Corporal Fanwell who was highly talented and the first African to pass the course. Fanwell was KIA a few weeks later (see below).

Elderkin recalls:

At the beginning of 1977 with the arrival of WOII Nick Heerden, outdoor riding schools were built. Nick took over from me as Chief Equitation Officer. We were then able to introduce a full training program. This lasted for six weeks and included infantry and riding tactics. RWS (Rhodesia Women's Service) Sergeant Anne Webb, an instructor who had trained Lipizzaners in South Africa, was also a member of the Training Staff. On the riding side the guys spent two to three weeks on the end of a long line whether they could ride or not. The rest was spent in the indoor schools where they were split. Those who could ride came over to me for advanced instruction. The remainder were taught by Nick, Corporal Dave McGillivray and Corporal Baker. When these were trained to ride the whole course were re-united for Mounted Infantry training. This was conducted by Infantry instructors Colour Sergeant Aubrey Brooks, Bruno Rabie (brother of the late legendary Selous Scout Andre Rabie) and Lance Corporal Mellett. This training program remained unchanged until 1980.

Nick van Heerden remembers:

... I took over riding instruction. We started outside in schools with a canvas surround made up from discarded old tents. This was okay but as training progressed and got tougher the going got as hard as hell for the horses. We had to use rubber chips made from old motor tyres; being black, these got hot as coal in the scorching Rhodesian sun. Realising recruits only had three weeks before deployment, all we could do was to make them as safe and confident on a horse as possible. For this reason during these first three weeks the recruits were paired off – each with his own horse. They were then taught how to lunge (long line) each other. The instructors stood by to assist both the rider and the lunger (the handler/recruit holding the line). We hoped this would improve their balance sufficiently so they could go on to some form of control. This depended to a large extent on the horse's own amenability. Horse amenability was created in no small measure by competent remount riders. This competence was expected from all our instructors. Fortunately McClelland saddles were well suited and easy to ride in. On my first patrol I had ridden in my own show-jumping saddle and learned very quickly how unsuitable it was. I might add here that FN rifles were also not easy to ride with and practically impossible without a sling. MAGs were equally difficult and damned dangerous and, quite apart from the hazard of an a.d., should one fall off the mount the sheer weight of the weapon was likely to injure the rider. We made a big fuss about this in the hope that we would be offered better alternative weapons, i.e., American carbines, South African R14s, Greener shotguns, Israeli Uzis, AKs or even the old reliable Stens. Personally we all preferred AKs but what we got were G3s with fragile plastic butts which broke off in a fall, rendering it useless. The unit was certainly effective as history records. How much better we could have been is debateable, for example, firing blanks in the training school to get horses used to gunfire was a futile exercise. In a contact situation to expect soldiers to control horses successfully under fire would be insanity. What we did try was to pair horses off with suitable riders. We felt this was more important. When I took over from Roy, the instructors were 'Smudge Smith (Stable Manager), and Rob Early, both sergeants. Later, when they left, I was joined by Dave McGillivray as my stick leader, Peter Ward and Rusti Henderson (in charge of the vet section). Ann Webb was with us for a while and was part of the first squad that went to South Africa for horses.

We were involved in travelling to South Africa for several trips to collect horses donated by the people of Harding in Natal. Some of the animals were very good, others pretty average and some were even more dangerous than the terrs!

Larry Jenkins, a member of the BSAP adds;

... I was involved with the Rhodesia Horse Society and knew Nick and Ailsa van Heerden who were well-known in the Rhodesian equitation world. I remember Nick being concerned about taking casualties during 'crack and thump' training because the RPD the Grey's were using in training lacked a foresight. It had been only pure good fortune that no man or beast had so far been killed.

I had contacts at 'Group 7' where the BSAP Special Investigations stored captured enemy

Chief Equitation Officer, WOII Nick van Heerden on a trip to South
Africa and beauty contestants, 1977. (Nick van Heerden)

equipment. From here I was able to get Nick a coveted RPD foresight.

Regarding Nick van Heerden's riding school, Dave McGillivray has this to add:

After one particular bush trip I got back to Inkomo and decided to look in at the Riding
School and pay my respects to WOII van Heerden. As I approached the school I could hear
his voice bellowing at some unfortunate recruit. I slipped unnoticed behind the kicking boards
and watched as Nick attempted to get the recruit to perform a particular movement. All his
instructions of 'it's a simple matter' etc. proved to be of no use. In frustration and in a show of
'I'll show you how it's done', he ordered the recruit to dismount. He then set about a physical
demonstration of how this 'simple' move was to be performed. To his own surprise the horse also
gave him a hard time and dumped him flat on his back. Unable to resist McGillivray called out:
    'Hands up the recruit who spotted the Sergeant Major's deliberate mistake.'

To which, van Heerden, spitting out a mouthful of sand retorted loudly: 'Fuck off Sergeant
McGillivray!'
Nick van Heerden concludes:

Military intelligence, like agricultural economics is a contradiction in terms. The obvious
advantage of being a mounted unit was the ability for rapid follow up. To this end we also
acquired fox hounds and, in a demo show for the brass, they completed a follow up in twenty
minutes. We had 14 hounds under Geoff Gainess Burrill who had hunted hounds in Ireland.
Unfortunately our adjutant, Lieutenant Allen, was a dog handler of note. On his advice a pair of
hounds was attached to each section which completely broke the 'hunting as a pack' principle.

These nine photographs are of Alan Collier riding Ligting, demonstrating a Grey's Scouts boerperd and horse furniture and carrying a 7.62mm G3. (Alan Collier)

LCpl Albert (Dick) Weidemann (second left, kneeling) training recruits
at Lake McLLwaine, Salisbury, late 1970s. (Dick Weidemann)

Left to right (mounted): WO2 Nick van Heerden, Corporal Dave McGillivray, Corporal Ed
Wandell: opening of Crippled Eagles or US goodwill embassy, 1977. (Nick van Heerden)

The mutts then simply became nice pets but bloody useless otherwise.

Sometime in April, Captain Cedric Tipping-Woods of 2RR (2nd Battalion, The Rhodesia Regiment – a TA battalion) was transferred to Grey's Scouts. He had already worked with the Grey's in the Fort Victoria area. Transferred with him also were Ted Wilmot and Roy Mathews. During the train journey to Salisbury, Tipping-Woods initially found himself less than impressed with these two arrogant beer-swilling individuals. These initial impressions were soon reversed. Tipping-Woods writes:

> Ted and Roy were to be outstanding horsemen and fearless soldiers serving right up to the final dissolution of the Regiment.

At Inkomo, Tipping-Woods met the OC Major Stephens and Lieutenant Allen, the Adjutant. He, under Colour Sergeant Smudge Smith, then underwent an intensive equestrian course on a horse called Frazer who performed side bites, kicks and had no brakes. Somehow he occasionally managed to stay in the saddle – all due to Smudge who ' ... performed wonders ... '.

At this stage, remembers Tipping-Woods, the unit consisted of one squadron –'A' – which comprised three troops. These troops were made up of a mix of regulars (ES and AS), TA and national servicemen. The splitting of the unit into two squadrons came later under Mick McKenna and Mike Wilson. These were then detailed as 'A' Squadron (regulars) and 'B' Squadron (TA). Tipping-Woods was then appointed 2i/c of 'A' Squadron.

In June 1977 Corporals Neil Johns and Mike Bradshaw signed up for service with the Regular Army. Both had formerly been national servicemen of Intake 156. After basic training at Bulawayo's Lewellin Barracks they had been posted to the 4th Battalion The Rhodesia Regiment at Umtali. After a short spell there they decided to join the Grey's Scouts – this decision being motivated by the fact that, during one scene, they had come under fire from their own side!

Both attended riding courses under Anne Webb, Sergeant Ward and other instructors. For a mount, Johns was given a gelding named Count Yorga. Count Yorga was destined to be his horse until mid 1979 when he had to be put down after being wounded in Mozambique during an external operation. Tactical and operational instruction was provided by Dave Sparkes, Aubrey Brookes, Bruno Rabie and John Mellett.

After this they both attended tracking courses: the first, a basic tracking course at Lake McIllwaine under Dave Sparkes, John and 'Baba' Wiggle and Tony Devenish, the second an advanced tracking course at Kariba on the Zambezi under John McNeilage, Aubrey Brookes, Kufa Buku and Mike Spies. This latter course included a four-day survival course at the Selous Scouts' camp at Wafa Wafa.

Shortly after mid-year, a leadership vacuum resulted during which operational and disciplinary standards, in some cases, deteriorated (see below). Charles Mosley, an NCO at HQ, was on duty when a couple of BSAP policemen brought in a trooper. The man looked in a bad state – as if he was high (on drugs). The Squadron Sergeant Major, WOII Jimmy Jamieson, ordered Mosley to escort the man to the barrack block to sleep it off. Mosley placed him in the 3rd block from the Guard Room. The trooper asked for something to eat. Mosley went to the 'Graze Hall' (dining room) and got him a steak sandwich and a cup of tea. On the way back Mosley heard a couple of shots coming from the block. He took cover uttering, 'Fucking hell!'. He then called out to a recruit across the way to go and get the SSM. Meanwhile he called out to the trooper to put down his weapon and come out. In return he received a string of biblical quotes. A member of Training Troop, armed with an FN, suddenly came up and offered to give the trooper a 'rev' if he fired again! At that moment Jimmy Jamieson thankfully showed up and began talking to the trooper hoping to bring him out. After a while a further two shots were fired followed by silence. Jamieson and Mosley went forward and found the man sitting on the bed. He had put two rounds through his right hand and kept repeating, 'If thy right hand offend thee cut it off'. As the medic rendered first aid it transpired that the trooper had broken up with his girlfriend. During the bust-up he had struck her with his right hand. He looked completely broken down.

During this unfortunate period in the unit Mosley says:

> There were a few weapons 'floating around' camp. I had to go to Norton police station to collect one of our farriers who had been arrested for trying to sell an AK to an American who was staying at Salisbury's Oasis Hotel. This American had attracted the attention of the CID after attempting to buy captured terrorist weapons from members of other Rhodesian Army units.

Operational log
Grey's in Operation Hurricane
On 15 February, on the border between the Mudzi and Ngarwe TTLs near Kotwa, a Grey's Scouts call sign led by Corporal Phanuel Ndokanga (Corporal Fanwell) was ambushed by ZANLA insurgents. Ndokanga took a round in the femoral artery. His 2i/c Steve Ziegler radioed for casevac. By the time the choppers arrived Dave McGillivray, who was in a stick operating nearby, heard Ziegler say that Fanwell was dead. Fanwell, highly regarded by all, was an unusually gifted individual. McGillivray adds:

> It was so very sad. We had lost a very special person.

Ziegler himself was KIA in a vehicle ambush the following year after transferring out of Grey's Scouts and serving with the very short-lived 7 (Indep) Company. This unit consisted of former French troops who had come to Rhodesia en-bloc.

Of Fanwell Keith Allan says:

> When I arrived at Grey's Scouts there were a dozen or so African Soldiers (AS) from Service Corps mostly employed in camp fatigues. One of them was Fanwell. He was a Shangaan, a tribe that were an offshoot of the Zulu. He was very proud of this fact and considered his fellow Service Corps AS, who were Shona, as merely one step up from a dog. He forcefully expressed his desire and intent to become a fully-fledged mounted infantryman. He wouldn't take no for an answer on this. By dint of his great charisma and perseverance he eventually got his wish. Fraser-Kirk and Stephens had long sorted out the fact that we would be a multi-racial unit like the neighbouring Selous Scouts. Fanwell was a really great guy to have around and to operate with. Tragically he made the supreme sacrifice and died in a contact after being shot through the upper legs.

Later in this year Dave McGillivray was part of a stick patrolling beyond Nyamapanda and into Mozambique. They were dismounted and leading their horses along when, detected by the enemy, they suddenly came under heavy mortar fire. The stick was ordered away from the area. McGillivray attempted to mount but his horse, Nutshell, began to panic. Encumbered by his rifle and pack, McGillivray was trying to calm the animal down so as to mount up. Noting his difficulties, and despite being under fire, Clive Freeman nearby came up and took McGillivray's rifle enabling him to mount. They then rode hard for the Rhodesian border. As they went along McGillivray noticed that Freeman's horse, Jim Boy, was bleeding badly having been hit by shrapnel. They took cover in a *donga* where McGillivray applied a field dressing to the injury to stem the blood loss. Freeman, who was known to love his horse, was for walking him back over the border but McGillivray ordered him to mount up as they were in dangerous territory. They made it okay. Jim Boy survived his wounds and was back on ops two weeks later.

Major Tony Stephens was obliged to give up command of the Grey's Scouts sometime after mid-1977 on the grounds of ill health. This resulted in a leadership vacuum during which the unit was indifferently led. Unfortunately, standards amongst some individuals dropped appallingly. An example of this is related by Brendan Girdler-Brown, one of the Grey's Scouts medics:

> It was around Xmas time and we were based up in Kotwa. One of our call signs was engaged on border control ops along a dirt road near the Mozambique-Rhodesia border. It was a blistering hot day. They saw a sparkling stream down in the valley below the road. The sight proved irresistible. They dismounted, tethered their mounts by the roadside, and stripped off. Then, taking only their rifles, went down the hill for a quick swim. Unbelievably they hadn't left anyone to guard the horses, radio, clothing, spare magazines etc.
>
> When, suitably cooled down, they returned up the bank to the roadside they were shocked to find that, apart from the horses, spare magazines and their single radio, everything had gone – saddles, bridles, clothing, etc.
>
> We received a very embarrassing call to come and resupply them. If I hadn't seen this myself I wouldn't have believed it! They were very lucky that their gear was obviously lifted by an army call sign. We knew that 'Eskimos' (SAS or Selous Scouts) were operating in the area. If a group of insurgents had stumbled upon them in such a vulnerable state the result would certainly have been tragic. I can't recall what disciplinary measures, if any, were taken against them.

Brendan Girdler-Brown went on to qualify as a doctor in the regular army and served in Umtali and at Gwelo's School of Infantry.

Grey's Scouts in Operation Repulse

At mid-afternoon on 18 March a Grey's Scouts call sign from 2 Troop, 'B' Squadron, commanded by Colour Sergeant Don Kenny was ambushed by a large group of ZANLA insurgents under the hard-bitten Nylon Ndela. Trooper Charles Johnson was fatally wounded in the engagement. Kenny got Johnson out of the contact area but he died later.[2]

Not long after this, when the unit was at Tswiza in the Gona-re-Zhou Game Reserve, insurgents derailed a train. Stephens detailed Don Kenny to lead a follow up on the group of six to ten insurgents responsible.

Dickson, the Ndebele tracker, led the troops westwards across the reserve. The tracks followed a depression leading into a basin near the Lundi river. The tracker dismounted and studied the spoor. He then went up to Kenny and reported that the tracks were very fresh. He reckoned the enemy would follow the riverline towards its confluence with the Sabi River.

They moved forward. A few moments later, two troopers on the right flank came under fire from the enemy concealed 30 metres to their front. Everyone dismounted and spread out. One of the troopers then saw two figures silhouetted on a rock feature. He fired instinctively while at the same time Dickson threw a grenade. Corporal Patrick Ollivier, a section commander experiencing his first contact, had also seen the figures. He cried out, 'Shit! They are women!'

Kenny ordered two men up to the feature to investigate. They quickly confirmed that they had found two dead women. Kenny called for air support. This consisted of a Gcar. The enemy were now in a ravine. With the chopper overhead the sweep went on. A 20-man Grey's stop group was positioned north of the ravine. Moments later Kenny's sweep line clashed with the insurgents. In the subsequent bloody firefight eleven insurgents were killed. When Kenny's assault group finally linked

---

2   See also Parkin, Jim. *Assignment Selous Scouts* pp115–116. Pub. Galago. 2006.

up with the stop group, he found that they had killed a further six insurgents and captured eleven insurgents along with six women.[3]

Grey's in Operation Thrasher

In Rhodesia's eastern highlands the small farming communities, such as Chipinga (European corruption of the Shona *Chipinge* meaning 'the obstructor' or 'impeder') and Melsetter, had begun to take the brunt of escalating ZANLA incursions into Rhodesia. These highlands, marking the border between Rhodesia and Mozambique, were made up of the Vumba, Inyanga and Chimanimani Mountains. This highland is spectacular and ranges from 2,500–3,000 metres in height. There was a JOC at Chipinga but the people of the small village of Melsetter felt isolated and forgotten. The insurgents were now making a determined effort to drive the farmers off the land. One way of achieving this was to make the main road to Umtali unusable. All the bus services virtually stopped. Armed convoys, composed of police and internal affairs personnel, escorted civilian traffic from Umtali to the eastern district towns. They could not, however, provide protection for the commercial companies in the area. In this year 12 heavy transport vehicles had been ambushed and burnt out. Melsetter, whose uplands all around were Forestry Commission, provided most of the country's timber. Border Timbers, faced with the inability of the government to provide their vehicles with armed escorts, decided to recruit its own. James MacBruce writes:

> They were all heavily armed with machine guns and it was quite a sight to see the six big lorries with their 20 tonne loads of timber leaving Charter every morning and evening. The convoys were attacked a number of times but these 'hot run' drivers always got through. Some were wounded. Later some joined the estate staff. They were even able to laugh about some of the incidents, blown-up bridges or rocket and machine gun attacks on them. They were quite remarkable men.[4]

The Grey's Scouts were one of the units of the fully-stretched security forces operating in the area.

Cavalry Fireforce – a fine concept but a missed opportunity

By 1977 the paucity of available fireforces was becoming apparent. During an air recce, Group Captain Peter Petter-Bowyer of the Rhodesian Air Force observed:

> On 22 March I found a plum target and counted 38 CTs moving out of their well-defined base camp. Unfortunately the Mtoko Fireforce was not available, so the Grand Reef Fireforce, led by Mike Litson, responded instead. An agonising fifty-five minutes elapsed before the Fireforce came into view. I put Mike onto the campsite first for orientation purposes and, considering the long delay, it was fortunate that my guess at where the CTs might be found turned out to be correct. In the action that followed sixteen CTs were killed, one was captured unhurt and seventeen escaped, most having been peppered with 20mm shrapnel from the Kcar.
>
> Although I read all the Air Strike Reports in Air HQ, it was not the same as seeing for myself the existing problem of having too few Fireforces. They had to cover many thousands of square miles in which ever-growing numbers of CT groups were operating. I wondered if employing a new approach might offset the shortage of Fireforces and allow air recce finds to be less dependent on their availability.
>
> Major Tony Stephens, commander of the horse-borne troops of the Grey's Scouts, listened to my ideas about using his Grey's Scouts as an alternative to the heli-borne Fireforce. He leapt at the opportunity and we made plans to give it a try the next day in the St Swithins Tribal Trust

---

3   See also Patrick Ollivier. *Commandos de Brousse* pp31–49. Pub. 1985. Grasset. Paris.
4   James MacBruce. *When the Going was Rough* p223. Pub. Femina. SA.

Land. This was to have a force of twenty horsemen moving along a pre-determined line at a gentle walk whilst I conducted air recce five kilometres on either side of their line.

I found the force immediately I arrived at the appointed RV, and the sharp accent of the Grey's Scouts major made me realise he was American. He confirmed the line he would ride and I confirmed the procedure I would adopt. Not ten minutes passed before I found a base under the trees on high ground, commanding an excellent view of surrounding grasslands in which were some bare maize fields, very few trees and three small villages.

My 1:50,000-scale map showed a shallow depression running west to east 500 metres to the north of the base but this was not obvious from my recce height. I had no knowledge of horse-borne tactics for approaching targets unseen. Having given him the relevant grid references, I asked the major's opinion on the cover the depression would afford him. He assured me he could get to a position 500 metres north of the base without being seen and said he would call me across two minutes before his arrival there. At the time I was about five kilometres away, having maintained a routine orbit line, but I could see the horses clearly even when they passed through tree cover. The speed at which the horses covered the ground was very impressive.

When the force turned right to move directly towards the base, ten pairs of horsemen surged forward, galloping at different speeds to place them in a wide crescent before the centre horsemen came to a halt and dismounted. In no time there were ten pairs of men surrounding the base site. The nearest troops to the base were about 150 metres away. No more than ten minutes had passed from finding the base to having it surrounded by men who had dismounted to commence a cautious approach towards the base.

Disappointingly the base was empty, having been vacated about two hours earlier. Nevertheless, it was clear to me that this silent force would have achieved complete surprise and total encirclement. Had there been serious opposition, a status quo could have been maintained for as long as it took for a regular Fireforce to reach them.

Unfortunately, the success of the trial ended abruptly. I had continued searching for another target when I saw smoke rising from two villages close to the base. I could not raise the major on the radio so flew back to see what was going on and was horrified to find all huts of the third village in the process of being torched. My presence overhead brought the major back to his radio set and we entered into a very heated exchange. The major maintained that the locals needed to be punished for feeding the CTs. I objected and insisted that these same locals, who really had no alternative but to feed CTs, would more willingly support ZANLA following this senseless action.

I terminated the trial even before the whole hour had passed because I needed to discuss Grey's Scouts procedures with Tony Stephens. He was very apologetic about his American Major's actions and assured me that appropriate action would be taken. Nevertheless, Tony was delighted to learn that, in my opinion, Grey's Scouts could be employed in a Fireforce role in support of air recce and Selous Scouts. Regrettably I never found another opportunity to pursue the matter personally and the concept was lost.[5]

The American was in fact Major Mike Williams a tall Texan who wore a Colt 45 and smoked large cigars. On operations he carried a cavalry sabre and rode at the head of his men on a black horse called Baguta. He affected a John Wayne attitude.

An anecdote concerning Williams' affected image relates that on one occasion, wielding his sabre, he charged into a kraal situated on a vlei line. He pulled his mount up sharply in the centre of the village, overbalanced and toppled off the right side of his mount. He repeated this approach in the next village this time firing his Colt into the air after which he promptly fell off the left side of the

5   Group Captain P J H Petter-Bowyer. *Winds of Destruction* pp 295-296. Pub. 30 Degrees South. South Africa, 2005.

horse which then ran off. Seeing this his men muttered 'Fuck him. He can catch his own horse we're out of here ... '

⊹╾━╼⊹

Neil Johns writes:

> In the second half of 1977 we were based up at Odzi. Our main operating area was in the Maranke TTL. I had my first contact here. We had tracked a gang of five gooks. When we caught up with them we killed the entire gang. Kufa Buku, who had become a great friend of mine, personally killed three of the enemy. I got one.
>
> 'At Odzi also our camp was subjected to a long range attack by a group of about 60 insurgents. It was later discovered that this group consisted mainly of women. This subsequently made the Grey's the butt of many jokes by other units – notably the RLI!

Grey's Scouts in Operation Tangent

Sometime in July, Captain Cedric Tipping-Woods was deployed to Manama Mission in the south western area of the Gwanda District of Matabeleland. Here he met one of the unit's vets, Captain Anthony Taylor. The deployment proved uneventful, the only excitement being provided by one of the African civilians vanishing into the jesse atop John Davison's large horse. He reappeared hours later. This civilian ended up joining the unit as a regular soldier and progressing up the rank ladder to eventually end up as Warrant Officer II Chipinga Makomaya, a fine farrier.

In September the unit became the subject of some very unfavourable international publicity. An American journalist, Ross Baughman, reported that he had witnessed members of the Grey's Scouts burning civilian huts in the Lupane District. Worse, he stated that the troops had beaten and tortured a local black politician, Mr Ncube, during interrogation. He added that the man's wife and teenage daughter had been whipped. The politician, claimed Baughman, subsequently died as a result. In the United States, Baughman's article was accompanied by a photo which depicted an African with a rope around his neck being held prisoner by Rhodesian soldiers alleged to be Grey's Scouts. Baughman's report stated:

> They fastened rope nooses around the necks of two prisoners and forced them to run or be dragged for several miles behind horses.[6]

Of course Baughman ensured he was not in Rhodesia when the allegations were published. The Rhodesian investigation into the matter revealed that some 20% of the report was accurate – Ncube had been interrogated. Pretty much everything else proved to be an exaggeration intended to cause sensation overseas where the name Rhodesia was a dirty word. They also revealed that Mr Ncube was very much alive and unharmed. Additionally they found that his 'teenage' daughter was in fact a toddler.

Cedric Tipping-Woods remembers:

> Prior to my arrival the infamous incident involving a German journalist, J Ross Baughman occurred. This journalist, having gained the confidence of both Army Headquarters and the Prime Minister was authorised to do what was presumed to be a positive exposé on the unit. Baughman also managed to hoodwink 'B' Squadron's OC Major Mike Williams, an American, as well as the troops. He then produced a sensational article putting the unit in an extremely bad

6   Pat Scully. *Exit Rhodesia* p73.

light with threats of prosecutions for war crimes!

Nick van Heerden writes:

I had been in the area before this alleged incident took place. The first I heard of it was when I was in transit at Johannesburg airport where I bought an American magazine because of the curious cover headline. This stated something about American vets serving in Grey's Scouts. I knew that the officer then commanding Grey's Scouts was an American major named Williams but I also knew that there were no American veterinarians in the Grey's Scouts. Imagine my surprise when I discovered that the word, in the USA, meant veterans! Within there was an article with a photo of a terr in a prone position being interrogated at gunpoint which, of course, as everyone knows, is the only sensible and safe way to question an enemy. The article failed to impress me.

Morale in the unit was pretty low at this time as Tony Stephens had left due to ill health, and the interim temporary leadership appeared to be unequal to the task. Cedric Tipping-Woods was flown to Lupane to assume his duties as 2i/c of 1 Squadron, then commanded by Major Mike Williams.
At Lupane, 2 and 3 Troops were based in an old house in the village just off the main Bulawayo/Victoria Falls road. To Tipping-Woods it appeared to be fortified like something out of the film *Green Berets*! He found mortars and MAGs (mounted in tandem) all in trenches with no fields of fire and surrounded by occupied houses. Tipping-Woods then went on to visit Don Kenny, the Squadron's Sergeant Major. He recalls:

Don Kenny was much respected. At this time he was commanding 1 Troop based up on the late Arthur Cumming's farm on the railway line, about 30 kilometres from Victoria Falls. Don was desperate for a briefing and contact with the rest of the ssquadron as Major Williams seemed to have forgotten his existence. I spent two days with the troop which I found to be extremely well disciplined, trained and enthusiastic. This was in direct contrast to the rest of the squadron which, under Williams, was completely shambolic.
It transpired that Major Williams had ordered the unit to open fire during a daylight stand to. The fire was directed at two RDU (Rhodesia Defence Unit) coloured soldiers based down the road. One of the men was killed. Williams defended his decision by claiming that he had warned them not to break the curfew! An investigation ensued after which Williams was removed from command as a result of the Baughman incident, and for general incompetence.[7]
I took over command of the unit. The excellent Don Kenny was Squadron Sergeant Major. I had some fine men – amongst them 2nd Lieutenants Geoff Armand and Graham Baillie both Troop Commanders. For Signals Officer I had 2nd Lieutenant Callum Graham (son of Lord Graham) and Corporal Patrick Ollivier (ex-French Foreign Legion). Ollivier, on an early deployment, radioed in for ammo resupply. He was asked to give details of the contact he had been in. It transpired that he had used up all the call sign's ammo by firing into every bit of potential enemy cover that they rode by ... There was also a trooper, Sir Hugo Seebbright, who was doing continuous call-ups to avoid being deported back to the UK where he was wanted for some misdemeanour.[8]

---

7   Williams later wrote a book on his Rhodesian Army experiences – the account being made up of inaccuracies and nonsense.
8   Author's note: it is possible that Cedric Tipping-Woods was unaware that Ollivier was performing Drake Shooting. This combat tactic was devised by Major David Drake of the RAR. It involves pouring intensive fire into every area of concealment which could contain ambushing enemy. The results can be startlingly positive and high kill rates can be achieved. The idea has since been adopted by other western armies, notably the US Marines and the British Army.

On 11 October, Trooper Mark Harris was killed in a contact with ZIPRA insurgents near Borehole No 2 in the Chamabonda Vlei area. He died of a gunshot wound to the chest allegedly fired by a ZIPRA female cadre. He had been part of a returning stick which included Martin Atkinson. They had just completed a four day patrol. WOII Don Kenny, however, needed to reinforce the outgoing stick of five with someone from the incoming call sign. Harris drew the short straw. Atkinson relates:

> Mark was a really good mate. He came from the Lowveld area. He was only out for a day or so before the contact. I was a member of Sergeant Patrick Ollivier's stick who were deployed on the follow up. We followed tracks for some distance before finally losing them on the banks of the Zambezi. I still have the last picture ever taken of Mark. It's a photo taken on the top of a train as we were moving from Gona-re-Zhou to France Farm.

On a lighter note, whilst based up at Lupane one of the sections had rescued a piglet at Sipepa. It was presented to the Squadron as 'Skidonks'. It was so-named for the sound it emitted when being tossed in the air by a horse and landing in the mud. He grew into a large and undisciplined hog. On Christmas Eve he broke into Tipping-Woods' tent and gobbled down the goody parcel Cedric's wife had sent him. He then had a good mud-roll before settling down to sleep on Cedric's stretcher! During all this Cedric was busy in the Ops Tent sorting out a sitrep from a call sign which had just sprung an ambush on a gang of gooks. Having dealt with the matter, Cedric made his way to his tent in the pitch dark and got the fright of his life when he found himself confronted by a huge grunting monster! Despite this, Tipping-Woods refused to let Don Kenny get rid of the animal. He writes:

> Don must have thought, 'Bloody TA Officers – soft in the head'.

Kenny got his way in the end. On a later call up, Tipping-Woods stopped at the forces canteen and one of the wonderful women volunteers (WVS) offered him a pork roll. When Tipping-Woods saw Kenny later that day he noted that he couldn't keep a straight face.

4

Rhodesia 1978

On 3 March, Ian Smith made an agreement with the following internal African leaders Bishop Abel Muzorewa of the UANC, Ndabaningi Sithole of ZANU (Sithole), Chief Jeremiah Chirau and Chief Kayisa Ndwini. The two latter individuals had large tribal followings. This agreement became known as 'The Internal Settlement' and had two main objectives – the achievement of international recognition and the ending of the war. Between them, these four men formed an interim government with ministerial portfolios being shared by joint white and black ministers. A constitution was hammered out with a proposed House of Assembly of 100 seats, 28 of which, for a period of ten years, would be reserved for whites. This, it was mutually felt, would allow the new, incoming African ministers time to gain experience of government. There would also be a Senate comprised of ten blacks elected by the black MPs, ten whites elected by the white MPs and ten tribal chiefs. Sithole summed up this temporary arrangement with:

> ... it is to allow the whites to adjust to a new situation ...

The agreement was not recognised internationally. 'Carter', wrote Smith of the American president, 'was incapable of handling the problems surrounding him, and his indecision and misjudgement succeeded only in compounding them by the day.'

For the enemy, the Patriotic Front, this year was another turning point: ZANU, with nearly 10,000 insurgents operating in Rhodesia, declared 1978 to be 'The Year of the People' – in this period they would organise the people politically (through intimidation, torture and murder). This preparatory work was intended to be followed up in 1979 which would be 'the Year of the People's Storm'.[1] ZAPU, for their part, through their military arm ZIPRA, shot down an Air Rhodesia Viscount near Kariba on 3 September,. Then they also hung around to murder ten of the survivors brutally (see below under Operation Tangent).

Regimental and Training

In March, Captain Mike Wilson was serving as course officer for regular army cadets at Gwelo's School of Infantry. Sometime during that month, he was surprised to find that he had been posted to the Grey's Scouts as that unit's second in command. He had regarded his present employment as a stepping stone to greater things. 'Grey's Scouts' he recalls 'was not even on my radar!'

He subsequently discovered that Major Mick McKenna, the Grey's CO and with whom he had previously worked, had specifically asked for him.

Both McKenna and Wilson were informed that the unit's reputation had plummeted after the unfortunate incidents in the Lupane District which the international press had picked up. General Derry MacIntyre, the Army Chief of Staff, was adamant that if greater discipline, leadership and professionalism could not be restored he would disband the unit. McKenna and Wilson had six months to turn things around.

Cedric Tipping-Woods writes:

---

1   *Gore re Gukurahundi* – 'The wind that blows away the chaff'.

Mike Wilkinson (on the left) and Dave Blair (on the right) in sand kit, Inkomo 1978. (Mike Wilkinson)

Major McKenna had taken over and he was not a man to be trifled with. He began the process of creating one of the Rhodesia Army's finest units. The wankers (jerks) were out. Those remaining found a new pride and determination. The new 2i/c was an unknown force but his battle scars suggested he was not to be messed with!

The present 2i/c, Mike Williams, was removed by McKenna. Wilson says:

It quickly became apparent to me that we had the makings of a very fine unit. The troops needed to get back to basics however. Most of them looked like characters out of the Wild West! There was an assortment of stetsons, holsters, cowboy boots, bandanas and the like. I decided that our first ten day deployment would be on foot. I reasoned that we needed to get back to being mounted infantry, and this was one way of seeing who the bad performers were. After a week of having to walk in the bush instead of riding, the effect was dramatic. The stetsons vanished as did the low-slung holsters and riding boots. What was emerging looked like the beginnings of a very fine unit of the Rhodesia Army.

As part of the back-to-basics policy it was necessary to ensure that each man knew how to care for his horse. Trooper Collin Wellensky was sent to DB (Detention Barracks) for failure to look after government property. After this signal lesson, Smudge Smith, the Stable Manager, never had occasion thereafter to charge anyone for failure to look after his horse.

The Grey's were then given a larger than usual allocation of national servicemen. This meant that, since its creation, the Grey's could now field two squadrons: 'A' Squadron staffed by regulars and national servicemen and 'B' Squadron staffed by territorials.

After a spell commanding 'A' Squadron on ops (see below), I returned to Inkomo to begin a new selection and retraining of all the TA troops, and formed 'B' Squadron. Again it was a back-to-basics program as well as refining tactics. In 'B' Squadron we had an exceptional body of men different in age, outlook and experience. This was in contrast to 'A' Squadron but what both squadrons had in common was that very special Grey's style and arrogance which comes from being well-trained and led. In 'B' Squadron the main TA personalities in command were Captain Cedric Tipping-Wood, Lieutenants Rory Hensman and Glen Campbell and WO2 Charlie Davies. Sergeant Adrian Kelly Edwards was the stable manager.

The unit was growing fairly rapidly now. Obtaining suitable horses wasn't easy. The usual supplier couldn't keep up with our demands so we decided to try and capture, school and ride the wild horses of Devuli Ranch.[2] The TA guys of 'B' Squadron comprised some of the country's finest horsemen whether it was polo, polo crosse, dressage or cross country riding. It just so happened that they were in the Devuli area so they were tasked with the job. Cedric Tipping-Wood was in charge with Rory Hensman as his 2i/c. I went down to visit them and witnessed just what difficulties they were having. My first impression was that the few horses then in the corral certainly did not resemble the mustangs one sees running free across the American western prairies. They looked more like oversized feral donkeys. But they looked tough and if we could do something with them they could be of great use. On the day I visited, Rory and Trooper Wilmot were in the corral attempting to rope a very wild and aggressive young stallion. A number of other troopers jumped in to assist but the stallion wasn't having any of it. He suddenly broke free and went for them. The corral was a good three metres high and the would-be captors vaulted over it with a speed and an ease that would put an Olympic athlete to shame! We all had a great laugh but finally decided that this route was too time consuming.

Cedric Tipping-Woods adds:

'B' Squadron was deployed to Birchenough Bridge from Odzi. It was based up in the old hotel area with Corporal G Lawton perched on the top of the bridge as relay for three days. I arrived from Inkomo and we relocated to the Devuli Ranch (one million acres) Headquarters. Routine patrolling continued with little success. We did however capture 25 horses which were shipped back and integrated into the horse pool. Intelligence resulted in the squadron moving south to Humani Ranch owned by Roger and Richard Whittle. Not a great deal of activity except for a contact along the Sabi River with no casualties to either side. The squadron then returned to Inkomo.

Deployment in these vast and sparsely populated areas covering great distances on the off chance of locating enemy spoor were seldom successful. There was little CT movement as there was no logistic support for them in the area. Later deployments in the Victoria Falls area covering known ZIPRA infiltration routes and utilising the troops as a reaction unit, tracking and engaging CTs as a Fireforce unit, yielded great success.

Mike Wilson concludes:

The sheer complexity and individuality of the Grey's made it unique. No other unit in the Rhodesian Army had such a diversity of support services. We had vets (both Government and private), stable managers (we had most of the trainers and jockeys from Salisbury's Borrowdale Race Course and Bulawayo's Turf Club), farriers, saddlers, mechanics, special vehicles such as HCVs (Horse Carrying Vehicles) and a dog section made up of foxhounds and coon hounds –

---

2   Devuli Ranch in the Sabi (Save) valley. The ranch's name derives from the nearby River Devure ('the spiller'). This area has the greatest concentration of baobab trees found anywhere in Africa; it is a scorching, dry-heat wilderness of *mopani* woodland and harsh thorn scrub. The silence here is broken by the ceaseless shrill sound of cicadas and the long plaintive calling of the small emerald spotted doves with their constant *doo, doo-doo; doo-doo, doo-doo, doo-doo, doo, doo, doo* ... said, by the locals, to be in lamentation for the birds' dead ancestors. The tribespeople here live on the granite kopjes (to avoid the termites) and herd goats. (See also T V Bulpin. *Discovering Southern Africa*, p1041)

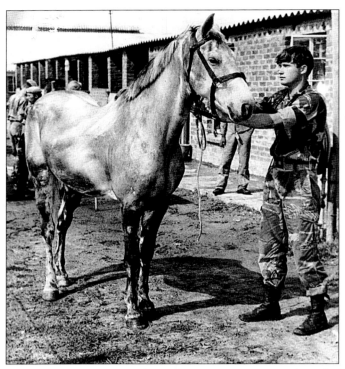

'A' Squadron's Lance Corporal Ben Vermeulen with Eagle, Inkomo 1978. 'Now hold it right there!' Sadly, Eagle was killed in action on 21 October 1979 in Operation Tangent. (Craig Fourie)

the latter breed derived from the North American raccoon-hunting hounds. The fighting troops themselves consisted of black and white regular army members, TA and NS personnel. The whole, for me, represented the most challenging, exciting and rewarding time of my whole career.

On 1 April, Captain Peter 'Pip' Erasmus joined the Grey's Scouts as OC 'B' Squadron. He had previously served as a member of the South African Horse Infantry.

At the South African Army College he had met Mick McKenna, CO of the Grey's whilst both were there on a course. Following this meeting, he resigned from the South African Military and joined the Grey's Scouts.

With the exception of himself, the CSM and the RQMS (Regimental Quartermaster Sergeant) and a handful of HQ regulars, the squadron was, at that time, composed of Territorial Army and National Service conscripts. He recalls:

The squadron leadership element was me and two National Service 2nd Lieutenants. The Squadron had 80 horses. Our Squadron HQ had the usual support services personnel such as signalers, farriers, clerks and cooks and so on, all of whom could ride if required.

The Squadron consisted of three troops of 24 men each. Each troop was theoretically made up of three sections of eight men each. These would occasionally be deployed in mutual support. In 'B' Squadron a section was commanded by a TA Corporal and a half-section by a Lance Corporal. Territorial Bruno Rabie (brother of the late legendary Selous Scout, Andre Rabie) was

Rusti Henderson, veterinary and remount section, 1978. (Neville Croxford)

the senior NCO of the squadron at this time.

The older European territorials were very good with their horses and most of them considered soldiering philosophically as a natural extension of life's problems.

The NCOs and Troopers were equally proficient. These men were mostly 'farm-boys' with a natural-born ability and confidence in dealing with men and handling horses.

Without the benefit of a formal posting and because of his former experience, later that year Erasmus was suddenly seconded from Grey's Scouts to Rhodesian Counter Intelligence. Erasmus was replaced, as OC 'B' Squadron, by Tipping-Woods.

Sometime in 1978, McKenna approached Russett Henderson and asked her to join the unit as a remount rider. Henderson was the daughter of a regular army officer, Lieutenant Colonel Dennis Ford, then the Commanding Officer of 4 RR in Umtali.

Henderson, who could ride, accepted and attested into the regular army as an RWS (Rhodesia Women's Service) in Intake 1/18 at the RLI's Cranborne Barracks in Salisbury. After training as a sergeant, she joined the team of remount riders under Nick van Heerden at Inkomo. Here she also met Corporal Norma Lambert who ran the Vet Section. Lambert was a qualified veterinary nurse who had trained in South Africa. Anne Webb was one of the instructors. Webb had trained in South Africa under Major George Iwanowski who had started the South African Lipizzaner stallions' equestrian establishment at Kyalami.

Henderson was allocated six horses. There was no groom so the remount riders did everything except muck out the stalls. The Grey's had the only indoor riding school in the country at this time. It was very good and most of the training took place in it.

All remount riders had experience of training horses and competing. Once the horses were saddle-broken and going reasonably well, they were ridden out into the open to accustom them to the outside world and what they could expect to encounter in it. Some of the horses were already rideable and did not require further schooling. Others were very young and had to be brought on from scratch. This required time and patience. Henderson found that some of the animals were other people's problems, others were simply too mean and bad-tempered. These animals were subsequently sold. She says:

We had a huge sale. We sold off all the unsuitable horses we had. We were actually looking for animals that were sturdy and that would convert easily, i.e., that could exist on the MIU cubes and still do a good day's work. Bush-type ponies and horses were the best. We weren't interested in thoroughbreds and hot bloods. Having said that, my own horse was a thoroughbred showjumper from Fort Victoria where Colour Sergeant Smudge Smith had bought him. He was named 'Mystic' and once he became my 'instructor's' horse he never again went on operations. (We had 15 years together. When he died aged 22 it was the biggest loss of my life. I had had him since my youngest son was three months old!)

There were a fair number of stallions in the unit. These usually came from South Africa. On one trip we drove to Messina to collect about 100 horses railed up from Natal. When we got them to Inkomo, we spent days getting them through the crush, vetting each one. There were two beautiful big stallions in this lot. After they recovered from gelding they went into training for bush operations. It was a fairly rapid turnover into remounts and then out on bush patrols. Horses were injured on operations and some were killed but many of them stayed with one rider for years. We got to know them and their idiosyncrasies. Because their lives depended on their horses the troops were, on the whole, pretty careful with them.

Mines accounted for more than a few deaths. Some horses were KIA. Others, caught in ambushes, ran off in terror and were subsequently eaten by tribesfolk or lions. Several runaways joined zebra herds, particularly in the Lowveld. Any tack they had on them either eventually fell off or caused problems. One horse which had bolted after an explosion at Inkomo was recovered several days later. The saddle had slipped under his belly and the girth had caused a nasty wound on his withers. It was full of maggots which do help the healing process. We, however, cleaned them off with peroxide and the wound healed beautifully, leaving only a few white hairs to show where the wound had been. Some horses were killed in vehicle accidents; others were stampeded in the lines at night by lions or elephant. One horse, Guiseppe, was found after two years running wild in the bush. We got him back to camp, de-ticked and de-wormed him and he was back on ops in no time.

When the TA guys of 'B' Squadron reported for call up, it fell to me to get their horses fit for bush ops. Some of the guys, like Gary and Rory Hensman who were polo players, brought their own horses. When the jockeys from Borrowdale Racecourse came in on call up they would have the job of riding 'B' Squadron's horses. They were a fun bunch who never took anything seriously and they could ride anything. They worked very hard. When they broke for tea some would head off to the Corporals' mess and tank up on 'voddies for the bodies' after which they would head out again for another riding session. They were a great help.

Jimmy Jamieson ran a tight WOs' and Sergeants' mess. He was very kind and tolerant. He even allowed my fox terrier, Tictac, into this hallowed place and granted her mess privileges. We had some great times in the mess. Many of the guys would semi-humourously recount 'war stories'. Some of these were hair-raising but you could sense that it was one way of coping with war stress.

Concerning runaway horses Major Don Price, BCR, then serving as OC 1 (Indep) Company comments:

Whilst on patrol in a very remote area during our first deployment to Mabalauta in the Operation Repulse area we came upon two beautiful horses. Both had numbers branded on their rumps. I reported this to JOC Repulse who became quite excited by our find. Apparently, some six months previously, a Grey's Scouts call sign operating along the Mozambique border were ambushed by a large group of insurgents. During the subsequent firefight a few of the horses were killed and a few fled. The Grey's eventually gave them up as lost until we found them.

My guys relocated the animals and succeeded in securing one of them. He was a big black horse. Grey's turned up and, together, after a five-day search, we tracked the other fugitive down. We discovered that he sported massive claw marks on his rump – evidence that he had been attacked by a lion. Both animals were pretty wild and had proved difficult to catch. Loading them into the horse box proved entertaining. I stood well back and watched the Grey's cursing and shouting as they took the odd kick from flying hooves before the horses were finally loaded

Corporal Simon F Austin.

up. I really was amazed that these two animals had survived for so long in a wilderness teeming with large carnivores such as lion, hyena and leopard, all of which were fairly active around Mabalauta.

My CQMS, Chalkie van Skalkwyk, (RLI) had approached me with a request to keep a horse. He said 'Hey sir, *Ek se*![3] Please can I keep the perd? If I can't learn to ride it we can always eat it, *Ek se!*'.

Once an RLI skate (scoundrel) always a skate!

New Zealander, Simon Austin, arrived in Rhodesia on 9 April with the specific intention of joining Grey's Scouts. Alas, there were no vacancies at the time so he served with 2RR until 3 October when he was finally accepted to attend a Grey's Scouts selection course which, oddly enough, had started eight days previously!

On a sweltering 5 October, Austin de-bussed at Inkomo where he was issued with an FN, two magazines, a saddle, bridle halter and blankets, etc. After this, he reported to CSM Nick van Heerden, the senior Equitation Instructor, who gave him the bay mare Gemini. He was told that the recruits on selection course were in three sections. After lunch van Heerden took Austin for basic trotting then told him that he would be joining Colour Sergeant Ward's class the next day. Ward instructed the more experienced recruits.

Austin found that the Grey's Scouts' barracks were very comfortable with a good canteen.

The recruits' daily routine, basically, consisted of:

05.45hrs: Stables (feed, water and rub down individual horses).
06.45hrs: Wash and shave and breakfast.
08.00 to 10.00hrs: saddle up for the day's lesson, e.g., on Day One it consisted of trot figure of

3   Afrikaans for 'I say'.

eight circles then canter circles.

10.00hrs: Tea break.

10.30hrs: Lectures. On Day One Lieutenant Graham, RSO, gave them a talk on voice procedure, radio mainly concerned with Grey's Scouts net security as they used TR48s not the small A76 (which came into use soon hereafter). CSM van Heerden then spoke to them on how to sit a horse properly.

13.00hrs: Out to the grenade range where they all threw an HE; followed by a demo on WP (white phosphorus), claymores and 32 Zulus (rifle grenade/rocket).

17.00hrs: Stables (feed, water and groom horses).

All recruits were taught how to care for their mounts. They were required to know how to treat their mount's injuries in barracks and in the bush. The first horse wounds they were taught to deal with were those inflicted by the rider. Below, and hopefully without labouring the point, these basic horse wounds were:

1. Saddle sores: prevented by having the saddle blanket correctly folded on the horse. The horse itself should be kept clean. After a riding period, off-saddle completely, dry off blanket and massage the horse for blood circulation

2. Girth galls: prevented by keeping the horse and its girth clean. Girth galls were treated with gall cure and cotton wool.

3. Rope burns: caused by poor picket lines and bad tying. Treated with lanolin.

4. Feet: at every stop check the mount's feet for cleanliness. Remove stones etc. Cracked heels were mainly caused by dirt.

5. Mouth sores: prevented by checking cheek pieces and making a rubber protector ring.

6. Eye infections: prevented by regular cleaning with a sponge.

The second category were war and environmental wounds:

Cuts: a) small cuts: clean with Savlon to prevent infection; then 1) add Terramycin, 2) inject Trycil (Penicillin), 3) dress wound daily. b) Bleeding copiously: apply pressure pad or heavy dressing.

Snake bites: respiratory problems can arise; apply Scancolin.

Bee stings: calm horse down then give Scancolin. This was not an uncommon injury. African bees are extremely aggressive. Al 'Dick' Weidemann recollects:

Victory was my horse. She was a grey mare and a fine horse who worked hard. We were on patrol in the Victoria Falls area and stopped for a break as the heat was very intense. A swarm of bees suddenly appeared and attacked some of the guys and their horses a short distance from me. I ran to help and we managed to get a couple of the horses away. When I turned about I saw Victory being swarmed by the bees. It was a very bad attack. She was uplifted and I was given another horse. When I returned to Victoria Falls I was told she had died. Apparently she seemed to be recovering nicely in an enclosed section; when she was let out, however, the excitement and adrenalin proved too much for her and she collapsed and died.

Heat stroke: get the horse to shade and water. Give glucose or sugar. Give animal complete rest. If any injections are given make a note of the amount, date and time and give these to the vet.

Colic: biggest single killer of horses. Characteristics: engorgement caused by consuming too much meal or green feed. Symptoms: drowsiness and head-pressing against the wall, the animal won't lie down. Prevention: do not overfeed on green mealies, sorghum or lucerne as these cause gas build-up due to fermentation. Treatment: try 20cc of Analate either IV or IM.

October 1978 Grey's Scouts Training Troop (No.2 Selection Course), passing out day. Standing: Cpl. John Mellet (Instr.),Trps. Simon Austin, Famie Noijie, Fred Van der Merve, Phil Clarridge, Phil Van Vuuren, Leon Kruger, Sgt. Dave Sparkes (Instr.) Kneeling, Tips. Sean King, Tim Reynolds, Sinks Hone, Vic Van der Heever, Ian Longworthy, Fred Sadie. (Simon Austin)

The course involved the usual training in infantry skills with Sergeant Dave Sparkes and Corporal Mellett. Daily riding instruction was usually provided by Colour Sergeant Ward and Sergeant Dave McGillivray. This consisted of mounting and dismounting with FNs progressing to walking, trotting, cantering and finally jumping also with FNs. This progressed to outriding, jumping on and off at gallop, patrol formations and sweeping, skirmishing and mounted anti-ambush drills and so on.

The course was strenuous and demanding. It didn't suit everyone; for instance, on 19 October Austin's diary records:

Sunny day until mid-afternoon. There was a stink today as all yesterday's AWOL blokes (eleven of them) went up on OC's Orders. Each received six days CB (confined to barracks) and docked one day's pay. Derek Bowhay, an RLI bloke, is leaving the course. Most of the TA on the course have also threatened the same. Today's lesson with C/Sgt Ward was outside the riding school, then in the lower paddock for some riding competitions. After morning tea we had a map-reading lecture from Cpl Mellet. After lunch we practised horse formations over obstacles on foot, wearing full webbing and carrying a rifle. Then stables. This evening we heard that security forces had raided Zambia and Mozambique simultaneously ...

Various members were either thrown off the course or decided to RTU (Return to Unit) such as Bowhay (above). Austin's diary records several such instances during this time. Three individuals were found to be unsuitable as late as 14 November – three days before the end of the course.

The course ended on 17 November with a passing out parade. Phil van Vuuren was awarded Best

Recruit. Sinks Hone was awarded Most Improved Rider and Austin gained the Best Shot award. They were all now entitled to wear the Grey's Scouts belt and beret but unfortunately there were no belts in stock on the day. The parade was followed by a celebration in the canteen attended by all officers and NCOs.

On Tuesday 24 Austin found himself part of 2 Section, 4 Troop, 'B' Squadron. The troop commander was Lieutenant Campbell and the troop sergeant was Chris Estherhuizen. Section members included Lance Corporal Norman Minter, Chris Russell, Nigel Bancroff and Gordon Cunliffe.

Near the end of the year, Major Chris Pearce, BCR, then nearing the end of a year-long South African Army Command and Staff Course at Voortrekkerhooghte in Pretoria, received the startling news that he was being appointed Commanding Officer of the Grey's Scouts. Pearce, who had joined the RLI in 1965, had been awarded the Bronze Cross for gallantry and leadership of 13 Troop, 3 Commando, 1 RLI in March 1968 during Operation Cauldron. As he couldn't ride a horse, the idea that he had been given command of a mounted unit left him somewhat flabbergasted!

Operational Log: Grey's Scouts in Operation Hurricane

During the first quarter of 1978, 'B' Squadron was based in Odzi. From here they patrolled the surrounding areas, notably the Maranke TTL. When a small SB OP based up in the neighbouring Zimunya TT, just south of Umtali, reported a sighting of a group of insurgents on a large kopje, Doug Kriedeman and his eight-man section were deployed to the area. Dave Rees was his half-section commander. Recalling the event, Rees writes:

The SB guys had moved from their OP to act as a stop group in an ambush position. We went into similar stop positions. The plan was that the Air Force would bomb the enemy position on the *gomo* (hill) and that we would deal with any escaping gooks that ran into our stop line. We all prayed the bombings would be accurate because we were pretty close to the target area; additionally, as there were only eight of us, there was a good chance the gooks would by-pass our stop line. Doug told us all to turn our combat caps inside out to reveal the orange day-glo flashes stitched to the inside for the airmen to see.

When all the stop groups were in position, the jets screamed in with a terrifying and deafening roar. The explosions followed. It all sounded closer than it really was. I remember thinking that, terrifying as it was for us, what must be the effect on the insurgents on the *gomo*?

Minutes later we heard someone running down the *gomo* at a high rate of knots. This was accompanied by a man's voice calling out to his comrades to regroup. The jesse bush was pretty thick. But then he burst into view running like a jack rabbit, darting from side to side. My half-section opened up and hit him. He screamed but ran on and vanished from sight. We held our positions in the expectation of further possible action. We then linked up with the SB call sign and began the usual extended-line post contact sweep. I was on the extreme left flank alongside an SB member. We found blood spoor and followed it cautiously to a clump of bush from where we could hear the sound of moaning. The SB guy and I, with adrenalin going, went in, located and dragged out the wounded CT. He was actually petrified and in severe pain and shock. We then saw that his arm was badly shot up. We patched him up and gave him a saline drip. We knew how fortunate we were – a captured CT was worth a lot more alive than dead. This one turned out to be the group's Political Commissar trained in Tanzania and China.

He was casevaced. On the following day, amazingly, he was back with us minus the wounded arm. We had found weapons cached in the camp but he proceeded to show us some further arms dumps. We uncovered AKs, ammunition, RPG7 rocket launchers, rockets and mines as well as documents and instruction manuals. I remember that he was quite composed, cooperative and

Assegai magazine, March 1978. (Tony Raft)

polite. Perhaps this was because anyone bearing arms against Rhodesia got the death penalty; if he cooperated (became a 'tame terr') he was spared? I also remember being impressed with the amount of equipment the CT cadres carried per person from across the Mozambique border and into the Zimunya TTL in a matter of days.

On the afternoon of 22 March, two call signs of Grey's Scouts under Sergeant 'Doc' Ward operating in the Zimunya TTL linked up with a tracker call sign which was on the tracks of an estimated 50–60 ZANLA insurgents. The tracks were of a Chinese boot pattern. The troops followed the tracks eastwards with Ward's call sign 5A in the lead, followed by Corporal Doug Kriedemann's call sign 5B. All the insurgents appeared to be moving in single file and were not bothering to anti-track, evidence that they were very confident and had local support. Some time later, Kriedemann spotted an African man moving stealthily along the crest of a kopje 300 metres to his south. Three carefully aimed shots were fired at him and he disappeared into cover. Kriedemann's c/s moved on and was approaching a mielie field when they came under mortar and small arms fire from an enemy position to their north-east. Everyone dismounted and returned fire. The mortars then fell silent but the enemy kept up their small arms fire. The undetected main enemy rifle group to the troops' south east then opened up and both call signs found themselves under heavy fire from an estimated 20–30 insurgents. Both call signs then charged forwards assaulting the enemy main rifle group. The insurgents ceased fire and bombshelled. The troops secured the area which appeared to be an enemy resting-up place.The area was well camouflaged but nothing was found. Follow up tracking proved impossible due to the rocky terrain. Ward concluded his contact logbook for the day with, 'Unfortunately Fireforce was not available to us – which, had it come, would have had a successful engagement'.

Shortly after this contact, 'B' Squadron moved to base up at Birchenough Bridge.

On a sunny and very hot 22 November Simon Austin and his stick mates loaded their horses onto the HCVs and headed for Marandellas, a small town 70 kilometers east of Salisbury on the Umtali road. Here, after lunch, they attended an 'O' (Orders) Group where they were told that they would be operating in the Soswe TTL, south-east of Marandellas. They would be operating as a highly mobile back-up Fireforce behind PATU (Police Anti-Terrorist Unit) and Intaf (Internal Affairs) sticks.[4] Their task was to sweep through the TTL and round up all the African males aged 14–25. The Squadron Commander on this trip was 'Pip' Erasmus.

At 01.00hrs the following morning the Grey's loaded up their horses and left for their FUP (Forming Up Point/Place) in the Soswe arriving at 05.00hrs. Here they off-loaded and saddled up. Austin wrote:

> The Patu sticks, on foot, moved ahead of us. We followed and searched the kraals sweeping northwards through very hilly country. We soon lost the foot patrols and, working our way along the western edge of the TTL, joined up with our reserve section at a deserted school. An insurgent had been sighted nearby but wasn't located. We moved back to our Tac HQ in late afternoon.

Still in the Operation Hurricane area, during late November to early December 'B' Squadron received intelligence that a gang of four insurgents was resting up on a hillside near a small kraal some five kilometres from base. The hill itself was somewhat horseshoe-shaped. A plan was devised using RAR troops as stops on the hillside's outer perimeter while the Grey's Scouts assaulted the enemy position. Corporal Nigel Ramshaw and his section were deployed to the area in pouring rain. This op involved a mixture of 'A' and 'B' squadron members – Steve Bradfield, Collin Welensky, 'Doop' DuPreez, Corporal Lovecross and Ian Wiggill. Fortunately the route was fairly direct for the first four hours. After this they cut through the bush until they neared the kraal. Here they dismounted, tethered their horses and proceeded the rest of the way on foot. Undetected, they reached the edge of the kraal at first light, the rain deadening the sound of their approach. They shook out into assault formation and had just begun to sweep forward when a shot fired by one of the members of the call sign initiated contact. Almost immediately fire began to pour down from the hillside as the enemy responded. Ramshaw noted the enemy green tracer mingling with his section's red tracer, accompanied by the sound of whirring ricochets as rounds struck the rocky hillside. Ramshaw recalls:

> I found myself lying in cover next to Collin Welensky. We both fired double taps into any likely enemy cover within our arc of fire. We couldn't have been better placed being right in the middle of the horseshoe. The contact went on for a couple of minutes followed by a brief lull before kicking off again for another minute or so. Ceasefire was then called. This went on and off for about forty minutes after which there was silence. We then did a sweep and found four dead insurgents on our side of the hill.

---

4   Internal Affairs personnel/cadets attended to the administration of the African population in the TTLs. As the Bush War evolved they became trained in the defence of keeps and kraals. With the escalation of the conflict, their role changed from defensive to offensive and they would deploy alongside regular troops and PATU units.

Captain Erasmus and Colour Sergeant Bruno Rabie arrived in a truck 30 minutes later. We had something to eat then were debriefed before being moved to another contact area nearby. This went on all day. We were finally moved out of the area at midnight, not having slept since 5am the previous day. An exhausting 43 hours.

Grey's Scouts in Operation Repulse

In October, 'A' Squadron were transferred from Victoria Falls to the Midlands. The entire squadron moved by train. It proved an exhausting undertaking. Fortunately the very competent Colour Sergeant Bill 'Smudge' Smith, the Stable Manager, and the Veterinary Officer, Captain Kevin Schulman, organised the entire affair. The trip, in the appalling heat of October, lasted two days with the horses requiring food and water every four hours. For this the train had to stop and the animals fed without being offloaded. Smith had been head of the BSAP equitation section at Morris Depot in Salisbury before joining the Grey's. He was a great and much-loved character held in grand-fatherly affection by everyone.

They based up on a farm belonging to 'A' Squadron's Corporal Mick Spies' grandparents in Somabula. The Squadron were tasked to operate in the Runde TTL north of Shabani. This TTL was considered, by ZANLA, to be semi-liberated and a no-go area for the security forces. The Squadron task was, basically, to dispell this illusion.

Here the Squadron's OC, Captain Mike Wilson, handed over to Captain Theo Williams. Wilson had been promoted to major and appointed 2i/c of the regiment. Williams, a former 'founder member' of the Selous Scouts, had just been posted in from Gwelo's School of Infantry where he had been 2i/c Tactical Wing. He remembers:

> I arrived at the camp on a cold and wet day to take over 'A' Squadron. What I found amazed me. Everything seemed to be doubled, e.g., for every soldier a medic, for every horse a vet and so on.
>
> I spent the first few days speaking to Smudge Smith, the Stables Manager, and C/Sgt Don Kenny who later became the Squadron's Sergeant Major (SSM). Smudge and Don became my sounding boards. Both were always frank and honest with me. From them I learnt a great deal about the men I was to command. I learnt who were the efficient soldiers and, conversely, who the 'skivers' and malingers were. When I asked what the single most serious problem was, Smudge replied that it was a known fact among some of the men that to lose your horse and equipment in a contact proved that you had been in action. When I asked how we could solve this problem Don, in his Yorkshire accent, replied, 'Let the fuckers walk!'

The squadron fell in and Wilson made his 'farewell and good luck' speech. He then asked Williams if he wanted to address the men. Williams declined with a brief 'They will soon get to know me'. Clive Midlane recalls:

> We had all been trying to work Williams out. This terse answer from him assured us that we were in for a hard time. Williams and Don Kenny ran the squadron with an iron rod which, in retrospect, stood us all in good stead.

From base camp the squadron deployed on operations into the totally subverted Runde TTL. The plan was for the Grey's to operate an HDF (High Density Force) with troops from 2RAR and 1RLI. Men from 2RAR had been previously moved into OPs (Observation Posts) in the area. On sighting/locating insurgents from their OPs, the RAR would call in the closest Grey's Scouts call sign as the initial reaction force. If the enemy were in large numbers, additional 2RAR or RLI stand-by Fireforce sticks would be para-dropped from Fort Victoria. Theo Williams recalls:

Clive Midlane, 1 Troop, establishing comms. (Neville Croxford)

I was very keen to keep abreast of what was happening and to monitor the conduct of my men during the operation. I sat by the radio and followed events. Sadly, within the first hour of the op, a horse threw a shoe. I was astounded to learn that an entire section was now out of action due to this. A few hours later a similar incident affected another section. I then overheard Lieutenant Colonel Ian Bate, CO of 1RLI, telling one of his Commando Commanders, Simon Haarhof that ' ... these Grey's Scouts are a bunch of wasters'.

'I immediately got hold of the farrier, a German-born individual, Sergeant Markoumb, and demanded a solution to this problem. He replied that we only did hot-shoeing and that troops could not possibly carry a forge! I then suggested that a farrier accompanied every patrol and did cold-shoeing on the spot. This was in line with modern cavalry where immediate and long-term maintenance was performed. I had now effectively solved one of the Squadron's most important issues.

The operation, overall, went off very well and over the next ten days the Grey's had contacts all over the Runde TTL. They had the local ZANLA on the run. The Grey's witnessed many para drops during this time. All these were from very low altitudes – 400 to 500 feet. Midlane, in 1Troop observed one jump on the side of a hill which was under 300 feet and injuries were sustained.

On the last day of the deployment, an RAR OP sighted a considerable group of insurgents resting up on a large hill feature. Lieutenant Geoff Armand's 1 Troop linked up with 3 Troop under 2nd Lieutenant Colin Davy and were tasked with sweeping the hill. Armand was an experienced officer with two years' service. Davy was a newly arrived national service subaltern, busy learning his trade by understudying his troop corporals Mike Bradshaw, Bobby Hay and 'Doc' Ward.

The sweep, for some reason, was called off. Both troops were instructed to leave the area and move to an uplift location for the following day.

It was late afternoon and both troops, spread out, cantered along a wide dirt road. As they came around a bend where Tom Chebie School was sited, they were ambushed by the large ZANLA group.

Clive Midlane along with the two officers was up front when the firing started. Midlane's horse, 747 Boeing, did a cartwheel sending him head over heels before taking off, never to be seen again. Meanwhile both Armand and Davy had leapt off their horses. The rest of the troops had wheeled off into cover to the right of the killing ground. Armand, Davy and Midlane, out in the open, were the focus of the enemy fire. Midlane says:

> My rifle was about four metres behind me. The only cover I had was the few inches of camber at the edge of the road. Everytime I arched my back to slide back I attracted RPD fire from an insurgent positioned about 30 metres ahead. I hugged the ground with my face turned away from the incoming fire. After a few moments I managed to hook my foot around my rifle and draw it up. During all this time I could see both Armand and Davy who were slightly up the road from me. Armand, incredibly was in the correct prone position normally seen on the rifle range. He was firing short controlled bursts despite the intense accurate fire churning up the dirt all around.
>
> Meanwhile the RAR OP had called up the Lynx which soon appeared overhead. The insurgents were also firing RPG7 rockets over us which were air-bursting behind the rest of the guys who were busy organising themselves in the cover of some dead ground.
>
> As I began to think that Armand and Davy's luck was about to run out, Bobby Hay and his stick came sweeping over the rise in a flanking attack firing into the enemy positions. Alongside Bobby was Mark Element and the bespectacled Sim Maberly. Sim let rip with a 42Z. He aimed it incorrectly and it struck near Trooper Danie Darvel's position. By great good fortune it failed to explode. We laughed about this for years afterwards!
>
> In the face of this, the insurgents began to pull back to the thick jesse along the riverline firing as they went. We followed up, sweeping through their ambush position. We followed a lot of blood spoor leading to the river.
>
> The light was beginning to fade and the Lynx pilot advised Lieutenant Armand not to sweep along the dense riverine vegetation of the streambed. He returned to Fort Vic.
>
> We moved away a few kilometres and based up for the night. Because the three of us had lost all our kit and horses, the rest of the guys shared out their food and blankets.

On the following day they walked to the uplift point. Armand, Davy and Midlane, however, were told to walk back to base through 'Indian territory' as chastisement for losing their horses and kit. It was a 65 kilometre trek. After this, for losing his horse and kit, 2nd Lieutenant Davy was posted out of the unit to RIC (Rhodesia Army Intelligence Corps). For the same reason Armand was given a punitive posting to Grey's HQ Squadron for a few months. Midlane ended up at the School of Infantry to see the MA3 medic to sort out his feet.

On 25 November, 4 Troop moved from Marandellas to the Police Camp at Wedza. They were briefed to round up all African males between 14 and 40 and to destroy all their farm tools/implements as the *mujibas* had been digging up the roads.

On the following day, 4 Troop, in an extended line, began riding at first light. They rounded up all the African men they could find and ordered them to carry all their picks and shovels to the pick-up point. At mid-afternoon, Austin and Russell had a good long distance chase of a probable insurgent who got away. A bit later, at Chidoka Store, they bought some cakes. While consuming these outside they noticed a figure creeping up on them. They shot at it.

> Turned out to be a piccanin (an African juvenile)' recorded Austin 'Probably a *mujiba* spying on us. My rifle jammed after the first round ...

October 1978 Wedza TTL Chris Russel and Nigel Bancroft at Chisisike Support Unit base. 'B' Sqdn. (Simon Austin)

December 1978 B Sqdn, 4 Troop about to leave Mukamba Keep,Wedza TTL, for a night patrol. (Simon Austin)

The next morning, having drawn two days' rations, the troop set off to patrol the area east of Wedza Mountain. They reached an African store where they discovered that the locals had just fed a few insurgents. The troops began an immediate search of the area and saw two men running. They were both shot dead and found to be civilians. They swept on but found nothing further.

The following morning, Monday 27, was overcast and windy. The troop set off at 04.00hrs moving north-west. They saw five insurgents running from a kraal and gave chase but lost them in the jesse. From here they swept up through the kopjes for about 12 kilometres. It was hard going. Nigel Bancroft however, captured three suspects. The troops then rode to the trucks and were recovered to Wedza. They were also told that their CO, Major Mick McKenna,was leaving on promotion to lieutenant colonel. McKenna had been appointed as CO of 2RAR (2nd Battalion the Rhodesian African Rifles). He was being replaced by RLI Major Chris Pearce.

At mid-morning two days later, as they were lazing around camp, 4 Troop were suddenly called

2nd Lieutenant Geoff Armand. (Geoff Armand)

up by RAR to go into the Wedza TTL as an extra stick. Along with the RAR, the troop attacked an enemy camp at first light the following day and killed four insurgents. The survivors bombshelled. All four enemy kills that day were by 4 Troop. They then did OP until dusk but nothing else was seen and they were trucked back to Wedza.

On 2 December both 4 and 5 Troop were given an evening briefing and told to go and set up a night ambush some ten kilometres south of camp. Austin's section was to be Stop 1, Corporal Pettigrew's section was Stop 2 while Lieutenant Campbell would lead the assault section. They reached St Barnabas School at last light then walked five kilometres to their ambush positions and set up their claymores. Nothing transpired but it poured all night. They tried to dry out the following morning before setting off east with Sergeant Esterhuizen in command. They rode for about ten kilometres then stopped at a school where they spent the night.

The next morning dawned cloudy with threatening rain. The Troop began sweeping east to south towards the Internal Affairs keep at Mukamba. Once there they attended a briefing which was interrupted when insurgents were reported five kilometres away by an RAR OP. The troops saddled up pronto and set off. Austin was in a three-man stick with Esterhuizen and Norman Minter. They were moving along a riverline when they suddenly came under fire. They dismounted and skirmished forward returning fire. They killed an insurgent and three women. The insurgent was then found to be a section or platoon commander as he had important diaries and record books on him.

After a night's sleep in the keep, Captain Erasmus arrived and told them that 5 Troop was going back but 4 Troop were required to do a night walk-in to an OP position. The OP proved uneventful and everyone was recovered the next day.

After muster parade on 7 December both troops were detailed back to Mukamba Keep for OP duty. They loaded up the horses at last light and set off. At midnight 5 Troop was dropped off to ride to their OP. 4 Troop reached Mukamba at 02.00hrs. After a couple of hours sleep, 4 Troop set off for their OP position south of the keep. When they got there they also found tracks for twenty insurgents which they immediately began to follow. They then heard RAR troops having a contact further away so they deployed into a stop line. Their c/s 25 (Bill Viljoen and 'Dup' du Preez) then ran into an ambush and the rest of the troop cantered up as reinforcements. The Lynx was overhead and there was a lot of firing going as the troops engaged small groups of insurgents. These then bombshelled. One of the horses had been killed and Trooper Leon Kruger was casevaced suffering from shock. Austin recorded:

> A very disappointing day. My stick fired at six insurgents and missed!

At 03.30hrs in pouring rain on the following morning, the Troop set off for Mukamba to re-occupy their positions of the previous day and deployed into a stop line. The RAR troops then swept towards them. At first light the troop heard the RAR sweepline having a heavy contact. The troops waited expectantly for fleeing insurgents to run into their stop line. Nothing like that happened, so they moved towards a kopje four kilometres to the north-west from where three insurgents had reportedly been sighted. They swept the kopje unsuccessfully. At late evening, Austin and eleven others were detailed to OP duty under Corporal Stu McGregor. They had a *mujiba* for a guide. The exercise turned out to be a lemon as they occupied the wrong OP. On the following morning, Sunday 10 December, RAR's Major Mann contacted them and ordered them to RV with his troops. He also got the Grey's locstat wrong – when his troops began mortaring a group of escaping insurgents, three of the bombs landed within 300 metres of the Grey's Scouts! Everyone was recovered to Mukamba by last light.

At Mukamba, after a few hours sleep the troop, in pouring rain, saddled-up at 01.30hrs and then walked out in the pitch dark. They went south for five kilometres to a deserted store towards the infantry stop lines. The RAR mortaring began at first light which initially made several horses jump as the bombs were being fired over their heads. Kevin Walsh's section then saw two figures running and opened fire, killing a man and capturing a woman. Nothing further transpired. 'B' Squadron was then split into three sections under Lieutenant Campbell, Lieutenant McIllwaine and Sergeant Wiggill. Austin found himself in Wiggill's section. They spent the next few days patrolling.

On a dry and windy morning of Friday 15 December, 4 Troop saddled up at 03.45hrs and set off to patrol north-east of the Wedza TTL. They were tasked with sweeping north then south-east along the Rusawi river which borders the neighbouring Chiduku TTL in the European farming area. They debussed at Morris Bridge on the Rusawi. They rode for about twelve kilometres then came to a mountain range where they captured a running insurgent. After this they walked the horses over a pass before mounting up again. Austin's diary notes for that day records:

> ... We were now on a plateau and in very rough country but the views were superb. At about 14.30hrs, just as we were coming out of the hills, we surprised a party of insurgents at a beer drink. We killed three and captured five. Late afternoon we set up a mortar to flush out insurgents for the PATU sticks but the shoot was cancelled. We were picked up and brought to Rusawi River Club which will be our base until Sunday ...

Grey's Scouts in Operation Tangent
Mike Wilson writes:

> I had the privilege to command the first full 'A' Squadron and we were deployed to Victoria Falls under command Headquarters 1 Brigade. This was in July. We were based at the Airport. 'A' Squadron had three troops commanded by Geoff Armand, a regular subaltern, Okkie Strumpher,

Operation Tangent LCpl Albert (Dick) Weidemann standing with horse Victory facing the camera – sadly her last trip. August 1978. See Roll of Honour. (Source Dick Weidemann)

a national service subaltern and Sergeant Patrick Ollivier, ex French Army. Alistair Hope was my 2i/c, Don Kenny was the SSM and Smudge Smith, as already mentioned, was the stable manager. Tragically, during this first deployment down to Panda-ma-Tenga, the recently joined vet, Captain Luis Vieira, was killed when one of our convoys was ambushed. His replacement was Captain Kevin Schulman – an exceptional vet as well as being a very strict Orthodox Jew. He seldom ate with us as his food had to be Kosher and his mother would send it to him by Swift Transport! On Fridays he would place lighted candles on his trunk and recite the Torah. We all respected him greatly for both his professional skills and his religious ideals.

'During this first deployment a number of contacts were had with ZIPRA insurgents crossing from Zambia to Botswana. In all cases they were well-armed and clothed and in large groups. Captures were very difficult and on two occasions we found bodies of insurgents who had blown themselves up rather than be captured. It was due, in no small measure, to the Grey's that ZIPRA eventually abandoned this route as too dangerous. Our contact drills had been refined. Once contact was made we would dismount. Often some of the horses would run from the contact area and flee back to base, leaving a trail of saddle bags, radios etc. strewn from the border to the fence that surrounded Victoria Falls. In one contact, a trooper named Chad Esterhuizen who was an engine driver for Rhodesia Railways, fell off his horse and it bolted. Asked why he didn't control it he replied 'It's easier to stop a fxxxxxx train than one of these fxxxxxx when they want to go!

Rhodesian Intelligence had uncovered information that heat-seeking missiles were being deployed into the country for the purpose of bringing down civilian passenger aircraft. At the Grey's Scouts, 1 Troop had just come off 10 days R&R after operating in Operation Repulse. One of the section commanders was Corporal Doug Kriedemann who remembers:

'A' Squadron on the way to France Farm to operate against ZIPRA
during Operation Tangent. (Martin Atkinson)

At Inkomo we were told that Combined Operations urgently wanted us to deploy into Northern
Matabeleland. We were to be based at the old Spray View airstrip at Victoria Falls. Intriguingly
we were further informed that our deployment had a special 'clandestine' connotation.

Our Troop Commander was 2nd Lieutenant Geoff Armand. When we arrived we were
briefed by Major Don Price's 2 i/c, Lieutenant Ian Gates. The charismatic and flamboyant Major
Don Price, BCR, was the 'area commander' based at Vic Falls with 1 (Indep) Company. Major
Peter Mincher, OC of 4 (Indep) Company was at times the JOC Commander. In essence Gates
told us that, quite recently, from an elevated area above France Farm homestead, two attempts
had been made by ZIPRA to shoot down the civilian Viscount aircraft at Victoria Falls. Gates
then added that he was handing over the search responsibilty for any missile sites to us.

From this it was realised that ZIPRA was, for the first time, deploying Strela SAM 7s (surface
to air missiles). It also confirmed earlier suspicions that the enemy were looking to launch these
missiles from within Rhodesia. Price's infantry troops had been frustratingly unsuccessful at
locating the ZIPRA missile site. Our task, as fast-moving mounted troops, was to search for and
recover these weapons. The briefing concluded with the usual 'There's a crate of beer in it if you
guys find anything.'

The terrain in this area is mainly wooded kopjes and jesse bush. The soil is mostly Kalahari sand.
There was higher ground to the west above France Farm. This, according to the subsequently recovered
launch commander's journal, was the only logical suitable site from which to launch ground-to-air
missiles. Lower terrain had proved disadvantageous as the nature of the Sam 7s require a targeted
heat source for a minimum time frame and the missile crew believed they would not be able to gain
this essential time-frame to 'lock-on' to the aircraft's afterburners. The earlier failed missile attacks

SCHOOL OF INFANTRY
REGIMENTAL WING
COURSE : INF/35(8) MORTAR FIRE CONTROL
6 MARCH — 23 MARCH 1978

Photography: ARTLIGHT STUDIO.

Back Row: Cpl Van Der Merwe I. J.; Cpl Jones G. A. F.; Tpr Cowell A. L; Tpr Bristow J. D.; Tpr Lambert J.; L Cpl Mosley G. A.

Third Row: Tpr Viljoen D. M.; Sgt Duffey W. A.; L Cpl MacGregor S. J.; Tpr Coelho V. M. C.; Tpr Le Roux J. J.; Tpr Cunliffe G. K.

Second Row: L Cpl Williams A. J.; Tpr Hugo B. D.; Tpr McAtter W. C.; Cpl Malden R. C.; Tpr Spies M. A.; Tpr Welensky C. B.; L Cpl Beckley

Front Row: Spr Smith M. J.; C Sgt Kelly-Edwards A.; Sgt McGillivray D. H.; Tpr Wiedeman A. J.; Pte Chirimunza J.; L Cpl Johns N. V.;
             Tpr Harcourt L. M.; Tpr Mitrovich W. G.

Sitting: 2 Lt G. E. N. Armand; Sgt Turner P. J. (Inst); Capt T. Simpson; Capt N. J. R. Galvin (Course Officer);
             Maj W. R. Winnal (OC Regimental Wing); WO2 Walker R. G. (Inst); 2 Lt C. I. Graham; Cpl Hutchinson D.
             Absent: Tpr Cowling S. A.; Tpr Hennen M.; Tpr Wawn W. S.; Tpr McIver I. G.

had already proved that.

Kriedemann continues:

> A mounted stick would be based at France Farm from where it would patrol the high ground. These patrols were to coincide with aircraft morning flight arrival and departure routines. This would be repeated with the afternoon flight patterns. All Grey's sticks involved in the operation were fully briefed that a major enemy camp and arms dump was being sought. Further, they were warned that these were no ordinary insurgents. These insurgents were likely to be a highly trained task force.

SCHOOL OF INFANTRY
REGIMENTAL WING
COURSE INF/31(10) : 81mm & 60mm MORTAR INSTRUCTORS
3 APRIL — 9 JUNE 1978

Photography: ARTLIGHT STUDIO, GWELO

(L to R):   Cpl Whitlie G. A; L Cpl Sellnick M. W.; Sgt Comber G. A.; Cpl Van Niekerk J. S.; L Cpl Smith R. J.

(L to R):   C Sgt Robey N.; Tpr Soutter G. B.; Sgt Dixon M. R.; L Cpl Campion P. B.; C Sgt Kenny D. A.; 2 Lt R. W. T. Revell.

(L to R):   Lt D. Havnar; Sgt Hutchinson D. G. (Instructor); Sgt Bruce L. (Instructor); Maj W. R. Winnall (OC Regimental Wing);
C Sgt Naested J. V. (Course Officer); Sgt Grantham W. (Instructor); 2 Lt D. Hoffman.

In support of this operation all 1 Troop call signs were brought into the greater Victoria Falls National Park area. Their specific role was to patrol and cross-grain this vast area. This was big game country. Apart from the Zambezi itself, the main feeding and water source for all living creatures in the area came from Chamabonda Vlei, Westwood Vlei and Kalisori Vlei.

'It was easy to see why Price's men were having a tough time of it. They had covered the France Farm area previously but their mobility was somewhat restricted due to the very rough country. Grey's Scouts took over and for the first four weeks we were not coming up with anything despite our greater mobility. It was now mid-June. My stick at this time comprised Troopers Al 'Dick' Weidemann, David Rees, Steve 'Pops' Bradfield, Colin Wellensky, Andre de Villiers and Sheppard, an AS.

Then, at mid-afternoon and just before the Viscount took off, we rode into a small open clearing. My attention was immediately caught by what looked like a grey tin. It looked like one of those old flour containers with the small push-in lid. When I then saw the funny writing on its side I realised we had stumbled into an enemy base camp. Leaping down I yelled out to everyone to take cover. They were great soldiers, debussing and rapidly tethering their horses in an instant.

Intake 159 Passing Out Parade, June/July 1978: most improved horseman, Gordon Forest, and best recruit Jeremy Morkel won awards at the same time. (Jeremy Morkel)

Then we were all in extended line sweeping forward. We combed the entire area then did it once more, just to make sure. There was no sign of the enemy. There was a lot of kit about. Then I heard Dick Weidemann call out a warning that there was a site with heavy tubes.

We secured the area. The insurgents appeared to have left in a hurry. I posted sentries and called up base on the A60 and gave them the sitrep. As usual I was hit with more questions than I could answer just then so I gave them the locstat. After this we began to investigate the camp first for booby traps and wires. We then began to investigate the tube site. Two of the tubes were empty which confirmed the earlier pilots' reports of flash-explosion activity. We then came across three intact SAM7s. All had removable and interchangeable firing mechanisms. One of them had the firing mechanism set and ready to go. We were pretty wary at this stage. We discovered that the missiles appeared to have an 'eye' in the front of the tube. This 'eye' was extremely sensitive – even to body heat! If we passed a hand over the front of the tube the 'eye' moved and focused on it. Unused to this we found it scary.

We also found the crew commander's journal as mentioned. It contained the names of the four crew members and the dates and times of their Zambezi River crossings. He went on to describe their walk to the site and the reasons why the earlier attempts had failed. He had been satisfied that the present site created the necessary close-up to any aircraft, thus eliminating the real effective time lapse required for the SAM 7 to 'lock-on' to its target. All the documents we found were handed over to 1 (Indep) who then passed them on to Victoria Falls' Special Branch.

Kriedemann and his men adopted a common sense approach and disarmed the missiles by removing the firing mechanisms. They then wrapped the weapons in blankets, loaded them on the horses and recovered everything back to France Farm.

A hot pursuit follow-up on the enemy group was begun by Grey's Scouts and elements of 1 (Indep). The Grey's also used their hounds. Sergeant Roy Wiggill and Geoff Gaines-Burrill brought the dogs out, keen to see how they performed in this big game country. Tracks were found and the dogs set off at a cracking pace. The insurgents had headed for the Zambezi River in an almost straight line. When

Grey's Scouts' officer group in the late 1970s. OC Major Tony Stephens,
front row, seated centre (with cane). (A. Weidemann)

the troops hit the river's flood plain, however, it became obvious that the enemy had long gone.
Kriedemann concludes:

Tragically the Kariba Viscount disasters were to follow. The first Viscount 'Hunyani' of Air
Rhodesia, Flight RH825, was shot down by ZIPRA on 3rd September 1978. There were fifty-
two crew and passengers on board. Eighteen survived the crash. Ten of them were mercilessly
bayoneted by ZIPRA on the ground, the other six escaped. The Flight's murdered air hostess
was Dulcie Esterhuizen, sister of Grey's Scouts Sergeant Chris Esterhuizen and Trooper Andre
Esterhuizen. The 2nd Viscount 'Umniati' was brought down by ZIPRA on 12 February 1979.
All fifty-nine aboard perished and included regular army officer Major John Teede and his wife
Mrs Sheila Teede. They were the parents of Grey's Scout Trooper Jan Teede. There was not a
single word of condemnation from the outside world concerning the murder of the one hundred
and seven innocent people involved in both these incidents.

Victoria Falls was encircled by a protective minefield. The men of Major Don Price's 1 (Indep)
Company manned ambush positions on the Victoria Falls-Kazungula road to the west. There were
also ambush positions set up on the bridge just out of the village on the main Falls-Wankie road.
These were the only openings in the cordon sanitaire.

One night Price was enjoying the sleep of the just when he was rudely awakened by an urgent
voice, 'Boss, please come to the radio. You are wanted on the small means sir'.

Wrapping a kikoi around his waist Price made for the Ops Room. There he found his CSM,
Tom van Rensburg, and Sergeant Geoff Brown, the Signals NCO. Brown said, 'The ambush on the

Kazungula Road has been sprung. The lads are standing by, Sir'.

Price grabbed the handset, '16 this is Sunray. Sitrep, over.'

The reply was immediate, 'Roger Sunray. Approximately 10 minutes ago we heard noises on the road to our front. I initiated contact with an Icarus and trip flares. When firing ceased I put up a further Icarus but couldn't see anything. Over.'

Price replied, 'Roger, well done. There is nothing more you can do now. Stay in position and I'll speak to you in the morning.'

At first light Price, van Rensburg and two sticks stood by. Price recollects:

I didn't want to hassle the ambush commander. At this stage he and his men would be cautiously moving forward checking out the kill zone. If and when he had something he would call me. A few minutes later the radio crackled to life, '1 this is 16 Alpha. We have picked up blood spoor on the road and scuff marks on the tarmac. We are moving out to the fence now'. Along with the two sticks the CSM and I set off to rendezvous with c/s 16A. When we caught them up we all moved along the mine field fence. Here we soon realised we were following an animal. The ground was very hard and difficult to read but the thought that came to mind was buffalo! The entire area, including Victoria Falls village, was part of the Victoria Falls National Park. Perhaps a herd of buffalo had walked into the ambush and sprung it? If my assumption was correct we could have a tricky situation on our hands. Wounded buffalo are notoriously dangerous.

I left both sticks on follow up whilst the CSM and I briefed National Parks. We had just rejoined the sticks when the radio came to life, 'Sunray this is 16. We've initiated contact. Over.'

I replied, 'Roger that! Go ahead.' (this anxiously), then the reply, 'Sunray, we have shot a horse!'

I couldn't believe my ears. 'A horse? Repeat, over.' The swift reply was 'Roger, a horse. Over.'

Well, my surprise was total! The follow-up had tracked the blood spoor for a short distance when they saw a brown animal obscured by bush. Thinking it was a buffalo they opened up. The horse was killed but the rider who was just then bending to tighten the girth strap miraculously escaped unscathed. It was a Grey's Scouts call sign which, supposedly on patrol to the north, had decided to sneak back into the village and in so doing had sprung the ambush. They really were extremely fortunate not to have taken casualties – initially when they were in the ambush kill zone and later on this follow-up in which the horse was shot.'

Price recovered his men back to camp. He then called Lieutenant Colonel Mick McKenna the Grey's CO on the phone. McKenna had been Course Officer when Price had been an officer cadet. McKenna wasn't happy, 'Don are you telling me your guys shot one of our members!?'

Price recalls being dumbfounded for a moment:

I thought to myself, 'Members? Was the horse a member?'. It obviously was because Mick then demanded its name and regimental number! I had no idea each animal had its own number. In mitigation I quickly pointed out that, if his men had been where they were supposed to be, the unfortunate incident would not have occurred.

I am sure Mick disciplined the defaulting call sign on their return to base as he was really pissed off about the affair. We met up sometime later and were able to share a laugh about the whole episode.

Sometime in 1978, the SAS 'D' Squadron of the South African Recces, dressed as SAS and under Lieutenant Douw Steyn, were deployed in an OP on the Zambezi about 20 kilometres above the Victoria Falls. Intelligence reports indicated that this area was a ZIPRA crossing point. The Recces set up an ambush on the area. Apart from their personal weapons they also had two 106mm recoilless rifles and LMGs. For support they had the 60mm mortars of Grey's Scouts, commanded by the mortar-trained ex-SAS Squadron Sergeant Major Don Kenny, who had set up their base plates about half a kilometre to the south behind a large kopje. Steyn had given them the required target grid reference for their ranging tables.

ZIPRA'S first appearance on the opposite bank was certainly not discreet! They moved about without any attempt at concealment, yelling and firing into the air. Lieutenant Steyn immediately notified the Grey's mortar team and everyone settled down to await the enemy crossing.

Four boats eventually hove into sight. They were all inflatables with a capability of carrying ten men with their weapons and equipment.

The four craft were launched – but not simultaneously! By the time the first approached the Rhodesian bank the fourth had only just become water-borne! The Recces hit the first one with their 106 just as it beached. Their LMGs then raked and punctured the inflatables which immediately began to sink. Surprisingly, few Africans can swim; these ZIPRA were no exception. Once in the river, they vanished beneath its fast flowing waters.

The Grey's mortar team dropped their bombs with deadly accuracy. Three of the craft were destroyed and turned into debris which was swept away. The fourth, writes Peter Stiff,

> ... bore a charmed life amid the storm of bullets, bombs and shells, disappeared downstream spinning out of control in the current, with no one still aboard. It was found on the sandbank the next day complete with weapons, food and rucksacks, but no ZIPRA. The Zambezi River is infested with crocodiles, which probably explains why.[5]

5   Peter Stiff. *The Silent War.* PP280-281. Pub. Galago.SA.

5

Zimbabwe-Rhodesia 1979

On 30 January the country's European electorate went to the polls to vote in a referendum on the new majority rule Constitution. On the following day the results were announced – an overwhelming 85% voted 'yes' to black rule. In effect the whites were voting themselves out of power. Both the British and American governments declared the result irrelevant.

On the evening of 12 February, the Rhodesia Broadcasting Corporation (RBC) reported the tragic news that a second civilian Viscount aircraft had been brought down by ZIPRA using a SAM-7 missile. Fifty-nine men, women and children were killed. There was no international condemnation of the heinous act.

On 28 February, Ian Smith, who had led his country defiantly against the world, ended his political career with a valedictory speech in the Rhodesian House of Parliament.

Two million of Rhodesia's black population (64% of eligible voters) turned out on 28 April to vote in the 'one man one vote' election demanded by Britain and the international community for so long. Bishop Abel Muzorewa's UANC (United African National Council) emerged as the winners. ZANU and ZAPU boycotted the election. The international observers all declared the election as having been 'fair and free'. Richard Wood writes:

> The guerrillas were stunned by the degree to which the tribesmen had defied them. The Rhodesian security forces mobilised every man they could muster to protect the election and to eradicate the threat to it. Two hundred and thirty insurgents were killed in the three days of the election and 650 in the month of April. The insurgents either went to ground or surrendered. The ZANLA commanders left the country for orders, and for six weeks their men did nothing. The war virtually stopped.' (Richard Wood. Chapter 14 page 378 of 'Challenge'Pub.Ashanti 1989. Ed. Al J. Venter)

On 1 June the country was given the interim name of Zimbabwe-Rhodesia and Bishop Abel Muzorewa took office as Prime Minister. The naïve Muzorewa, a man of God and totally without political acumen, now eagerly awaited the international recognition which had been promised as the country had fulfilled all the required pre-conditions demanded by Britain. Alas he had not counted on the fact that Britain and the United States were determined to see Robert Mugabe in power. Margaret Thatcher reneged on her promise of recognition. Both countries, in fact, withheld recognition of the new state. Because of this, Muzorewa allowed himself to be persuaded by the British to attend an all-party Constitutional Conference at Lancaster House in London. The leader of ZAPU, Joshua Nkomo and ZANU, Robert Mugabe would also attend under their recent (and very uneasy) joint alliance named the Patriotic Front. Here Muzorewa, on 4 December, was tricked into agreeing to hold another general election in which the Patriotic Front would participate. Before this, however, a ceasefire was declared on 28 December which involved the movement of all ZANLA and ZIPRA insurgents into 16 huge camps spread around the country. These were named Assembly Points and would be monitored by 850 soldiers of a British Commonwealth Monitoring Force consisting of detachments from the United Kingdom, Australia, New Zealand, Fiji, and Kenya.

By July 1979, reflecting Rhodesia's critical position, security forces on actual deployment was stretched almost to the limit viz:

33 infantry companies[1] in the Operational areas	3,300
3 RLI commandos on Fireforce duty	240
2 squadrons of Grey's Scouts	80
SAS	250
Selous Scouts	420
Security Force Auxiliaries	8,000
Guard Force	7,000
Internal Affairs	5,000
Rhodesia Defense Unit	6,900
British South Africa Police	9,000
BSAP Reserve	30,000[2]

For a country, which by now had a population of only about 200,000 (or fewer) whites who, in addition to everything else, were also providing military leadership the situation, in the long-term, would be unsustainable. Cilliers, with the benefit of hindsight, reckoned that by the end of 1979 Rhodesia had effectively lost the war.

Regimental and Training

On Wednesday, 23 January Major Chris Pearce, arrived at Grey's Umgusa Barracks to take over from McKenna as CO. He had done some preliminary research on the unit and had several lengthy discussions with Major Mike Wilson the unit's 2 i/c. From this he realised that he had touched down running. McKenna and Wilson had transformed a dispirited and badly-led unit into a very viable and energetic fighting force. Wherever Pearce looked he saw signs of vibrant and purposeful activity. Pearce says of his first impressions:

> This was clearly a place with energy. There was much work in progress and signs of efficiency everywhere: recruits were performing foot drill on the Parade Square, others were learning to ride in the Indoor School, and there were riders exercising, training and re-training horses in the Remount Section. Farriers were busy shoeing horses and mechanics were fixing vehicles in the new MT workshop. Admin staff were busy and canteen and kitchen staff were preparing lunch for the troops ...
>
> My Handover/Takeover with Mick was brief and to the point. He had been promoted to Lieutenant Colonel and was taking over as CO of the First Battalion, The Rhodesian African Rifles. By the end of the week, when Mick bid the unit farewell, I was in no doubt that thanks to him and Mike I had inherited a very fine unit. They had weeded out the uncommitted and unprofessional and re-installed the unit's pride and confidence in itself. There was no question in my mind that the regular European and African soldiers, the TA and the National Servicemen had been welded into a unit with great potential and with a belief in themselves as a fighting unit. McKenna and Wilson between them had changed a demoralised unit into a force to be reckoned with. Their legacy is this history.
>
> The barracks themselves were located near a small railway siding that serviced a number of

---

1   Eight companies each in Op *Hurricane, Repulse and Tangent*, 7 in Op *Thrasher* and 2 in Op *Grapple*.
2   These figures are taken from JK Cilliers' *'Counter-Insurgency in Rhodesia'* pp54-55. Unfortunately Cilliers makes no mention of the two RAR battalions who, along with the RLI, performed Fireforce duty. Furthermore, there is no mention of the six Rhodesia Regiment (Independent) Companies composed of highly effective and aggressive school-leavers actively undergoing their National Service.

farms in the area. There was a relatively new office block serving as Regimental HQ. There was a Quartermaster's Store and a veterinary clinic adjacent to the new Farrier's Shop. Across from HQ was a home-built affair housing the Officers' and Warrant Officers' and Senior NCOs' Mess. Central to all this was the parade square behind which was an asbestos roofed hangar that was the Indoor Riding School – a place I was soon to become very familiar with.

The unit had been founded as an experiment and as such much of the equipment was cast-offs from other units. By the time I took over we were well on the way to getting a proper establishment of new vehicles and equipment. The unit had also undergone a logistics overhaul. All this thanks to Mick. I later wrote a recommendation for him to receive an award for distinguished service in recognition of what he had achieved with the unit. To my regret no award was made.

Learning to ride was a basic necessity. I met with WOII Nick van Heerden the Chief Equitation Instructor and said 'Look Sarn't Major, I'm afraid you will have to teach me to ride'. He replied that he couldn't envisage a problem with this request. 'I'm afraid you don't understand Sarn't Major. I'm not too sure around horses ... ' Nick didn't bat an eyelid and merely repeated that there was no problem.

I subsequently spent many a lunch-hour in the Riding School under Nick's careful tutelage at the end of which I was able to at least ride well enough to stay on a horse ...

What many people were not aware of was that Grey's Scouts were designated as 'Army Troops – Special Forces'. We, in effect, came directly under the command of Combined Operations (Comops) Headquarters for operations but were under the command of Headquarters Salisbury District for administration. This meant that we were not part of any Rhodesian Army Brigade, e.g., 1RLI came under 2 Brigade, 1RAR came under 1 Brigade etc. The Grey's on the other hand could be deployed to any JOC where Comops decided we could be of best use. This had its advantages and disadvantages. The advantages resulted in our ability to leverage material and logistical support from a variety of sources. By and large the unit got fully re-equipped to operational scale in 1979. New HCVs (Horse Carrying Vehicles) were built and delivered based on actual operational requirements. These had an armoured and mine-proofed cab and carried eight horses. Coupled with these were a number of MAPs (Mine and Armour-Plated vehicles) to be used as TCVs (Troop Carrying Vehicles). The disadvantages were that at times some inevitable overlapping occurred.

In this year both routine matters and operations became hectic, the latter very intense at times. Both 'A' and 'B' Squadrons continued their operational commitments as dictated by Comops. The nature of their deployment was such that both squadron commanders, Theo Williams and Cedric Tipping-Woods, respectively operated autonomously under the JOCs they were seconded to but copying-in Grey's HQ and receiving admin and logistics support from them. Discussions were held with Comops as to the Grey's potential for cross-border operations into Mozambique making the best use of the tactical advantages that mounted infantry have. As a result, Theo Williams and his 'A' Squadron carried out several external test operations into neighbouring Mozambique as related below. The ability of horses to carry reasonable loads of ammunition and other equipment at speed over various types of terrain by day or night presented many advantages over deep penetration operations on foot. With sound logistical planning the concept of deep penetration patrols using horses presented considerable advantages over infantry recce patrols that, once compromised, would have great difficulty evading large enemy pursuit parties. Unfortunately these ideas never matured due to the fast moving political changes taking place.

On 8 March, recruit D Herselman along with his 29 fellow recruits of Intake 164 hopped off the

HCVs as they arrived at Grey's Scouts Inkomo barracks. At first glance they appeared to be somewhat cocksure of themselves, some chewing gum and several with long hair. They were, apparently, looking forward to a few easy months of riding around the countryside. The notion was soon disabused. The gum was swiftly discarded and the hair was quickly shorn off. Their instructors introduced themselves as Sergeant Wiggill and Corporal Devenish. The instructors' two theories were briefly explained, (a) they were always right and (b) if they weren't always right then (a) would apply ...

Just to make their lives a bit jollier two further instructors loomed out of nowhere – Corporal 'Bones' Forde and Corporal 'Sandwich' Wheeler. Between these four instructors, the lives of the unfortunate 30 recruits very soon became almost unbearable and the word SLEEP vanished from their dictionaries.

The day began with the assault course at first light. A very brief event called 'breakfast' followed. After this they discovered that they were constantly required to be in several different places at the same time. They became addicted to doing endless press-ups and also enjoyed constantly doubling about the place in four teams, each team toting a large telephone pole/log, each named after an African nationalist leader, viz: Nkomo, Sithole, Mugabe and Muzorewa. Of these Alan Collier, a member of the previous 163 Intake says:

> **Nkomo**: a petrified telephone pole about 45 cm in diameter at one end and 30 cm at the other. It weighed a ton. I'm quite certain that this pole was so old and petrified it had turned to stone – a fearsome burden for the eight unlucky guys that were too slow to grab a place on one of the other three logs!

> **Mugabe**: a really nasty log in itself. Slightly warped it was covered in knobs that dug into your arms and back. But still better than either Nkomo or Sithole. When doing sit-ups with this log its warped structure stuffed up the sit-up rhythm of the eight-man team as they tried to come up together. Also if the guy at the thick end of the log held on too tight the log would twist out of the arms of the guy on the other end and mess everything up!

The riding school was particularly pleasurable and it was where they developed a taste for the floor's rubber chips and horse-dung. Weapon training and lectures followed. After this they found that they could hardly wait for 4 o'clock because blessed relief was offered in the form of PT and its four mile run ... the boring evenings in the barrack room were regularly enlivened by visits from one RP (Regimental Policeman) or another who demanded that they perform 300 star jumps each, followed by a similar number of sit-ups.

Herselman recalls that amongst the highlights of the course was field craft and skirmishing. They learned, spurred on by a devilishly grinning Devenish, to 'lizard crawl' around Inkomo Camp in a record two hours. They even had a song, performed by their star vocalist, recruit Kietsman, about their prowess at this:

> We are the lizards – slither and slide
> We move about like we want to hide
> We came to Grey's Scouts and thought it would be a skive ...

Further highlights included the hilarious sight of recruit Worswick running about like a madman desperately trying to kick off a cobra which had entwined itself around his boot during a compass march, and the sight of copious amounts of blood flowing everywhere when applying drips to each other at a medical lecture.[3]

3   From the recollections of recruit Herselman in *Mahachi* July 1979 pp8-9.

January 1979, 'A' Sqdn, Mbizi, Rodef 45 horse-carrying trucks waiting to uplift a patrol. (Simon Austin)

January 1979, Matibi 2: TTL, mustering cattle from the TTL, to deny Cts a food source. (Simon Austin)

Another new arrival and part of an original 200+ intake was Graham Longstaff. He had wanted to be a Special Forces soldier. He baulked at joining the RLI after seeing the selection intake performing 100 press-ups before being judged good enough to join. The Selous Scouts were at full quota as was the SAS. This left him with Grey's Scouts as a final option in the Special Forces category. The Grey's were looking for 60 volunteers. The instructor asked if any of them could ride. Those who could raised their hands and were then told to fall out as they would not be required. Noting Longstaff's confusion Corporal Dan Brandt, standing nearby, told him that the unit trained soldiers for combat riding; any show-jumping and dressage riders only brought their fancy riding habits and styles with them which were difficult to eradicate.

Longstaff was given Casper, a big brown gelding. Casper was difficult but as nothing compared to Longstaff's fellow recruit, Pete Stappa, who was allocated a mount appropriately named Hellfire. Stappa found that he had to be up an hour before anyone else every morning for Stables just to feed and groom the animal. The Stables routine was enacted morning and evening. During this time grooming was performed, hooves were cleaned and any ticks removed. Most members instinctively inspected their mount's rear from the side to avoid any possible 'double-tap' (a lashing kick from both

January 1979, Matibi 2: TTL, patrolling, very green, rainy season. (Simon Austin)

January 1979, Matibi 2: TTL, burning a kraal to deny terrorist use. (Simon Austin)

hooves). Recruit Ed Trevenan overlooked this precaution one morning and took a double kick to the testicles and was laid off for over a week.

At roll-call on muster parade every morning the recruit had to sing out his horse's name and number. To Longstaff it appeared that they were up at 2 a.m. every morning preparing kit, cleaning weapons, grooming horses, attending muster, performing marching drill and weapon training. This was followed by lessons in map reading, bush craft, tracking, range practice, firing and grenade practice, assault courses, physical training and night exercises. The day ended at 10 p.m. or 11 p.m. They were in a state of constant exhaustion. The aim was to break them down and make them want to give up. If it didn't, it built them up into fighting horse soldiers who then learnt to stay in the saddle for six hours a day, who knew how to ride army style – mounting and dismounting at the gallop; firing at the gallop and also able to do a 'comrade's pickup' if their mate's horse was down and he required a fast lift-up.[4]

Alan Collier of Intake 163 recalls:

---

4   See Graham Longstaff: 'Where Flamelilies Grow' pp72-74. PublishAmerica. 2005.

We had several Rhodesian-born Portuguese guys in our intake; there was Pete de Sa, Tony Machado and Jose De Abreu. They were all in Barrack Room 1. They were real characters with typical Iberian charm. They had serious girlfriends which meant they were always scheming on how to bunk out. National Service was a serious impediment to their romantic inclinations. Before we got our first pass after eight weeks of training, both Pete and Tony had managed to jump the fence during a weekend to get to their girls in Salisbury. Some of the guys were furious at this as we'd all be in trouble if their absence had been discovered.

And then we had foreigners such as American Pat Frey in Barrack Room 1 and Australian Bill Thurman in Barrack Room 2. They both added enormous value to our Intake. Pat was ex Vietnam. He was very laid back and laconic – nothing phased him. His cool and calm attitude kept us all focused. When things were going bad he was always there with a joke or he would produce his guitar and get us all singing. When we were given the lyrics of the Grey's Scouts Song it came without the tune. Pat quickly adapted it to the lyrics of Johnny Cash's 'Ghost Riders in the Sky' so we sang our Regimental Song to the wrong tune! But it was fun. Pat had great leadership qualities and the respect of all including the hard-bitten training staff. Bill Thurman was a down-to-earth Aussie. He was even more foul-mouthed than the instructors! He was full of Aussie slang and other sayings so unique that he often had the instructors squinting askance at him.

Also in March, the newly commissioned Lieutenant Patrick Ollivier rejoined the unit from Gwelo's School of Infantry after successfully completing his Officer's Course.

On 10 April Mike Wilkinson was promoted to Sergeant. He writes:

There were three Troops in 'A' Squadron. I was Troop Sergeant of 1 Troop. Buster Shipster was Troop Sergeant of 2 Troop and Dave Blair was Troop Sergeant of 3 Troop. All three of us had been in the unit since mid-1977 and we all served right up to April 1980 (the advent of Zimbabwe).

Second Lieutenants Tennant and Loxton joined 'A' Squadron at the end of May. Tennant was ex-RLI and Loxton was from 4 (Indep) Coy RR. On joining both attended a crash riding course with intake 163's squad. Both affirmed that it was a crash course in more ways than one. WO2 van den Berg was squadron SQMS.

Mahachi[5] recorded the following:

Major Chris Pearce, the new Commanding Officer extended his sincere appreciation to all members of the unit for the professionalism and cheerfulness they displayed when deployed over the April (Muzorewa) election period. Pearce added that several unit projects were in process of being instituted to improve unit efficiency, amongst them:

1. Light weight rations: as the Regiment's horses each have to carry between 280lbs – 320lbs any weight reduction would improve their efficiency. Ammo and radios could not be pared down but rations certainly could. Using SAS endurance rations as a base an investigation was in progress to produce a light weight ration pack for the Grey's.

2. A proto-type riding denim is to be user-trialled. It is hoped that the new item if successful will solve saddle-sore problems.

The unit extended its congratulations to C/Sergeant Zinyoro and his wife Julia on the birth of their

---

5   The Grey's Scouts' newsletter.

Newly-commissioned Lieutenant Patrick Ollivier mounted up. (Neville Croxford)

Patrick Ollivier instructing an African recruit on the use of a rifle grenade. (Neville Croxford)

son Simon on 23 March. Sergeant Norman Minter and his wife Charmayne were also congratulated on the birth of their son Sean born on 9 May. Lieutenant Rory Hensman was congratulated on his recent marriage to Miss Suzanne Start. Everyone wondered where he had found the time to attend to such frivolity.

Congratulations were also extended to Reid 'Patski' Patterson (a professional jockey in private life) for winning Rhodesia's Premier Horse Race, The Castle Tankard, on Taranaki.

Allan Roy, a recent addition to the Remount Section was seen to bite the dust six times. Not an unusual occurrence of itself – but off the same horse?

Alan Collier continues his reminiscences and, concerning remounts, recalls:

As remounts we used to try and make a habit of going on an outride three or four times a week. Here we would ride the entire Inkomo Estate and get the horses to work as if on patrol. Now and then a good gallop would get the blood pumping. The guys would shorten stirrups jockey style and race each other through the bush. Great fun! Towards the end of 1979 I received a beautiful boerperd donated by a farmer from Harding in Natal. He was lovely to ride and ideally suited to the bush. When he cantered you felt you were in a rocking chair. He had been taught to triple-

March 1979, survivors of Inf.39 (30)at School of Infantry, Gwelo. SA second from right, front row. (Simon Austin)

trot which takes a lot of schooling. This meant one could sit him easy at the trot. I was grateful to the farmer who had raised him. For that he was re-named Ligting and I became very attached to him. This attachment was such that when Captain Fitzgerald asked for horses for active service I always had an excuse not to let Ligting go!

Leaving the unit during this year, after more than two years' service, was WO2 Nick van Heerden who had been hugely instrumental in imparting horse-sense to members at all levels. The Remount Section had benefited a great deal from his experience. His replacement was Captain Fitzgerald (a former RAR Malaya veteran) who took over Training Troop. The pipe-smoking Fitzgerald, incidentally, was not only a horseman but also a fluent Shona linguist. Leaving after nearly three years' service was Sergeant Dave McGillivray. A sad loss of two very experienced and virtually irreplaceable individuals. The loss of experienced NCOs and troops across the board in the Rhodesian Army was to have an effect on the faltering front line. These losses were replaced, in the main, by black conscripts and SFA (Security Force Auxiliaries).

Chris Pearce writes:

In June Army HQ decided that we should send a representation in force to South Africa to demonstrate our gratitude to the Natal communities of Harding and Underberg. Both these towns had generously provided the unit with many horses. The driving force behind the initiative was the amazing Maureen Belbin who was held in very high regard and still remembered with much affection. Major General Derry MacIntyre, Brigadier Tom Davidson and I flew down for the occasion. The Grey's contingent itself arrived at Harding for the two day celebrations which comprised meetings and dinners. The whole culminated in the official presentation to the unit of horses which were then escorted back to our Umgusa Barracks at Inkomo. The presentation ceremony was held in the Harding Community Hall which was packed to the rafters for the occasion.

Two other ladies whose generosity and hard work supported the unit were Doris Garner in Rhodesia and her friend Meme Walker in South Africa. They worked primarily to provide medical equipment for the Rhodesian Army. Doris was invited to the unit to discuss the possibility of providing us with much needed veterinary equipment. The visit marked the

March 1979, SA on Gemini, near the Botswana Border, west of Victoria Falls. (Simon Austin)

beginning of a tremendous friendship and support between these ladies and the unit. They did so much for us procuring shoeing nails and medical and veterinary equipment. They even raised funds to enable us to construct a further number of stables.

Our logistics continued to improve during this year. Services Corps' Major Rob Anderson helped us secure additional vehicles, radios and tentage. Thanks to him we also received, from a South African supplier, specially designed and manufactured webbing waistcoats for the squadrons.

One thing that didn't work, due to sanctions, was the attempted acquisition of the lighter 5.56 calibre US M-16 armalite rifles (Mick McKenna had sought a weapon better suited to mounted infantry than the standard and heavier 7.62 FN or G3). We did, however, get an issue of captured Russian 7.62 intermediate RPD light machine-guns. These were much lighter than our own conventional NATO MAGs (the equivalent of the British GPMG). The RPDs were a useful addition and could also be used with belt-fed ammo or drum magazines.

In about August I was called to ComopsHQ (Combined Operations HQ) where the Chief of Staff (Operations) advised me that the Grey's were about to be given a large sum of money – nearly a million rand – to spend in South Africa purchasing horses and key equipment. He told me to go away and return when I had devised a plan as to how this would be organised. He added that none of funds was to be spent on air fares or hotels.

I could hardly believe our good fortune. This was a very substantial sum and its buying power would be tremendous. Mike Wilson and I sat down and planned how we would implement the operation. We finally decided that Mike would head the team which would include:

Mike Toff, veterinarian
Lieutenant Vince King, quartermaster

March 1979, McClelland saddle
and equipment on horse near
Botswana Border. (Simon Austin)

March 1979, loading
horses onto the new
MAPP HCVs, along the
Victoria Falls-Kazungula
road. (Simon Austin)

Sergeant Mostert, caterer.
Sergeant Hattingh, mechanic
Sergeant Rusty Leggett, saddler, plus two remount riders.

For transport Mike's team had an army VW Kombi and a Datsun pick-up. Both had been fitted with civilian number plates, despite the fact that their green army colour was an immediate giveaway!

On arrival in Pretoria Mike had a one-to-one meeting with a senior military person who handed him a briefcase containing the cash. No doubt feeling he was participating in a bizarre real-life undercover assignment Mike then had the briefcase chained to his wrist. The feeling was accentuated when he was told that no paperwork or receipt accounting would be required for any expenditure. He was to simply return any unexpended cash.

For the next three weeks Mike slept with one eye open and the briefcase attached to his wrist. What little sleep he got was filled with nightmares in which he was attempting to explain how the money had been stolen.

The team worked the area of the Orange Free State and Northern Natal. They did an amazing job. When all the purchases were completed they were reinforced by the Horse Transit

March 1979, Victoria
Falls, 3 Troop patrolling
the Chamunzi area.
(Simon Austin)

March 1979, 2 Troop
leaving for a patrol,
north of the Victoria
Falls-Kazungula road
(good camouflage).
(Simon Austin)

March 1979, 3 Troop
unsaddling while
awaiting uplift, Victoria
Falls-Kazungula road.
(Simon Austin)

March 1979, Dave Blair on Goshawk, near the Botswana Border. (Simon Austin)

March 1979, watering horses on patrol inside Botswana. (Simon Austin)

March 1979, 3 Troop patrolling the Panda-ma-Tenga road, Botswana on left, Rhodesia on right. (Simon Austin)

March 1979, 3 Troop patrolling in the Panda-ma-Tenga area. (Simon Austin)

April 1979, approaching Victoria Falls, negotiating the Police roadblock by the minefield. (Simon Austin)

April 1979, horses in the MAPP on Victoria Falls-Kazungula road. (Simon Austin)

April 1979, 4 Indep, Coy. RAR trackers and our horses doing the "drag", Victoria Falls-Kazungula. (Simon Austin)

April 1979, Scotty Scott and his 4 Indep. Coy. Tracker team in their 25, doing the drag. (Simon Austin)

April 1979, refuelling a MAPP at the main filling station in Victoria Falls. Sgt. Buster Shipster right. (Simon Austin)

May 1979, Cpl. Dave Blair with some 2 Troop guys, along the Zambezi River, west of Victoria Falls. (Simon Austin)

May 1979, 1 Troop on a truck being deployed, SA third from left. (Simon Austin)

May 1979, general view of the Sprayview airfield camp. (Simon Austin)

Party and the horses were railed up to Salisbury. All the animals arrived in good shape and were soon in the Remount Section. Master Saddler Sergeant was delighted to receive numerous sides of good leather and his skilled team was soon not only refurbishing saddles but also making them from scratch using locally made fibreglass saddle trees. There were various other purchases ranging from shoeing nails to veterinary equipment. Everyone agreed that it was 'like Christmas'.

On 14 June, Simon Austin was informed that both he and Trooper Kufa Buku were to pack their kit as they were detailed to a six day Observation Post operators Course at Gwelo's School of Infantry. On arrival they found themselves part of a group of 22 others from various units including RLI, RAR, 10 RR and 5 and 6 (Indep) Company National Servicemen as well as two other Grey's Scouts – Dan Brandt and C/Sergeant John McNeilage. Their Course Instructor was Selous Scout WOII Dennis Croukamp BCR, one of the Rhodesia Army's major reconnaissance exponents.

The Commandant, Lieutenant Colonel Charles Aust, welcomed them to the School of Infantry's first OP operators Course Inf/9(1).

Day 1 of the course itself consisted of how to plan and use an OP. There were lectures on the interpretation of air photography followed by a talk on lines of advance and a practice using maps and air photos. Croukamp then took them out to the nearby hills for a practice on the day's lessons. This was conducted at night in the rain and some of the candidates got lost.

On Day 2 Croukamp lectured on the occupation and setting up of an OP using two films with the emphasis on 'what the enemy sees'. After morning tea Lieutenant Adams, the Course Officer, briefed them on the Reporting Procedures required by an OP when calling up Fireforce. The afternoon was taken up on a demo on types of kit to take when detailed for OP duty.

The morning of Day 3 was spent on GAC (Ground-to-Air Control), first using a sand model then the real thing with a Lynx firing live ammunition. In the afternoon Croukamp lectured them on terrorist tactics using his Selous Scouts debrief notes.

On the following day, they were given a talk by an SAS Captain Bob McKenzie on aspects of OP work and small team operations.[6] That afternoon Croukamp talked to them about mine-laying and followed this up by taking them all out to a nearby gravel road where they were taught how to physically lay a mine. Adams then took them to the range for a demo on ambushing using five claymores and cordex for simultaneous discharge.

On the final day, Adams moved everyone out to the Selukwe TTL to do a clandestine walk-in followed by a night-time occupation of a pre-selected OP site.[7] Having spent the night in the OP the candidates were then tasked to select and plot two GAC targets and call in the Lynx. This was accomplished with ' ... middling success' recalls Austin.

The scribe of July's issue of *Mahachi* wrote:

With the growth of the Regiment comes the finalisation of our dress. The proposals put forward to Army HQ are:

a.   **Bush Hat.** A grey Bush hat, with side flap. Encircling the brim is a plum-coloured band. There is also a plum-coloured stripe up the centre of the flap, in the middle of which is placed the badge. This has already been approved and production has started.

b.   **Hackle.** A single black feather hackle has already been approved for the Bush hat; however

6   Years later, Bob McKenzie served in the conflict in Sierra Leone. Here, when wounded by rebels, he was deserted by his men. His captors strung him up, butchered and ate him.

7   Aware that locals could quickly detect their tracks, Rhodesian Army troops had taken to walking to their OP positions at night. This meant being dropped off barefoot, at evening, from a moving civilian van or truck then marching to their position in the dark over some very rugged terrain. No modern western army would today contemplate such tactics. The Rhodesians did and with great success.

the following changes have been put forward:

Single hackle – Troopers to Corporals

Double Hackle – Sergeants to Colour Sergeants

Triple Hackle – Warrant Officers and Officers

c.   **Competitive Riding Dress.** White breeches, black boots, green jacket. This has always been the 'unofficial' dress and it is hoped to standardise it. Purchase is at members' own cost at this time. Please note that any member wishing to ride in this dress, Regular or TA, need only apply to the CO who encourages individual participation in mounted events.

d.   **Dress No1 (Greens).** Basically the Greens (Army Ceremonial dress) remain the same, except for a tapered trouser cut away at the bottom to permit spurs to be worn. This only applies to officers and the RSM.

e.   **Mess Dress: Warrant officers and senior NCOs.** To comprise a dove-grey monkey-jacket with plum facings. A plum cummerbund and grey trousers with plum stripe.

f.   **Mess Dress: Officers.** Basically the same as at the moment except that all facings on the scarlet jacket will be dove-grey. There will be a grey waistcoat, a grey trouser stripe and spurs will be worn.

In addition to the above, production has commenced on silver badges and collar-dogs for the officers. Should there be a demand for these, they could be made into ladies regimental brooches.

―――――

In September, the 22 year-old Paul Kirk arrived in Rhodesia from the UK with the intention of joining the RLI. Kirk had served in the Royal Air Force Regiment for five years which included an operational tour in Dhofar in Oman in 1975.[8] At the recruiting centre in Salisbury, however, he met John Turner, a fellow Brit who had served in a tank regiment. Turner told Kirk that a mounted infantry unit named Grey's Scouts was looking for trained soldiers.

With curiosity piqued, both men made their way to the Grey's Scouts Umgusa Barracks to find out more. The unit's 2 i/c Major Mike Wilson interviewed them. Obviously not dissatisfied with what he saw, Wilson told them that he was looking for potential NCOs for a new 'C' Squadron that was to be formed. If they successfully completed a conversion course covering drill, weapons and bushcraft he would accept them into the unit as Lance Corporals.

Both men were then assigned to Major Fitzgerald's HQ Squadron. Here Lieutenant Rod Garnett was in charge of Training Troop. His senior Drill and Weapons Instructor was Colour Sergeant Ian Wiggill whose right hand men were Sergeants Martin 'Stretch' Atkinson and Tony Devenish. Junior NCOs were Ken Walker, Dan Brunt and Mark Ellement.

RWS Sergeant Rusti Henderson was in charge of the remount riders. Their job was to train and exercise the many horses that the unit had now accumulated. Riding instructors were Lance Corporals Bradley Grove and Bowyer who, between them, tried to ensure that Kirk and Turner were able to stay on a horse without falling off.

Having successfully completed the conversion course Kirk and Turner were employed in training up the recruits of Intake 167.

For the ten days from 26 October to 4 November, 'A' Squadron underwent intensive retraining. This was because the OC, Captain Williams, was less than impressed with its recent performance. The squadron had impromptu barrack-room inspections ('like a bloody recruit course' laments Austin in his diary note for 30 October), map-reading exercises including night compass marches and speed compass marches, weapon training and drill revision, and lectures on calling in artillery

8   This regiment, whose members are nick-named 'Rock Apes', are the RAF's soldiers.

The Officers' Mess (Corps Training Depot), Inkomo Garrison, in August 1979 on the occasion of the visit by The Hon. Josiah Gumede, President of Zimbabwe-Rhodesia. Left to right: Captain Alistair Ball (Adjutant), Lieutenant Alexandre Binda (Paymaster), Lieutenant Simon Chiwocha (Admin Officer), The Hon. Josiah Gumede MBE, GMLM, Major Alexander 'Sandy' Ward (Officer Commanding), Captain Peter Piggott (Training Officer), Lieutenant Patrick Muzanenhamo (Quartermaster). (Alex Binda)

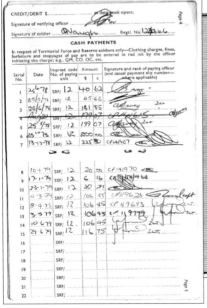

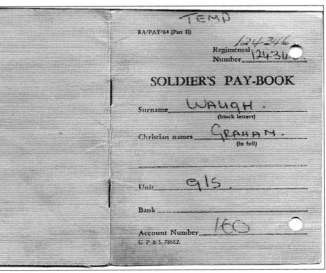

Pay book. (Graham Waugh)

May 1979, followup with 4 Indep. Coy. Trackers near Chamabonda Vlei. (Simon Austin)

May 1979, 1 Troop at the Main Roads Camp on the Kazungula road. Buster Shipster, Neville Croxford, Bugs Hill, Graham Waugh. (Simon Austin)

May 1979, foot patrol along the Zambezi, west of Victoria Falls, Zambia in background. (Simon Austin)

May 1979, section on foot patrol along the Zambezi. Paul Davis, Buck Rogers, Vince Wharren and Graham Waugh. (Simon Austin)

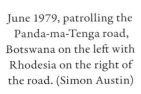

May 1979, L/Cpl Shadreck, resident tracker with a tiger fish he caught in the Zambezi. (Simon Austin)

June 1979, patrolling the Panda-ma-Tenga road, Botswana on the left with Rhodesia on the right of the road. (Simon Austin)

June 1979, evening
relaxation in the troopie
pub at the caravan park
camp. (Simon Austin)

July 1979, troopies and
drivers at the sadza pot,
Main Roads camp whilst
on drag. (Simon Austin)

and camouflage and concealment. All this retraining ended in an inter-troop competition. 3 Troop won the Drill and Weapons competition with 1 Troop second. 2 Troop came top in the ten kilometre battle march and shooting with 1 Troop again coming second. But 1 Troop won on points overall and were awarded the Loxton Buku Trophy by the CO Major Pearce.

Operational Log... The Grey's in Op Repulse

On 8 January Simon Austin noted that of Training Troop only he, Phil van Vuuren, Phil Clarridge and Fanie Nortje were left. Suddenly they, along with the other regulars and NS from 'B' Squadron, were detailed to Rutenga. They had to exchange their FNs for G3s then loaded their kit and seven horses and set off. They had an overnight stop at Fort Victoria and, at first light, headed for Bob van de Sande's Oerwoud Ranch. Here the OC Captain, Theo Williams, set them to work building a mortar pit. At mid-day Austin and Ron Taylor rode shotgun for Bob van der Sande in his armoured Land Rover on an inspection tour of the nearby Ironwood Ranch. They then drove past Nuanetsi Ranch and found 150 cattle that had been slaughtered by insurgents. On return to base, Austin found that both he and van Vuuren had been posted to 2nd Lieutenant Armand's 1 Troop. Armand and his 2i/c Sergeant Beckley were out on patrol just then and due back the next day.

At midnight the following day, 1 Troop, under Beckley, was ordered to a locstat in the Matibi No 2 TTL to act as stop groups to intercept a group of approximately 106 insurgents. It turned out to be a lemon.

On a very hot morning of 12 January, 3 Troop and 1 Troop were deployed to Stelmarcoe Ranch for OP duty on the African compound. 3 Troop were dropped near the homestead. 1 Troop were driven a further six kilometres then debussed and began walking. Beckley and the section leaders did a moonlight recce after which the Troop based up for the night.

At first light Nos 2 and 3 Sections began patrolling. Austin, with No 1 Section, remained in the OP position and logged all movement in and out of the compound. It was dreadful work as they were tormented by tsetse flies attracted by the horses. Again nothing transpired so they returned to base.

During the next few days C/Sergeant Kenny kept them all busy, starting at first light with a five kilometre run in full kit and rifles followed by camp-cleaning, bricking the mortar pit and digging slit trenches. Some of the horses' hooves developed hoof cracks requiring the application of Stockholm Tar and Neatfoot oil to reduce the cracking. This monotony was broken when Austin was informed that he was to attend a five weeks weapons course at Gwelo's School of Infantry in February.

On 18 January, Lieutenant Okkie Strumpher took over 1 Troop from Beckley who, having completed his three year commitment was leaving the regular army. The Troop then began a four day cross-graining patrol on the western border of the Matibi No2 TTL. They patrolled by section burning a couple of kraals along the way. The sections then headed north riding side by side but 150 metres apart in a wide sweep until they reached the Edenvale Ranch boundary fence where they based up for the night. On the next day Austin's call sign came across 50 head of cattle and were ordered to bring them in. As a former ex-ringer Austin was put in charge of the muster operation and the herd was driven to the Stelmarcoe yards. Lieutenant Strumpher's with the other sections brought in a further 23 head.

Strumpher decided that the following days would be spent looking for more cattle. All sections set off and by dusk had mustered a further 259 head. Further mustering resulted in a round-up of over 400 head of cattle.

This trip ended shortly afterwards and everyone was back at Inkomo on 24 January.

On 2 February, Austin loaded his kit onto a Land Rover preparatory to leaving for Gwelo to attend his six week weapons course. Six other Grey's Scouts would also be on it. As he did so he watched the latest intake of 70 newly arrived national servicemen from Llewellin Barracks in Bulawayo falling in for drill. 'Poor buggers' he recalled 'Being put through their paces today by the drill-pigs (instructors). The start of a hell of a life. This is their third week in the Army.'

On 16/17 February 'A' Squadron's 1 Troop killed six insurgents in a contact in the south-east operational area. 'B' squadron, operating in the same area had a contact with an insurgent gang and in the ensuing firefight killed three and captured one.

In March Corporal Mike Wilkinson, his 2i/c Ron Taylor and their four-man section were deployed to the Sengwe TTL. The whole area was crawling with ZANLA insurgents who pretty much had the run of the TTL. Most of the tribes folk had been removed to PVs which meant that any activity observed in the bush would be suspicious and require investigating. Wilkinson's call sign would be set off from farmland. Once in the TTL the feeling of being watched was somehow always unsettling. There was no sign of animal life and the bush was very thick due to the rains. They rode down various trails into the dense jesse and tried to follow several leads. There was spoor everywhere, mostly scattered or old but nothing definite.

On the cold and cloudy morning of 13 March, Wilkinson and his section were riding down a track leading through very dense riverine vegetation near a small stream when he thought he detected movement ahead. It appeared vague and unclear, as if someone had broken cover and then quickly vanished. Wilkinson instinctively felt that there was something ahead. He pulled his men off to the left of the track. Everyone dismounted, tethered the horses and waited. It was dead still and the troops were all 'switched on'. The tension was palpable. Wilkinson remembers:

I kept Vince Warren and Scotty McTeer with me and told Ron to take Kevin Fitzgerald and Paul Davis and go on our left flank along the river line. He was to move along the stream just in case he was required to cross over in a flank attack. We shook out into an assault line – both Vince and Scotty were to my right. After a brief pause we began to move slowly forward out of the thick cover and through the long grass towards the dense jesse along the stream. We followed the path where I thought I had previously seen movement. When we reached the streambed we found it was only about 20 metres wide, with the opposite bank being slightly higher so that we looked up at it. We were all nervous. As we crouched down, the enemy opened fire from the jesse bush on the opposite bank to our immediate front. The three of us dived into the streambed returning fire at the same time. The firing was deafening and we could actually smell the smoke and gunpowder as well as dust. The firing to our front stopped after a while but we could hear firing from slightly further back. I remember thinking that these were fighting terrs and not the usual 'hit and run' variety. I also realised that we had to move forward. There was still firing to our rear, so I thought Ron and his guys had come in from the flank and were giving the terrs a thumping. But rounds were still coming over us. I leapt up and shouted to Vince and Mac to follow. A barrage then opened up, this time from over the top of the bank; there was a big tree to the left of the path about 15 metres away. I made for it. As I ran up to the tree I saw three terrs to my right lying on the top of the bank in thick bush. As I came level with them I very nearly stepped on the closest one; I opened up and emptied my magazine at them. I jumped back behind the tree to re-load. These initial three terrs were now about five metres behind me and there were more to my front. I now found that, because of my crouching position, I couldn't get a magazine out of a pouch on my chest webbing. Because of a design fault, the webbing incorrectly covered the whole magazine. I was now well ahead of my men with no immediate firepower to hand. I tugged desperately at the webbing, expecting one of the terrs from my initial contact to come up behind me at any moment. I then decided to pull out a grenade. Even this stuck! When I got one out I realised it would be of no use – the enemy were so close I'd blow myself up as well.

I then heard Vince shouting for me. He obviously thought I'd been hit. I dared not reply. Behind me and between me and Vince were the three terrs I'd hit. If these three saw how vulnerable I was it would be curtains. Additionally, if any of the terrs to my front resumed firing, both Vince and Scotty would assume a new assault was being made and would return fire. I'd be caught in the middle. After this quick assessment I decided my only option was to stand up and free the magazines from the webbing. As I did so my field of vision expanded. Two of the terrs behind me were now crawling past unseeing. They were so close I could have reached out and touched them. The third wasn't moving having been killed by my first burst. From my standing position I then saw three terrs to my front also crawling to join up with four or five others some twenty metres further back. This group were still firing. The tactic had been that one row of three covered the other and so on.

To the right I saw the enemy commander, about fifty metres away, directing the attack with his AK in one hand resting on his shoulder almost casual-like. With his other hand he was waving his assault group back. He turned to indicate the other way and I saw his right section move up to assault our right flank. Worse, he now motioned forward a further group behind him that I couldn't see. I had originally planned for Ron to come in from the left flank. The terrs were about to go right-flanking on us.

Innovative before their time – The Grey's Scouts, Rhodesia's
Irrepressible Mounted Infantry. (Tony Butler)

Squadron transport and open horse boxes en route to the operational area. The self sufficiency of the Grey's Scouts made them highly effective. (Neville Croxford)

On patrol – kinetic and lethal ... Cpl Kufa Buku, left, armed with a 32 Zulu rifle grenade and, right, L/Cpl Colin Wheeler. (Tony Butler)

The ability to cross most terrains quickly and quietly made the Grey's a valuable asset to the Rhodesian military. They could be upon a terrorist position before the enemy is able to react. (Tony Butler)

Operating light was the norm for the Grey's Scouts – both mounts and Troopers worked off what they could carry. Bivouacs like that shown were simple affairs. (Neville Croxford)

1977; Sgt Doug Kriedemann adorns an Alouette Fireforce helicopter. The Grey's Scouts were occasionally deployed as Fireforce Troops.

1977; Inkomo Barracks, A and B Squadron, Recruits Course Passout: Back row L to R: Shepherd Chirimanzi, unknown, Ian ?, Van Der Merwe, Tom Coid, Titch Harcourt, Dick Weidemann, Mike Bradshaw. Middle row: Mike Gibson, Clive Small, Dan Brandt, Joe Leroux, Buski, Mike Braham, Unknown. Front row: Cpl George Zeeman (Best Recruit), Cpl Joe Barnard , C/Sgt Roy Elderkin, RSM Jimmy Jamieson, WO Nick van Heerden, Sgt Pete Ward, Cpl Jon Mellet, Unknown. (Robin Griesel)

1978 – Mine laying operations with the SAS in Mozambique: Left to right: Rory Thomas, Gavin Woest, Saunders, unknown Greys Scout (sitting), Don Kretzman (holding .50 cal), unknown Greys Scout (sitting), PJ Smith (standing between legs), Jerry De Lange (sitting). Herman Conradie (standing), Frans Botha (sitting far right) Unknown SAS Trooper, Tony Johnson (standing far right). (Frans Botha – SAS)

1978; Frans Botha prepares his mount for mine laying activity in Mozambique. Operations with the SAS were a common occurrence. (Frans Botha – SAS)

1978; The dog tracking section. Nigel Ramshaw with Duke. The dog section was variously attached in a combat tracking role to B Squadron and to other Grey's Scouts details on operations in Sengwe, Grand Reef, and Victoria Falls. (Collin Welensky)

Yet another day, yet another patrol. Grey's Scouts leave their laager. The patrol commander with his radio set hand-piece at affixed to his left webbing strap. (Paul Kirk)

1979; Liam 'Bones' Forde points at the camera as the Grey's Scouts prepare to deploy into Mozambique from Mount Selinda. On this operation, the Grey's worked with black Shangaan trackers who, unusually, were also mounted. (Gordon Forrest)

Limber and horse box – the Rhodesians excelled at fashioning specialist vehicles and equipments from commercial and agricultural chassis'. (Clive Midlane)

1981; Inkomo Barracks. Left to right: C/Sgt. Rusti Henderson on Helsinki 116. Cpl O'Toole, Veterinary Section on Hotspot 101. (Paul Corser)

2010, Dunstable: From left to right; SSM Don Kenny (A Squadron), Lt Colonel Chris Pearce BCR, the last CO of the Grey's Scouts, Lt Colonel Mick McKenna, former CO of the Grey's Scouts. (Dick Weidemann)

Operation Repulse area: Mike Wilkinson, third from left wearing a watch, next to him in the centre is Clive Midlane (blonde hair), 1979. (Mike Wilkinson)

By now I had freed up my four magazines. One on the rifle, one in each pocket and the fourth tucked into my chest. Vince was still shouting for me. I killed the two crawling terrs near me as I called out to Vince to come to me. Knowing that Vince was on his way made me feel back in control. I knew I had to stop the enemy right-flanking attack; to do this I initially fired at the enemy commander. I don't know if I hit him but he got a hell of a fright because he immediately ducked down and started a fast crouching run back, waving all his men to retreat. Potential disaster had been averted. It was a very fortunate break and enabled us to attack the group twenty metres to our front as they were still firing. I know I hit one of them. They all began to move back as Vince joined me. We both left the cover of the tree and attacked the three terrs to our immediate front, killing all of them. We then made for the next row of three but they were now up and running. The commander and his right-flanking group had vanished in the face of our now concentrated firepower.

We did a quick clearance and found blood spoor. The three of us then got back to the tree to assess things. Ron had come up on the flank. I felt really stupid and angry about the magazine fumbling issue; in addition I was so pumped with adrenalin I was shouting at everyone for no apparent reason. I guess I was just simply relieved that we had survived without casualties. We piled the captured weapons by the tree. We were all pretty low on ammo so were not inclined to do a follow up just then. Bobby Hayes' eight-man call sign was a few kilometres away and he came up a couple of hours later to attempt a follow up but found the terr tracks had bombshelled.

For our part we stayed by the streamline from where we had a fair view of the country around us as we waited for helicopter uplift. We kept calling but the chopper just wouldn't come. We had been in the area too long and needed to get away before dark. I felt uneasy as we all knew these ZANLA terrs were organised and bold enough to attack us conventionally. My fears were justified.

At mid-afternoon the terrs came back for us. It was the same big group I'd seen first-hand.

March through Victoria Falls (with the rising spray of the Falls in the background), column leader Captain Theo Williams and Second Lieutenant G Armand followed by troops. (Geoff Armand)

We were ostensibly on stand to but not really expecting to be attacked. They came at us with very heavy automatic and rocket fire. I was by the tree and this time had Paul and Fitz with me. We got the brunt of the attack as the terrs knew the terrain and its layout. The firefight went on for some time. Fitz eventually ran out of ammo. Paul had a few rounds left so I ordered him to cease firing. I only had one full magazine. I crawled to where the radio and captured weapons were and tried to get support. I called repeatedly and remember someone answering but comms were very bad. I gathered up the terr weapons and rejoined Paul and Fitz. The enemy barrage seemed to slacken but rounds were still striking the tree branches above us. We still expected an attack so kept the AKs ready. Having seen their earlier combat tactics I was dreading any similar attempt now and kept a wary eye on our flanks. After a long while the enemy firing faded away and it sounded as though they had withdrawn. We, however, did the obligatory charge through their former positions just to make sure. We were relieved they had gone.

We regrouped and took stock. One of our horses had been shot dead. This was our only casualty. The chopper eventually arrived and dropped us some ammo and left. We then moved as far from the enemy camp as possible in the darkness. We didn't post a guard that night as we'd just performed the longest stand to possible ...

For his performance during this engagement Wilkinson was awarded the Bronze Cross of Rhodesia.[9]

Wilkinson adds this amazing series of uncanny coincidences:

I was inducted into National Service Intake 155 on 15 December 1976. Twenty-one members of

---

9   See Citation in the Honours and Awards appendix.

Corporal Kufa Buku (centre) and members of 'A' Squadron's 2 Troop with landmined vehicle, Operation Repulse area. (Tony Butler)

this intake were selected for National Service Officers Course at Gwelo's School of Infantry on 20 December 1976. I was one of them along with Graeme Rae and Neil McLaughlin. The Course Officer was Captain Theo Williams who, later, was to command Grey's Scouts 'A' Squadron. The three of us were later awarded the Bronze Cross of Rhodesia in July 1979 at the same Award Ceremony.

Neil McLaughlin and I became friends and opted to attend the Regular Officers Course on 10 January 1977. For this we attested into the Regular Army. I was issued with Regimental No 728271 and Neil's was 728272.

During the course we both got lost during the 'survival' phase and both failed the course.

We both opted for Grey's Scouts when we left Gwelo to attend training at RLI in Salisbury.

We both passed out of RLI training on 24 June 1977. I went to Grey's Scouts and Neil stayed with the RLI.

On 13 March 1979 we were both involved in separate contacts in different areas for which we were both awarded the Bronze Cross. Our two names are the only ones on the same General Order No17/79 dated 3 July 1979. I wonder if Neil has ever been aware of these uncanny coincidences.

The Grey's in Op Tangent

In early March, Neville 'Star Wars' Croxford of 'A' Squadron's 1 Troop and his stick mates were patrolling the Zambezi shoreline between Victoria Falls and the Kazungula border post. Corporal Mike Wilkinson was the section commander. Looking across the river at the Zambian town

2 April 1979, Manjolo TTL, Alouette chopper landing to pick up two Cts shot and wounded on the Kamativi operation. (Simon Austin)

2 April 1979, Manjolo TTL, loading the two Cts shot and wounded on the Kamativi operation. (Simon Austin)

2 April 1979, Manjolo TTL, Alouette taking off with the two Cts shot and wounded on the Kamativi op. (Simon Austin)

April 1979, 3 Troop practising Fireforce drills at Sprayview aerodrome, as they were FF for the Elections. (Simon Austin)

April 1979, 3 Troop practising debussing, when tasked as FF for the elections. (Simon Austin)

of Katombora they noticed two Russian T54 tanks parked up and facing them. They relayed the sighting to JOC HQ. They were then ordered to meet up with three SAS and a South African recce mortar teams on the Kazungula road. Leaving an OP in position they reached the RV at midnight. Here 'Operation Katombora' was devised. The six mounted Grey's Scouts carried the 60mm mortar tubes and bombs back to the OP position. Here the SAS and SA Recce mortar teams set up the tubes in pits quickly excavated in the river sand. An SAS team in two canoes, meanwhile, crossed over to the Zambian shore and mined all roads leading out of Katombora. Everything was ready just before first light.

At 05.30 the mortars opened up on the tank positions. Moments later, however, the enemy returned fire with two 50mm anti-aircraft guns. They were fairly accurate. Croxford says:

We returned fire. But it was pretty ineffective. They pinned us down for over an hour. Their shrapnel and tracer were flying everywhere. The only available cover was the mortar positions. The SAS, however, got us out of the shit. Without thought to themselves, they continued a steady and accurate mortar bombardment on the enemy positions. They were pretty methodical and very accurate. First one of the 50mms went silent and then, moments later, the other. I think the SAS used up over 60 bombs but they took out the AK gun and tank positions. The gooks then began to flee. We heard the explosions as their vehicles hit the SAS mines when they sped out of Katombora.

We checked our immediate shore area afterwards. It was riddled with shrapnel. I don't believe I've ever been closer to death than on that day. And all we had were G3s and a couple of FNs!

On 19 March Simon Austin was back at Grey's Scouts having passed his weapons course and been awarded a 'C' grade Instructor's pass by the School of Infantry's Lieutenant Colonel Charles Aust. Reporting to Captain Wilson, Austin and two other members, were detailed to Victoria Falls. Victoria Falls was in the Op *Tangent* area and the Grey's were to work with 4 (Indep) Coy – school leavers undergoing national service – who were based there. The village of Victoria Falls itself was a very picturesque resort with hotels, stores, curio shops, a rest camp and a caravan park as well as a few bungalows – all of this within the rain-forest mist cast by the waterfall. From here boat cruises and game-viewing flights could be chartered. The Falls themselves were originally named by the Kololo people as *Mosi o a Tunya* meaning 'smoke that rises' which was later, incorrectly, but more popularly, translated as 'the smoke that thunders'. The Victoria Falls Hotel faced the famous bridge spanning the Zambezi. To its left was Sprayview. The path from the hotel to the bridge was more than one kilometre and the distance from the hotel to the famous Big Tree (via Livingstone's statue) was somewhat less than three kilometres.

On arrival at the Falls, the trio was immediately ordered by the OC, Captain Theo Williams, to take a TCV and an HCV and pick up 2 Troop who were patrolling along the Zambezi towards Kazungula. Kazungula, in the extreme north-west of Rhodesia, operated a vehicle ferry service between Zambia and Botswana. It is a point on the map bordering Zambia, South West Africa's Caprivi Strip (now Namibia) and Botswana.

Present at the Grey's camp was C/Sergeant Don Kenny now a WO2 (Warrant Officer Class Two) and Squadron Sergeant Major for 'A' Squadron. Alan Collier writes:

Don Kenny, 'A' Squadron's SSM, was fearsome. To this day, the words 'pack drill' still send shivers through me. Pack drill was punishment meted out for any operational misdemeanour. It involved two to three hours of leopard-crawling, press-ups and running up and down an anthill; all of these performed in full kit and a pack full of sandbags It was brutal and guaranteed to knock the shit out of anyone.

Of this punishment Graham Longstaff writes:

Nuanetsi was where I received my first pack drill punishment. I had not heard the call to 'fall in' one afternoon and was late. Displeased, SSM Don Kenny detailed Sergeant Patrick Ollivier to take me through it. A rucksack was filled with sand with the top few inches layered with bricks or rocks. It was tightly strapped to my back. I was then made to run in a circle, stop, do a forward roll, crawl back onto my feet and resume the run. The routine continued non-stop for ten minutes and, with the temperature at nearly 40 degrees Celsius, absolutely exhausting. It was designed to break you down.

Alan Collier continues:

All three Troops of the Squadron alternated between Call-Out, 10 day patrols and Stand By. Those on Call-Out loaded their horses onto the vehicles and performed the 'drag' – the patrolling of the sand road alongside the Victoria Falls–Kazungula main road. This sand road was 'dragged' daily with tractor tyres to a smooth sandy surface in which tracks would be instantly discernible.

Austin was pleased to be reunited with his original mount, the bay mare Gemini. He now found himself in Corporal John Coast's section (Coast was later awarded the Silver Cross) and they spent the next week patrolling the Panda-ma-Tenga (more correctly *Mpanda Mutenga* – lit: Mutenga's rain trees) Road, also known as 'the drag'. This road borders onto Botswana. Patrolling the drag was to become routine border control from now on.

On 2 April, a Tracker Combat Team of 4 (Indep) operating in the Kamativi area reported being on tracks for 15 insurgents. Grey's Scouts were deployed to the area as reaction troops. They spent the night at an abandoned mission. On the following day they set off hoping to cut spoor ahead of the 4 (Indep) trackers. At midday 4 (Indep) made contact with an enemy gang of some 25 insurgents. The enemy bombshelled. Austin's call sign 1.3C were sent in to try and cut spoor south and east of the contact area. As they moved on they heard the Lynx attack with Frantan on a group of over 80 insurgents. The Hunters were called in for a re-strike. Austin saw them come out of their dive directly over his position. His call sign moved forward and came across a big enemy camp containing a large quantity of ammunition, land mines and RPG rockets. On the way back the call sign, following up and looking for tracks, had a fleeting contact with five insurgents but lost them in the very thick jesse bush. On the following day they patrolled 25 kilometres up to the fly gate on the old game fence in the Manjolo TTL. They moved on for a further eight kilometres then based up for the night. At mid-morning on the following day they captured what they believed to be two *mujibas* (young insurgent supporters). Two hours later they approached a kraal and saw three men. On being challenged the three broke and ran. Troopers Sean Coles and Schaap shot and wounded two whilst Austin and Brown captured the third after a hectic chase. The chopper casevaced the wounded and the c/s continued on, returning to the fly gate where they linked up with c/s 1.3A and 1.3B who had located tracks for four which were followed then lost in the jesse. All call signs then returned to Kamativi.

⊹⊱──⊰⊹

Peter Stiff writes:

On 22 March 1979 the Selous Scouts captured Elliot Sibanda, ZIPRA's senior Intelligence officer for their Southern Front, in an ambush laid within Botswana.

Sibanda's interrogation revealed that the Soviets had decided to revitalise ZIPRA's failing war effort, bringing the organisation on to a conventional war footing with five battalions of mixed motorised infantry and armour. Their idea was to work towards preempting the Red Chinese-backed ZANLA, which was purely organised as a guerrilla army, by invading Rhodesia and capturing Salisbury within a time-span of twenty four hours.

The plan involved seizing two bridgeheads over the Zambezi River, one at Chirundu and the other at Victoria Falls, and sending two armoured columns, 9,000 strong, across to capture the airfields at Kariba and Wankie. Libyan transport aircraft would fly in ZIPRA reinforcements to consolidate their gains, while the armoured columns continued with a pincer movement on Salisbury.

Soviet MiG fighters, piloted by Libyan or Cuban 'volunteers' and Soviet-trained ZIPRA pilots would provide air support. The MiGs were shipped to Zambia but were left in their crates and eventually expropriated by the Zambians for their own air force.[10]

Back at Victoria Falls on 6 April, Austin's diary records that the Grey's were given a talk by the OC Captain Theo Williams on what to expect from over the river. Williams informed them that things appeared to be hotting up. The Grey's would be standing by as Fireforce reinforcements. To this end three choppers would be arriving soon to train them in Fireforce drills. Austin and Troopers Sean Coles and Schaap became part of a four-man stick under Lance Corporal Neil Johns. Conversely, if the stick were to be suddenly required as a horse call-out or mounted reaction call sign, they would be joined by troopers Brown and Davel. The Grey's were nothing if not versatile! Austin added that, additionally, 'The OC Captain Williams gave us an hour's intensive PT in full kit and webbing – blokes not amused.'

Williams, seemingly determined to have his men at their peak, gave them another dose of the same the following day but, as Austin recorded, it was ' … taken in good spirit this time'.

On the following morning a company of army engineers arrived with barbed wire. In the afternoon two squadrons of Elands and Ferrets from the Armoured Car Regiment arrived, as did a company from 9RR and mortar teams from 2RR (both 9 and 2RR were Rhodesia Regiment Bulawayo battalions). Later a half squadron of SAS also arrived. The troops at Victoria Falls were now at about battalion strength.

When the choppers arrived on 8 April the Grey's began practicing fireforce drills. This went on all morning and involved much emplaning and deplaning – the latter sometimes from uncomfortable three to five metre hovers. In the afternoon the whole troop did a stand to, then trucked past the Big Tree to a river location as insurgents were reported crossing over in boats near the 16 kilometre peg.

The story is taken up by Lieutenant Tony Ballinger of 2nd Battalion Rhodesia Regiment Support Company:

> I remember that episode as if it was yesterday. I commanded a platoon of 2RR Support Company troops based behind the ruins of the Elephant Hills Hotel. I had three 81mm and two 60mm mortars under my command as well as an anti-tank platoon armed with American 106mm guns mounted on German Unimogs.
>
> Sometime in early April of 1979 I was called to an urgent meeting at the A'Zambezi hotel which was now devoid of tourists and served as sub-JOC headquarters for that part of Matabeleland.
>
> Seated at the conference table, behind guarded doors, was Captain Theo Williams of the Grey's Scouts plus the OC of 4 (Indep) Company, a Brigadier, the OC of a company from 9RR whose troops had been moved into the area and the OCs of the Artillery and Armoured Cars, plus the JOC commander, Ron Barker.
>
> The topic that was announced literally made the hair on the nape of my neck stand on end. We were told that upwards of 20,000 ZIPRA troops were about to invade Rhodesia. A substantial number of these would be coming through Victoria Falls and the remainder through Chirundu. We were placed on a conventional war footing and most of the troops out on ops or on routine border control had been notified to return to Victoria Falls immediately.
>
> We were briefed on the defensive plan, specially the forces to be positioned at the Victoria Falls bridge itself.
>
> From the air, the spit of land that ran up to the bridge looks like a lizard's neck and head. The tip of the nose would be where the bridge was located and two or three hundred metres back, by the 'neck', was a Customs and Immigration post building that was allocated as a Forward

---

10   Peter Stiff: *The Silent War*. Pub. Galago, S.A.

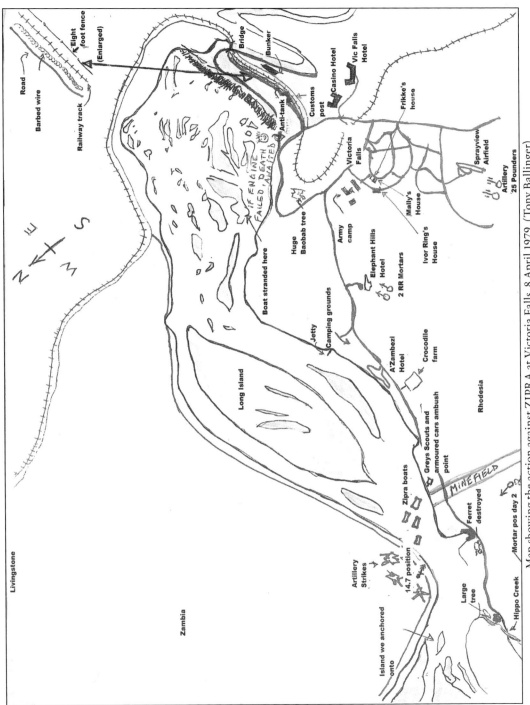

Map showing the action against ZIPRA at Victoria Falls, 8 April 1979. (Tony Ballinger)

Control Centre (see sketch).Within was a closed circuit television that had been hooked up to a camera that faced the bridge spanning into Zambia. The idea was that it was too dangerous for troops to physically watch the bridge, so it was to be done by this remote camera.

Along the right-hand, or southern side of the neck, several defensive positions were dug into the soft, wet soil. This included a big, heavily fortified bunker that housed at least a dozen men with machine guns and a B-10 recoilless rifle thrown in for good measure. An eight-foot fence separated the bunker from the railway line which ran down the spine of the 'lizard head/ neck' spit of land. This had various nasties attached to it by two engineers based in Victoria Falls village, Keith Samson and Charlie Small.

On the immediate left-hand or northern side of the railway line was a coiled barbed-wire fence that ran for its full length from the bridge to the Customs post building. Bunkered by the building and behind 44-gallon drums were my two anti-tank vehicles facing down the road that ran parallel with the rail track. Our task was to take out any armour that attempted to cross the bridge.

The second bit of news explained the defensive measures being taken. A large number of ZIPRA troops, reportedly 1,200, were to come over in a train – Trojan Horse fashion – to help take out the village. The fences on either side of the tracks were designed to slow down or stop them from de-training and going on the attack. Any that attempted to do so would be blown up by the nasties hanging on the fences as well as being blasted by my anti-tank guns, the B-10, MAG and small arms fire. They would also be bombed by my mortars sited up on the hill and by the artillery based at the airstrip. It would be a massacre even though we might eventually lose the initiative against the overwhelming ZIPRA on the train.

Over to the west of the village was a point where the minefield which surrounded Victoria Falls entered the Zambezi River. Here, Captain Theo Williams, who was the Operational Commander, decided to position two armoured cars and some Grey's Scouts troops in ambush position. This was because intelligence reports indicated that a large number of ZIPRA would cross the river in dingies to the west of the bridge with the intention of unlocking its defensive positions with an attack from the rear, i.e., from the village itself.

On the night of the attack, sometime near mid-April I think it was, I was at my girlfriend's flat when I heard a high volume of machine-gun fire rip into the night from the minefield area. I raced back to my platoon behind the Elephant Hills hotel ruins and in the process nearly collided with my anti-tank guns which were speeding down to the bridge.

I waited with bated breath to bring my mortars to bear on what now appeared to be developing into a major enemy crossing at the minefield/river interface. I stood on the edge of the ruins, high on a hill overlooking the Zambezi River and watched tracer zipping this way and that – red from our side and green and white from theirs. The white tracer came from a 14.7 gun mounted on the Zambian shoreline and was being used to great effect to cover ZIPRA as they crossed the river. Artillery was brought to bear to neutralize the 14.7. I remember dozens of rounds whistling over my head. It was like a WWII movie! The rounds, with red flashes, exploded with thuds and rumbles inside Zambia.

Captain Theo Williams now takes up the narrative:

The most interesting part of the night was the planning. Once the intelligence was received, I sat in my ops vehicle which was at the Caravan Park; my radio operators were Burt Caneza and Peter Chadwick. From where I sat I could see the river and its bends. If ZIPRA used the current and the natural bend that ended at the beginning of the minefield they would end up entering the area within the minefield, i.e., the safe zone. I decided to put an ambush in that area consisting of two armoured cars and a section of my Grey's Scouts troops. Nothing happened on the first night but on the second things began to occur. The first enemy boat containing between 30 and 40 ZIPRA paddled into the killing area. This was followed by others. My men and the armoured cars opened fire. ZIPRA boats and bodies dissolved into the river.

With that the Zambian side opened up with a 14.7 from their boat embarkation point. The troop commander of the armoured cars got such a fright he tried to back his car into safety. Alas, he backed into the other armoured car. This might appear funny in retrospect but not at that particular moment. I requested the 25 pounders at Sprayview to open up at a 'slow' rate. Unfortunately the very keen battery commander ordered 'intense'. This meant eight guns, each firing five rounds per minute, were pounding the gooks on the Zambian shore that were waiting to be ferried across to Rhodesia.

I then ordered the 81mm mortars to bring support on the defensive fire zone but added 500 metres to the range. This gave me a larger beaten zone. Once things quietened down, we reduced the rate of fire but kept up a creeping barrage on to the Zambian side and on to the fleeing enemy.

We killed an unknown number of bad guys that night but for a week a large number of bodies surfaced which were an embarrassment to the tourists on the Falls Booze Cruise a few days later.

It was subsequently rumoured that we killed between 300 to 500 ZIPRA infantry on the Zambian side. They had planned a brigade attack on us but we had hit them hard at their embarkation point. It was never confirmed but a Special Branch informer by the name of Kenny got information that Livingstone was awash with bodies and that many days were spent burying the dead there.

Ron Barker and I collected bits of bodies. The main capture of survivors took place a day later on the Kazungula road by Grey's Scouts. The Grey's along with the SB informer, Kenny, took to boats and scoured the river for bodies. They also found a lot of survivors on several of the Zambezi islands

The intelligence about a ZIPRA brigade attack was proved correct and verified. If they had captured Victoria Falls their leader, Joshua Nkomo and his Russian sponsors would have scored a political and military success.

Tony Ballinger adds to this account with:

On the next day I went down the hill to the booze cruise jetty. There I saw a dozen or more ZIPRA being offloaded from a tour boat which had been commandeered to search for insurgent survivors downstream. Under the guns of the troops these survivors looked scared and dejected. Some hobbled about bearing horrific wounds. Even though they were the enemy, at that moment I pitied them.

A few hours later I was tasked with covering river-front searches for further survivors. We drove through the minefield and up a steep hill. My mortar detachment had orders to be on call if our infantry lower down got into difficulties or were targeted by the 14.7 of the previous evening.

We had no sooner got into position with mortars pointing north and ammo boxes cracked open when a long line of mounted Grey's Scouts came out of the bush to our left. They looked at us and we smiled at each other. They were all blacked up and looked bloody rugged. I thanked God I was not a gook being hunted by these guys. I got an inkling then of the terror that infantry in a bygone age must have experienced when charged by cavalry. Perhaps these were the Grey's who had rounded up the ZIPRA survivors on the Kazungula road? They certainly looked the part of a corps of men with a very proud Rhodesian tradition.

August 1979, in the "Bit Inn", the troopie pub at the A'Zambezi, Victoria Falls. Neville Croxford, Sgt. Mike Wilkinson BCR, Cpl. Chris Steyn. (Simon Austin)

Simon Austin concludes with:

I was sent out a few days after the battle with three BSAP members, one of whom was a woman. We had been ordered to collect some bodies that had been seen floating in the river. We found them and they were pretty bloated having been in the water for a couple of days. The two male cops refused to touch them so it was up to the policewoman and me. We pulled several to the bank. The bodies actually came apart. At one stage I was left with an arm and a head. The stench was appalling as can be imagined. The policewoman was amazing – she dragged all the bits to the bank. We then loaded them on to her Land Rover and she drove off with them back to Victoria Falls.

A few evenings later, Austin, now back in Lieutenant Strumpher's call sign 1.1, was manning the minefield roadblock on the Kamativi road in support of the Armoured Cars who were deployed for a night attack.

On 12 April members of 1 and 2 Troops were deployed with police on a midnight raid on the African township to pick up known enemy sympathizers. It was very successful and everyone was back by dawn.

Mike Wilkinson was promoted to Sergeant and Austin, who was part of his section, was made up to Lance Corporal. The entire section had to parade in full webbing for the benefit of some visiting South African army officers. This was followed by a demonstration of horse combat tactics.

On 17 April, the first day of the Elections, Simon Austin accompanied the OC, Captain Williams, to Kazungula. The OC was due to parley with Zambian and Botswanan officials but the latter failed to arrive so the meeting was called off. Despite not having resided in the country for more than two years, Austin was allowed to vote. At the Victoria Falls polling station he voted for Chief Chirau of the moderate ZUPO (Zimbabwe United Peoples Organisation).

On 18 April the unit was told that their camp area was to become a JOC. This entailed a complete move. The new location was the holiday camp near the Zambezi River just beyond the A'Zambezi River Lodge which was closing down. On the evening of the same day 1 Troop took over patrolling from 2 Troop at the 16 mile peg. They followed the cut-line to the river before walking on and setting up a semi-permanent base camp about one kilometre from the Zambezi.

August 1979, Call Sign 1.1 Bravo, near the Zambezi, west of Victoria Falls. (Simon Austin)

August 1979, follow-up on communist terrorist tracks at The Pause farm, south of Victoria Falls. (Simon Austin)

August 1979, section on patrol, leaving Paradise Ranch HQ, near Kazungula. (Simon Austin)

August 1979, Section on patrol, west of Victoria Falls. (Simon Austin)

August 1979, SA with horse Gemini, at Paradise Ranch HQ, overlooking the Zambezi, Kazungula. (Simon Austin)

August 1979, watering horses near Westwood Ranch HQ, west of Victoria Falls. (Simon Austin)

August 1979, approaching the Zambezi, west of Victoria Falls. (Simon Austin)

My section with captured CT weaponry by the Zambezi, west of Victoria Falls, after an attempted crossing in strength. L/Cpl Shadreck, White, Mossison, Desa, Smith, Cpl. Steyn, Henderson. (Simon Austin)

August 1979, SA with a captured RPG7, west of Victoria Falls. (Simon Austin)

September 1979, Smudge Smith and Tony Wilkinson on our OP on Zinunyi Mt, north of Chisumbanje, in the south-east. (Simon Austin)

September 1979, 'A' Sqdn moving into Gaza Province, Mozambique, to attack a terrorist base camp. (Simon Austin)

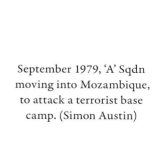

September 1979, 'A' Sqdn moving into Mozambique, to attack a terrorist base camp. (Simon Austin)

September 1979, SA's stop group position to stop armour from Espungabera, while the Sqdn was attacking a Terrorist base camp. (Simon Austin)

On the following day they were informed that 3 Troop were on tracks for four insurgents who were heading for the river. 1 Troop quickly detailed three sticks as stops. At 1500 hours 3 Troop reported capturing two AMA suspects. Nothing further occurred so 1 Troop returned to their base and spent the rest of the day swimming, fishing and hippo-watching.

The next few days were spent on OP and ambush duty. Game was everywhere – Bobby Hay's section walked into an elephant herd and had to 'gap it' post haste! Hippos were plentiful and lion could be heard roaring nearby most nights, no doubt drawn by the smell of the equines.

On 23 April Grey's Scouts c/s 4.3 had a last light, long distance contact with a group of 15 to 20 insurgents who were moving by boat to an island east of their position. No casualties were reported. Unhappy about this Mike Wilkinson gave everyone a 'rev' (dressing down) for being 'switched off'.

On 28 April Armoured Cars call sign 2.2 saw a boatload of insurgents and opened fire on it. A hit was scored and some enemy was killed. The Armoured Cars c/s then came under immediate mortar fire from across the river where a Zipra/Zambian force was set up covering the enemy's crossing. The surviving enemy made it to the Rhodesian bank but walked into a minefield where many got blown up. Others were reported as having bombshelled, discarding their weapons and running for their lives.

On 1 May Colin Waddel's section of 2 Troop had a contact with an unknown number of insurgents and killed two. Both were young men and armed with SARs using Tokarev ammunition (7.62x25mm).

On the evening of the following day, eight insurgents were observed on Princess Island. The Grey's captured them all without a fight. Apparently the group was totally demoralized as they had not eaten for five days.

The Grey's now received an issue of newly designed webbing. Austin commented, ' ... it's made of light nylon and is South African. The webbing was specially procured for the Grey's by RhASC's Major Rob Anderson. The camo is very gaudy. Interesting to see how it stands up to work.'

On 4 May Simon Austin's section, consisting of Troopers Davis, Wharren, Paxton and Zacharias, was out on armoured cars escort duty after which they set up a night ambush position on the other side of the minefield. Nothing transpired so they were recovered back to camp the following morning. They had been there a mere ten minutes when they were called out as reaction force for 4 (Indep) trackers who reported finding spoor for four insurgents near the camp. The Grey's deployed on follow up. By mid-morning they estimated being five minutes behind the insurgents. Shortly afterwards one of the horses whinnied and the nearby enemy broke cover and bombshelled. The troops then spent two hours following the tracks up to Chamabonda Vlei. As they began to cross the vlei, the trackers spotted the enemy who were now to the rear of the troops, about a kilometre away. The Grey's did a mounted assault but the insurgents vanished into the thick jesse bush. The Grey's and the 4 (Indep) trackers then based up for the night. No spoor was found the following morning and all troops were recovered to base.

On 12 May Sergeant Wilkinson's section reported finding tracks for about six insurgents in the Grey's base camp of 5 May. The tracks led out of the camp heading west. Then 1 Troop's call signs 1.1 and 1.2 were deployed and began to cross-grain towards Wilkinson's position. It proved very difficult without trackers as the grass was very tall. They moved back to Chamabonda Vlei and based up. On the following morning Dave Blair's section located tracks for two heading south towards the main road. They began to follow up but the tracks were lost.

After a bitterly cold night, at 0730 hours the next morning, 2 Troop under Lieutenant Patrick Ollivier who had been conducting a follow-up, caught up with the group and killed two. Three were seen to escape. Wilkinson's section did a backtrack and established that it was the same gang who had rested in the Grey's old base camp.

Two days later, on 15 May, the Troop celebrated the grant of the Bronze Cross of Rhodesia to Mike Wilkinson for the action he was involved in the Sengwe TTL.[11]

Routine patrolling and OP duty occupied the next two weeks. On 26 May John Coast's section on OP by the river were mortared and bombed with 12.7s. During this period WO2 Don Kenny instructed everyone on the new support weapon. This was a 60mm Commando mortar which was hand-held with a simple range table attachment which each Troop would carry from now on. The unit then returned to Inkomo for R&R.

After a spell of R&R, 'A' Squadron was back at Victoria Falls' A'Zambezi Lodge on 8 June. A new regular army subbie, 2nd Lieutenant Tennant, had joined Grey's. Buster Shipster was promoted to sergeant and took over 2 Troop from Ollivier. The move meant that Lance Corporal Clive Midlane got made up to full corporal and became Lieutenant Strumpher's 2i/c in 1 Troop (call sign 1.1). The events were not celebrated in the canteen because Captain Williams closed it as a disciplinary measure following a row with 2 and 3 Troop.

On the following day trucks arrived bearing 1 Troop's new recruits and their horses.

Two days later four sections from 1 Troop and their new additions were deployed. Each section was made up of eight men command by Strumpher Austin, de Villiers and Lance Corporal Ellement. They were to operate in the area bounded by the Botswana border to the west and Westwood Vlei to the east with the drag to the north. The exercise was also intended to break in the new recruits and familiarise them with the area.

From Westwood Vlei they moved to Triangle Dam where they based up for the night. On the following day the troop split up with de Villiers' section heading south and Austin's section going west towards the cutline. At the cutline, the section followed it south-eastwards to Stoffel's Vlei which they crossed and arrived at Missis Airstrip alongside the border. From here they travelled on to the Panda-ma-tenga road and linked up with c/s 1.1A. Both call signs then made for Kakulwane pan to water the horses before basing up.

The new boys were doing OK and on the next day everyone moved back to the start point. By 14 everyone was recovered to base.

The unit had, since being based in Victoria Falls, integrated very well with the local community. Teaching the local folk and their children to ride was one of the pastimes troops performed. The activity was enjoyed by both sides. It livened up the time when the troops were not on stand-by for ops. Austin's diary entry for Sunday, 1 July reads:

---

11   See the Honours and Awards appendix.

Cold night, sunny day. Morning: Mark Ellement's section is doing the drag. Arvo: a whole span of local kids and girls arrived to ride horses. Evening: PT followed by volleyball.

On 3 July and back at Victoria Falls, a vehicle detonated a landmine on the road to Jambezi Keep injuring Captain Robinson who was currently in charge of operations in the area. Three European policemen accompanying him were seriously injured. On the next day a sighting of 80 to 100 insurgents in the Jambezi Keep area was reported. Lieutenant Strumpher deployed two sections from 1 Troop – one mounted and one afoot – as well as two Artillery 25 pounders. They arrived at a suitable spot about five kilometres from the sighting where the guns were zeroed in. A Hunter strike was requested. The pilot came overhead at midday and reported nothing to strike at. The troops then moved on to Jambezi Keep and cast about for spoor. Nothing was found. The 25 pounders fired a couple of rounds into likely concealment areas. At 1800 hours everyone returned to base. It had been another lemon.

Shortly after this 2 Troop was based at Sprayview when a report was received that a farmer had been assaulted by a gang of five ZIPRA insurgents at Pause Farm. They took his 357 Magnum and his gold watch. They also took a poisoned bottle of brandy and a transistor radio which was fitted with a Bekker homing device.

Corporal Neil Johns and Corporal Mike Bradshaw were detailed to lead their sections on a follow up. The farm was situated just off the Bulawayo–Victoria Falls main road. Spoor was located and followed. Johns' horse, named John, then had to be sent back as it had severe colic. On a borrowed horse Johns went on.

The Air Force Lynx, from Wankie, had picked up the Bekker homing device signal and directed the call signs towards the insurgents who had a 12 hour lead. A couple of hours later the Lynx was able to relay a positive grid reference for the enemy position.

When they reached the approximate position the troops dismounted in the cover of some thick jesse bush and began sweeping forward. They found three packs but no sign of the enemy. The Lynx then left to refuel and its place was taken by a Gcar three minutes later. The chopper picked up the Bekker signal which now emanated five kilometres from the troops sweep line. The pilot added that the insurgents were on the run. The troops mounted up and went in pursuit. When they had closed the gap they dismounted near a line of low kopjes. The Lynx then arrived and stonked the enemy position which was in a tree line at the base of which was dense cover. The Sneb rocket strike failed to flush the insurgents out.

Johns and Bradshaw then decided to move towards the tree line. Their sections shook out into assault line and moved forward. After about 50 metres the insurgents were seen and the troops opened up. Johns, armed with an RPD fired it from a crouching position. The Gcar overhead was also firing into the enemy position. The firefight was very brief and at the end the troops went forward and found three dead insurgents. Johns recalls;

They were pretty well kitted out in Russian type webbing. They were armed with an AKM, an AK and an SKS as well as grenades. One of them had the magnum and the gold watch on him which I took for myself. (At this stage I didn't know these items belonged to the farmer so I claimed them as war spoils.) We were all pretty chuffed with ourselves.

When we got back to Sprayview, Captain Williams and Don Kenny had Mike and me in for the usual debrief. Williams shat on me for not having indicated the gook position with white phosphorus but otherwise both he and Kenny congratulated us on the result. They added that we deserved a few beers. As we were about to leave Don Kenny asked quietly: 'No sign of a magnum and a gold watch then?'

I 'fessed up immediately and reluctantly handed the items over. I then went to attend to

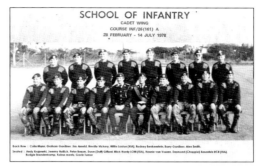

SCHOOL OF INFANTRY
CADET WING
COURSE INF/26(161) A
28 FEBRUARY – 14 JULY 1978

Lieutenant William "Willie" Loxton, 2 Troop, 'A' Squadron Grey's Scouts, KIA from a gunshot wound in a contact near Chomabonda Vlei, Victoria Falls, Operation Tangent. Corporal K Buku was also killed in this prolonged contact with a large group of ZIPRA, 1979. (Gordon Forest)

B. SQUADRON   GREY'S SCOUTS

Back Row:
 Tpr. Reynolds, T. P. Sgt. Mills, G. A. Cpl. Palmer, G. R. Tpr. DuRand, L. A. Tpr. Perrett, F. A. Tpr. McIlwaine, E. G. H. Cpl. Pettigrew, D. A. Sgt. Hatting, C. Sgt. Johnstone, W. Tpr. Rodgers, B. G. Tpr. Bancroft, N. F.

Third Row:
 Tpr. Fraser, C. P. Cpl. Somerville, I. R. Tpr. McLean, D. W. L/Cpl. MacGregor, S. J. L/Cpl. Van Schalkwyk, P. R. Tpr. Maberly A. Cpl. Watt-Pringle, J. D. Sgt. Viljoen, W. P. Sgt. Brown, D. A. L/Cpl. Matthews, R. M. Sgt. Minter, N. P. Sgt. Hopper, H. Tpr. Rendall, G. F.

Second Row:
 Tpr. Olds. M. Tpr. Honiball, T. P. Tpr. Edwards, D. R. Tpr. Sutton, K. S. Tpr. Vant, C. P. Sgt. Ziemann, R. G. Tpr. Bristow, J. D. Sgt. Dardagaan, B. A. Tpr. Nieuwenhuizen, H. J. Cpl. Harper, D. G. Tpr. Saul, R. D. Tpr. Greeff, J. N. Sgt. Campbell, L. R.

Front Row:
 Sgt. Esterhuizen, C. J. C/Sgt. Rabie B de W. W.O.2 Davies (S.S.M.) Lt. A. H. Moore Lt. R. M. Hensman (2 i/c B. Squadron) Capt. C. J. Tipping Woods (O.C. B.Squadron) Maj. C. J. Pierce, B.C.R. (C.O. Grey's Scouts) Capt. M. G. H. Wilson (2 I/C Grey's Scouts) Capt. P. J. Blignaut Lt. G. A. Campbell 2nd Lt. R. L. McIlwaine C/Sgt. Coutts, W.C. Sgt. Byford, A. R.

Cpl. Lawton, G. D.

'B' Squadron Grey's Scouts 1979. (Dick Weidemann)

October 1979, Section on patrol on Nuanetsi Ranch. (Simon Austin)

October 1979, SA on horse Bengal, near a dip tank on Nuanetsi Ranch in the south-east. (Simon Austin)

October 1979, 1 Troop deploying, one section by vehicle, one riding out, at camp on Nuanetsi Airstrip. (Simon Austin)

October 1979, Lt. Ockert Strumpher's section on the Bubye River Ranch, in the south east. (Simon Austin)

October 1979, Lt. Strumpher's section plus Shangaan trackers, on the Bubye River Ranch. (Simon Austin)

October 1979, 1 Troop, under Lt. Strumpher, plus Shangaan trackers, deploying on the Bubye River Ranch. (Simon Austin)

October 1979, Lt. Ockert
Strumpher of 1 Troop,
at Nuanetsi Ranch
camp. (Simon Austin)

October 1979, horses watering
at a cattle trough on Nuanetsi
Ranch. (Simon Austin)

John, my sick horse. I walked him around Sprayview to keep his blood moving etc. but it was of no use. He was pretty sick. The colic had got to him and he died in the early hours of the following morning.[12]

The following few weeks were spent on normal border control patrolling, OP duties and night ambushes. A lot of time was spent on stand-by as reaction force for 4(Indep) trackers who were constantly cross-graining[13] the area. On 7 July insurgents murdered a tribesman at Ndlovu Keep near Victoria Falls airport. On 16 July Clive Midlane's section were called out to the Keep to investigate

---

12   The above is an example of a 'RoadRunner'. Rhodesian security forces had taken to inserting homing devices into transistor radios. These were placed in inviting locations such as small rural shops/stores in the hope that they would be picked up by insurgents. The results with 'RoadRunners' were very hit and miss but in this case it was successful. See also Alexandre Binda: *The Saints. The Rhodesian Light Infantry,* pp305-306. Chris Pearce adds here the interesting observation of the fact that the farmer was obviously given the radio; perhaps he was an SB agent? Or perhaps he was happy to take the radio as it could have been useful had he been ambushed and escaped or if he had been kidnapped.

13   Sweeping back and forth across a suspected or known enemy flight direction.

two further murders of tribesmen by insurgents. They found spoor which was followed up then lost. A man in civilian clothes then attempted to jump into the HCV and was shot. Midlane recalls:

> We rode into the kraal and came across a horrific sight. In the centre of the kraal, surrounded by women and children, lay two naked dead men. They appeared to have been subjected to the most barbarous cruelty. Both had their hands tied behind their backs with 'gussie tambo' (tree bark rope). Their ankles were similarly bound. ZIPRA had bayoneted them hundreds of times. It must have been a gruesome and agonizing death with all their families and fellow villagers forced to watch.
>
> Doug Kok, our top 1 Troop tracker, got on to spoor. The tracks were chevron pattern and we tracked them for hours to a large kraal encircled by low reed fence and cattle pens. The atmosphere was very tense as I remember, but the place was deserted. ZIPRA had exfiltrated the area. Doug lost the tracks here as they got lost in the cattle spoor. I called for vehicle up-lift. As we drove through the narrow bush track towards the Jambezi road I saw, through my wing-mirror, a black guy clad in denims running alongside the truck. He had no shirt on and was carrying a blue cooler bag. He tossed this into the back of the truck and then began to sprint away. We slammed on brakes and my 2i/c, Lance Corporal Mark Ellement who was a dead-shot, jumped out and fired a double tap at him from over 60 metres. The man dropped down. We came up to him to find he was lying face down. His right arm was nearly totally severed just above the elbow. As I approached he roused and greeted me with a cheerful grin and said something to the effect, 'Don't worry. It is just war.' We then recognised him as an ex-school teacher who had gone bonkers and was known as the 'mad man of Jambezi'. He added that he was Ian Smith's prophet and now merely required a gallon of water and a lift to Victoria Falls! We checked out the cooler bag and found it contained his shirt. The medic applied first aid and a tourniquet and we took him to the clinic at Vic Falls where his arm was amputated.
>
> Twenty years later, in 1999, Mark Ellement, now a professional big game hunter was guiding an American client through the area. They stopped at Jambezi Business Centre and of all people Element saw the 'mad man of Jambezi'! Mark, fluent in the local dialect, introduced himself and told the man that he had shot him way back in 1979. The 'mad man' was absolutely thrilled to meet Element and went on to explain to the crowd that had gathered around that this man was a brilliant marksman! What Mark's American client thought about all this has not been recorded.

Two days later 1 Troop were back in the Ndlovu keep area tasked with making their presence obvious while Selous Scouts trackers followed up on tracks left by a resident gang of insurgents. This gang, according to SB, had spread it about that they were going to execute all sell-outs in the area – this terror tactic was designed to bring the locals on side. The idea was that the enemy, on detecting the Grey's, would lie low in cover thereby allowing the Scouts to close in on them. The Troop spent the afternoon and evening riding around for some 25 kilometres before returning to camp. They were not informed of the outcome of the Selous Scouts' follow up but, on the morning of 20 July, jets and helicopters overflew the Grey's camp on their way to hit an insurgent base camp north of Livingstone in Zambia. In the evening they heard a huge explosion on the Zambian side and were told that the Selous Scouts had blown up an ammunition dump. Later that evening a security forces communique announced that security forces had killed 183 auxiliaries who had refused to comply with requests to lay down their weapons.

Simon Austin's call sign 1.1A of 1 Troop arrived at Westwood Concession on 21 July and relieved c/s 1.1B. They began patrolling eastwards to Lookout Point before moving on to Kacole Falls where they had previously had an OP camp. Here they established comms with c/s 4.1B (4 Indep trackers) who were in an Op 2 kilometres to their east. The call sign based up for the night. Later that evening,

Corporal Kufa Buko, killed in action at Chamabonda Vlei on 18 September 1979. (Tony Butler)

an elephant walked into their position and Chris Steyn tried to frighten it off with a miniflare which failed to function. Everyone then had to stand to until the pachyderm finally decided to move off. The c/s set off at dawn and had its first stop for a break at the Sansimba River, after which they pressed on until they reached the Jena River where they stopped for lunch with c/s 4.1C (4 (Indep). From here they set off, still unsuccessfully cutting for spoor, until they based up in Chundu Loop.

At 1400 the next day, they reached Kandahar Island and were about to give their locstat sitrep when they saw a group of eight to 10 insurgents on the other side. The call sign moved quickly on to Hippo Creek to watch and report. On the way they found an AK, an SKS and an RPG7. An ambush was set up for the night but nothing transpired.

On 10 August 1 Troop handed over to Lieutenant Loxton's 2 Troop of 'A' Squadron preparatory to setting off on R&R.

At first light on 18 September, 22 men of Lieutenant Willie Loxton's 2 Troop of 'A' Squadron were undertaking the 'drag' – the long, monotonous routine of patrolling the Kazungula Road. The troops were in a four-vehicle convoy with a Pookie[14] up front.

A few miles after setting out the Pookie stopped. The troops saw the driver hop out and examine the roadside. He then gestured to them to come forward. He had found enemy tracks for 40 to 60 ZIPRA in the Kalahari sand on the roadside. The tracks appeared to be about eight hours old.

The troops debussed, mounted up and began to follow up at a brisk walk through the mopani woodland. The sun was up and the trackers, with heads down, were following an easy spoor line which appeared to be heading for the Botswana border. The spoor was so obvious that the walk turned into a canter and by last light, when they based up, they estimated that they were an hour behind the enemy.

14   A Rhodesian mine-detecting vehicle resembling a skeletal moon buggy. The very vulnerable sapper-driver was seated in an armour-plated cab mid-chassis. The huge tyres were water-inflated to cushion a mine blast.

In the darkness of pre-dawn they fed their horses, checked weapons and equipment and resumed the follow up.

At 0800 they came to the edge of Chamabonda Vlei. Loxton halted his men and dismounted to study the terrain. As far as he could see the land was typical flat dry season *vlei,* i.e., vast stretches of waist high savannah and seas of yellow flowing T'wa grass with the odd clump of stunted trees growing around termite hills. The enemy was not too far ahead. Deciding to take the tracking lead himself, Loxton mounted up and moved on. One hundred metres behind came his call sign in file led by his 2i/c, the very competent Corporal Kufa Buku. Everyone was at the ready and very tense. The sweat on the young troopers' faces had caused streaks to run through the camouflage cream. None of them had ever been in a firefight being a mere 12 weeks out of basic recruit training.

Bringing up the rear was Trooper Bren Stanford. As he walked his horse along, his sharp eye suddenly caught a glimpse of camouflage uniform and webbing in the grass 30 metres to the right. He leapt off his horse in instant reaction with a yell of 'Contact! Contact!' and raced for cover, firing as he ran. At the same time ZIPRA, concealed in a semi-circle position around the call sign, opened up. Pandemonium ensued. Horses reared and men shouted as they lost control of the mounts. Many animals were hit in this initial contact. Loxton, ahead and out of the kill zone, whirled about, urged his horse, and headed back to his men. As he did so a burst hit him in the stomach and chest knocking him off his horse. Seeing this, Kufa Buku with a roar of *Pamberi ne Hondo*[15] ran to assist his commander who was calling out. He in turn was then killed by a further burst of fire which struck him in the hip and head, killing him instantly. Pete Kabel, the Troop medic saw Buku fall and made for him in a crouching run. He too was hit, taking a round in his lower back. The slug travelled up his body beneath the skin, miraculously missing his spine and exiting by his shoulder. Loxton was now also dead.

The young leaderless troops began to regroup. After springing the ambush with the initial hail of fire, ZIPRA went strangely silent for a brief while. This breathing space enabled the 15 surviving troops to round up the 14 remaining horses, mount up their five wounded and begin a tactical withdrawal. The respite was brief, however, as the enemy, suddenly apparently aware how vulnerable and outnumbered the call sign was, resumed firing. The troops moved off, heading for the tree line at the *vlei's* edge, their rearguard holding off the insurgents with concerted volleys which kept the enemy at bay. But the enemy follow up continued with their troops using controlled fire and movement, pepper-potting each other forward (running forward in ones and twos under covering fire).

It was a long withdrawal. By nightfall the troops had not reached the tree line. They had a sleepless night as the enemy all around called out insults and taunts. The men responded initially but then decided to remain silent and track the enemy positions by sound before firing in the direction of the enemy voices. They scored at least one hit, judging by the screaming response to one of their volleys. Trooper Graham Longstaff, a member of the stricken call sign writes:

> The night never seemed to end. Our eyes burned from lack of sleep and as the sun came up we made our move. The Troop needed to get into the forest for decent cover. We took stock of our predicament. We had lost eight horses killed or missing including my own, Fencer.
>
> ' ... We set off, a rearguard covering our retreat. Still ZIPRA followed, intent on wiping us all out or at least inflicting further casualties. Just before midday the tree line became visible and we halted in all round defense as we tried the radio.

Longstaff and his mates were in luck, as it happened, because a Hawker Hunter returning from a raid into Zambia was diverted to assist them. They were also told that 'B' Squadron would come to their relief. The men turned their caps inside out to reveal the Day Glo flashes stitched inside for the

---

15   Shona for 'on with the fight'.

airmen to distinguish friend from foe. The aircraft came overhead and stonked the enemy positions. At the end of the action the enemy casualty count, according to Longstaff, was 23 dead and three captured wounded.[16]

Brian Griffiths, a member of 1RHA (Rhodesian Artillery), was stationed at Victoria Falls at the time. The RHA had a battery of four 25 pounders positioned at the end of the old runway. These had been in set gun position for several months. He recalls that the evening before the tragedy, Loxton had been invited by WO2 Terry Kelly and Lieutenant Ged Smith to visit the RHA makeshift mess tent for a few drinks.

He told us he would be leading a patrol out in the morning. The following afternoon we heard the sound of distant gunfire. An hour or so later we, along with some RLI guys, were hurriedly drafted in as fireforce. Loxton's call sign had been ambushed by a gang of over 60 insurgents at Chamabonda Vlei. We boarded the choppers for a follow up. The chopper pilots were using the leap-frogging tactic to try and catch up with the insurgents who had bombshelled into smaller groups. They were all fleeing in the general direction of Wankie.

I was part of a stick which was dropped at Chamabonda Vlei near the contact area. We did a sweep of the ambush area at first light and found the insurgents' cooking spot. This was near an anthill from where they had launched their ambush. There were several AKs and SKS scattered about as well as a lot of brand new gear. I took a water-bottle and a camouflaged cap for souvenirs, both Russian and which I still have.

We established where the contact had actually occurred. It appeared that the mounted Scouts had entered the open *vlei* and, once in the middle, came under fire from the large ZIPRA group concealed in the thick jesse at the other end of the *vlei*.

Apparently Corporal Kufa Buku was killed in this initial burst of fire. The remaining Scouts, caught out in the open, took heavy fire. They did well and we were able to see where a skirmish had taken place around the anthill. As the Scouts sought cover, Loxton, who was closest to the enemy position, was hit and died instantly. The surviving and now leaderless young troopers, who were experiencing their first firefight, could only try to re-group in the flat exposed *vlei*. Five had been wounded. For some inexplicable reason the insurgents failed to follow up on their successful ambush and finish off the vulnerable survivors. Having knocked down two members of the security forces, perhaps they thought enough had been achieved and, possibly believing that there were more troops around, they decided to extricate the area.

The relieving stick that found the surviving troopers described them as all being in a totally traumatised state.

The pursuit of the surviving enemy gang continued. They had now split up into pairs, discarding equipment along the way. Some of these joined up again. Two days later an RLI call sign walked into one of these groups in an LUP near Wankie. Obviously exhausted, they were all asleep having failed to post a sentry. They were shot dead where they lay.

'We were told later that ZIPRA's plan was to blow up Wankie airport. Later unconfirmed information was that the ZIPRA group had been commanded by a Cuban who wore a beret similar in colour to the SAS beret. The beret and his remains were later found not far from the contact area, seemingly the victim of a lion attack.

Of this contact 1 Troop's Doug Kriedemann says:

It was a long and extended firefight. Kufa was hit in the head and died instantly. Willie took a round in the chest ... Kufa had originally been a labourer/stable groom along with a fellow

---

African named Sheppard. Both desperately wanted to become Grey's Scouts. After much intercession by many fellow Grey's (with whom both men were popular), the HQ SSM Jimmy Jamieson relented and sent them off for basic training. Both passed their course and returned to the unit to undergo the Grey's Selection and Riding Course. After successfully completing this they were attested into the regular army. Kufa turned out to be a fantastic and absolutely fearless tracker. He was hugely respected by everyone in the squadron. He was in my section as a trooper on many a patrol before he became an NCO. What we all remember of him particularly was the smile he always wore ...

Rusti Henderson recalls the following:

Losing any member of the unit, in action or otherwise, was the most heart-wrenching time. Willie Loxton was a great guy. He was a Bulawayo boy and his body was taken there for burial. A lot of us flew down for the funeral service. We were asked for a horse to accompany the funeral cortege. We sent Follower, a big grey. On the day of the Service he was decked out in funeral gear, complete with black plume and backward turned boots in the stirrups. As the coffin went past, there was Follower moving slowly and gently after it with that noble and quiet dignity that only an equine is capable of. It was incredibly moving and many of us were in tears.

Kufa's horse was Hashish. They loved and understood one another completely. When Kufa was tragically killed, Hashish pined for him and it was four months before he resumed eating properly.

Shortly after this tragedy the Troop was relieved by 'B' Squadron.

On a slightly overcast 21 October, Lieutenant G A Campbell and 14 of his men of 4 Troop 'B' Squadron Grey's Scouts began a follow up on tracks for a large group of ZIPRA insurgents along the cut-line. The tracks had been discovered across the Kazungula road. It appeared the group, commanded by Richard Mataure,[17] were en route to infiltrate the Victoria Falls TTL. Campbell had three trackers – one from 4 (Indep) and two Shangaans. (The OC of 'B' Squadron at this time was Captain Cedric Tipping-Woods who, with his 2i/c Rory Hensman, was in the control tower at Victoria Falls for comms.)

The terrain was mostly flat with sparse, burnt jesse bush. At mid-afternoon they saw two insurgents ahead and to their right. In the Contact Report Campbell subsequently wrote:

We opened fire on them which they returned on the run. We swept the area and lost sight of them. We regrouped and followed the two main tracks heading south-east. About 500 metres further on we came across three dozen packs which had been dumped.

We dismounted. As we were tying up the horses the insurgents opened fire on us. They were about fifty to seventy metres to our front. We skirmished forward in extended line for about ten metres and took cover. We then found we couldn't advance as their fire was low and very accurate. We were pinned down.

Fireforce deployed from FAF1 – Forward Airfield 1 (Wankie). A Kcar and the Lynx were airborne and about three minutes out when the main contact started. I gave the sitrep to the Kcar commander and placed maps on the flanks of the Flot.[18] I threw a white phosphorus grenade to indicate the enemy position. The Kcar, then having them visual, started firing. From this point the following took place:

---

17   *Nom de guerre:* Richard Ngwenya.
18   Front Line of Own Troops.

1. The Lynx made several runs using Frantan, Snebs and Brownings. Two members of c/s 21 were wounded by the enemy's rifle grenades. Wounds not serious.
2. Kcar and Gcar were circling and firing into likely enemy positions indicated by c/s on the ground.
3. The Lynx had to withdraw after taking heavy flak and losing his rear engine.
4. The Gcar took over air support while the Kcar left to refuel.
5. The heavy fire from the enemy ceased and the Gcar left to refuel.
6. The Kcar returned and gave cover while we skirmished through the area.
7. Two further members of c/s 21 were wounded by enemy rifle fire. One of the insurgents was killed by c/s 21 and the other ran into Stop2 injuring their machine gunner before being killed.
8. We cleared the area and cut an LZ for the Gcar to uplift the two injured.
9. We remained near the LZ in ambush and killed a further two insurgents at 1900hrs.
10. Next morning we linked up with Stop2 and swept back through the area killing two more insurgents and capturing one wounded.
11. We then joined up with all stop groups and swept the area again, collecting enemy bodies and packs into a central point.

Page 2 of Campbell's contact report shows thirty-four insurgents killed and one captured wounded. Of the twenty-five estimated escapees, ten were believed to be wounded. There were five security force wounded – all Grey's Scouts and detailed as Troopers T P Honiball, N J D Halliday, J M Coast, C H M Lane and P E Frey.

The ground troops involved in the action were:

Grey's Scouts: Twelve members of 6 Troop 'B' Squadron;
Grey's Scouts: Fourteen members of 4 Troop 'B' Squadron;
4 (Indep) Company Rhodesia Regiment: Eight members;
I Engineer Sqn Rhodesian Engineers (stop group): Eight members;
School of Infantry(stop group): Four members.

Under 'Ammunition Expended' Campbell accounted for the following:[19]

2,000 x FN 7.62 ball;
2,000x RPD 7.62 ball;
12 x 970 Grenades;
11 x 42z Rifle Grenades;
20 x Mini Flares;
12 x Coloured Smoke Grenades.

Under the 'Potential Honours and Awards' section of his report Cambell signaled out the exceptional conduct of Corporal John Coast:

113816 Corporal J M Coast was wounded in the beginning of the main contact but still led his men in taking out a group of insurgents that had them pinned down.

---

19   The accounting for ammunition spent had become routine to Rhodesian security forces by this time. Everyone was aware that the nation was desperately short of foreign exchange and every round was precious. For example, a 20mm round from the Kcar's cannon cost R$35 (about GBP£20 in 1979). This meant, as previously mentioned, most gunners had to be fairly good marksmen as they fired short three-round bursts.

He skirmished forward and killed the insurgent that had wounded two of his men and gave them cover and assisted in their evacuation.

He showed exceptional leadership under fire and led his men aggressively accounting for several insurgents.

Under 'Observations/Recommendations' Captain C Tipping-Woods, OC 'B' Squadron wrote:

An efficient and successful combined operation. Lieutenant G Campbell's efficiency saved the lives of his men and enabled them to achieve the success they did.

Under 'Any Further Comments' by Debriefing Officer/Contact Commander Tipping-Woods wrote:

My personal feeling is that most of the higher command element plus an element of personnel carrying rocket launchers, mortars and DPs left the area after the air support left, leaving the juniors to contain us as long as possible.

In other words – Richard Mataure and his senior hardcore members escaped.[20]

Below is the personal narrative of this engagement featuring John Coast with additional detail by Neill Halliday (now Neill Hales) who was also a participant.

At first light on 21 October Corporal John Coast, a Territorial member of 4 Troop, 'B' Squadron, was in an open 4 (Indep) Coy 25 (a Unimog) travelling along the Kazungula road. They were conducting vehicle aerial tracking looking for spoor of ZIPRA gangs crossing the road from Zambia en route to Victoria Falls or Botswana. In the vehicle were Conrad van der Merwe, two members of 4 (Indep) and another Grey's Scout.

This tracking system was routine. The vehicle moved at speed with two of the men doing the actual aerial tracking by scanning the road from over the top of the windscreen. By now they knew every corner, bump and overhanging branch on the 70–80 kilometres of graded dirt road. The sides of the road were regularly and specially prepared with disc harrows, graders so that the surface would show up any tell-tale indentations which denoted signs of enemy crossings. Tyres were also dragged across the dirt track to achieve the same effect.

On this day, when they reached the 30 kilometre peg, they noticed something odd about the sides of the road. They stopped, de-bussed and walked to the very obvious and plainly visible indentations. They followed them to the edge of the bush. By now they knew they had come across the tracks of a large group of insurgents. They were using anti-tracking devices such as walking over blankets or cut branches to break up the boot print pattern. But it had proved to no avail – the sheer number of the group, over 100, made the ruse quite hopeless.

The call sign immediately radioed their FOB (Forward Operating Base) for a Troop deployment. There then followed an unavoidable delay as the horses were loaded into the HCVs and the troops driven to the scene. Once they arrived and after a quick briefing the three Shangaan trackers got on to the spoor. This was very easy to follow as the terrain in the area is Kalahari sand.

At approximately 1200 hours they came under fire from a lone insurgent acting as the enemy rearguard. The troops went to ground and skirmished forward and killed him. They then got back on the tracks which now led southwards across the Kalisosi and Chamabonda Vleis. From previous follow-up experience the troops were aware of both of ZIPRA's modus operandi for large groups crossing through the area. The first was to move due south, then veer west to the Botswana border where they would get transport assistance from the Botswana Defence force; after this they would

---

20   See also sketch map of this action.

deploy into Matabeleland. The second was to go east and infiltrate the Victoria Falls TTL. Today it appeared that the enemy was adapting the latter option. This route would take them close to the Spray View airfield. Fortunately for the troops, on this day there happened to be a potential Fireforce at Spray View as the aircraft had just returned from an external operation into Zambia.

At around 1500 hours the Shangaan trackers informed the call sign that the enemy was close ahead. They found an enemy pack and all three trackers went to ground. The troops then saw packs littered across the area to their immediate front. These had been discarded by the insurgents upon hearing the first contact. The enemy then opened fire. The troops leapt off their horses to begin deploying. Some managed to tether their horses quickly. Most of the horses simply took off. Coast recalled:

> The initial barrage was very intense. There was RPG7s, AKs and RPDs fire as well as rifle grenades and G3s. Wheeled tracks for a heavier weapon were also found later. We couldn't see them but they were no more than 30 metres from us. Their fire was coming at us from all sides and they were very well controlled as we could hear whistles being used and commands being issued. Lieutenant Glen Campbell's section with me as 2i/c was on the right hand side and Sergeant Billy Viljoen's section on the left. I was armed with an RPD. We'd walked into an ambush and the enemy was in very good defensive positions.

Trooper Neill Halliday (now Neill Hales) recollects:

> I recall that we were in straight line formation. The gooks had us surrounded. We put our heads down and I think the gooks actually shot at each other for a while. Then a rifle grenade exploded between me and Pat Frey, an American guy, and I saw blood suddenly flow down his face.

Coast continues:

> We called up Fireforce. With Spray View so close they were with us pretty quickly. Captain Mike Wilson, our OC at Vic Falls, was in one of the Gcars and became Fireforce commander. From the air they could see that we were completely boxed in. The Lynx came in and stonked the enemy positions with Sneb rockets and Frantan. These seem to be landing right on top of us!
>
> The Kcar, piloted by Cocky Beneke came over and his tech/gunner Bruce Jameson opened up with the 20mm cannon, laying down three round bursts to our immediate front. We could hear the comms between Captain Wilson and Cocky. The terrs seemed to be everywhere around us; the terrs were shooting our horses ... and so on. We then heard that the Lynx had taken several hits and that the tail engine was damaged forcing it out of the battle.
>
> Twenty or thirty minutes into the contact, Cocky Beneke told our section that we needed to skirmish forward to a clump of fallen trees to our immediate front. By now we had split into four-man sticks. Billy Viljoen and his section were conducting their own battle to our left and centre. Beneke told me that there was a large group of terrs in the clump that would have to be flushed out. I got to my feet and called out to the guys that we needed to charge the position. I had barely moved two paces when an RPG type grenade exploded a few feet behind me. It splattered shrapnel over my whole back and head. The blood immediately poured over my face blinding me temporarily. I dropped down, quickly wiped my face whilst shouting that I'd been hit. Then I was up again and running forward. My adrenalin must have been on overdrive because I covered the 20 or so metres in seconds. As I got to the clump I saw the terrs looking at me in complete shocked surprise. There were about six to eight of them and they had been taking cover from the Kcar above. I shot them with my RPD before any could react. I was by myself but the section came up behind me. My ammo was low so I replenished the belts from the dead

CONFIDENTIAL

5

Appendix A to Part II

SKETCH MAP OF SCENE OF CONTACT

Notes

1. The legend is to be used.
2. A north pointer must be included.
3. The following information must be shown.
   a. Relevant topographical detail.
   b. Positions of any dead and wounded SF.
   c. Positions of any dead and wounded civilians.
   d. Positions of any dead, wounded and captured CTs.
   e. Directions taken by escaping CTs.
   f. Positions of SF and CTs during the contact, including directions of any manoeuvres executed by both sides.
   g. Scale line.

CONFIDENTIAL

Contact of 21 October 1979. 4 Troop, 'B' Squadron, Grey's Scouts sketch. This is the contact for which John Coast was awarded his Silver Cross. (Sketch by Lieutenant G A Campbell)

terrs' AK magazines. We then shook out into a sweep line and resumed the assault using fire and movement. The firefights on all fronts were still intense but not as before. Beneke then informed us that the Kcar had run out of ammo and he was returning to Spray View for resupply, and that Mike Wilson would take over air support and control with his Gcar's twin mounted Brownings.

We had moved about 20 metres from the tree clump when Tom Honiball was shot. The round knocked him down right in the killing ground. He had been hit under the shoulder. He took several further hits to both calf muscles and to the lower bicep and was screaming in pain.'

Neill Halliday writes:

As we went forward I saw Tom Honiball fall as he was hit. He fell about four metres to my right. I also saw that the insurgent that had shot him was firing from an antbear hole. He had an RPD. He was no more than ten metres away. We stared at each other. I ducked down just as he opened up on me. The rounds sprayed the ground alongside me churning up the sand so close and violently I got a mouthful of it. I was lying spread-eagled, hugging the ground, when I took a round in my left ankle. The pain was so agonising I remember hoping that his next round would finish me off.

Coast takes the account to its conclusion:

Initially we could not locate the gunman but I had the general area and ran to where I believed he was. This drew the fire away from Tom and Neill as the gunman turned his weapon on me. As soon as I located his position I dropped down and let off a long burst and killed him. We were then able to get Tom out of the immediate area and administer aid. This consisted of three ampoules of Sosagon. He was in dreadful pain having been shot through the joints and the analgesic seemed to take forever to be effective.

The contact continued for about three hours. The Kcar had returned and, assisted by the Gcar, dealt with several skirmishes. We had RAR troops as stop groups by now and they dealt with further insurgents who were trying to exfiltrate the area. During this two of the RAR guys were wounded.

At last light a casevac chopper was able to pick up our four wounded. It was unable to take me also. Throughout the night we continued to have isolated contacts, and at first light we did a sweep and counted forty-two dead insurgents and recovered about 100 packs. (The number of enemy casualties for this contact is listed differently in my Citation but I was there and the count was 42.) We found that most of the terrs had pockets full of Propon (pain killer) as well as *dagga* (marijuana). Being 'goofed' on drugs may have accounted for their decision to stay and fight it out. Some packs contained two landmines as well as loads of ammunition and the massive weight must have been exhausting and painful to carry about for long distances. This may have been another reason for the drug/pain killer fix.

I was flown to Wankie Hospital where the Catholic nurses did a great job of removing most of the shrapnel which was aluminium (this is usually RPG). I still, however, carry some to this day.

Cocky Beneke was awarded a Silver Cross of Rhodesia for his performance that day. We are all indebted to him and Bruce Jameson for their support. Likewise to Captain Mike Wilson for his control of the battle. On the ground we had all fought as a team and supported each other throughout the incident. This teamwork went a great way to ensuring our survival.

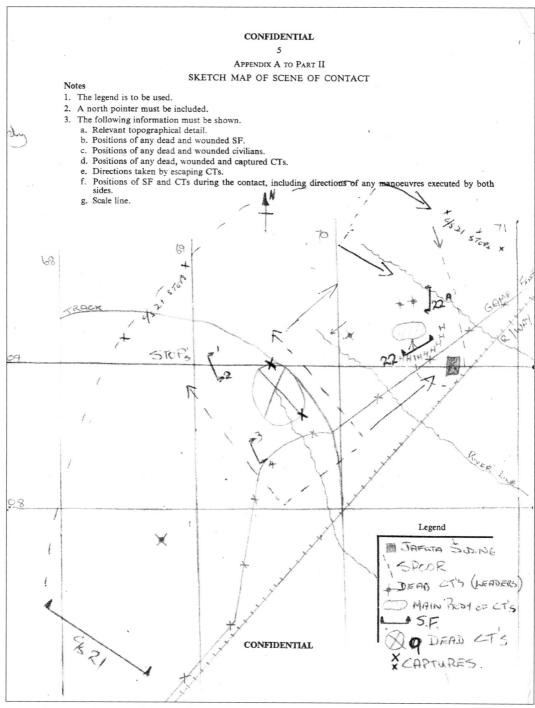

CONFIDENTIAL
5
APPENDIX A TO PART II
SKETCH MAP OF SCENE OF CONTACT

Notes
1. The legend is to be used.
2. A north pointer must be included.
3. The following information must be shown.
   a. Relevant topographical detail.
   b. Positions of any dead and wounded SF.
   c. Positions of any dead and wounded civilians.
   d. Positions of any dead, wounded and captured CTs.
   e. Directions taken by escaping CTs.
   f. Positions of SF and CTs during the contact, including directions of any manoeuvres executed by both sides.
   g. Scale line.

Legend

◼ JAFUTA SIDING
SPOOR
+ DEAD CT's (LEADERS)
⬭ MAIN BODY OF CT's
S.F.
⊗ Ǫ DEAD CT's
× CAPTURES.

CONFIDENTIAL

Contact of 3 November, Grey's Scouts, featuring Sgt D A Brown and 6 Troop, 'B' Squadron.

It was indeed fortunate for the ground troops that Kevin 'Cocky' Beneke was the Kcar's chopper pilot that day. Beneke, already a holder of the Defence Cross for Distinguished Service, was possessed of the most incredible eyesight. He was able, from the air, to detect enemy hidden in thick jesse bush and dense riverine vegetation. This ability had made him a major exponent of aerial reconnaisance. On medical examination by the Air Force's Dr Brian Knight, it had been discovered that Beneke's vision was abnormal in the green–brown range, enabling him to see dark objects concealed in the vegetation below him that others with normal vision could not.

The author is quite convinced here that Beneke's pointing out the position of the insurgents hidden in the bunch of fallen trees to the front of Coast's section is another example of his uncanny visual abilities.[21]

John Coast was initially recommended for a Bronze Cross for his outstanding performance during this contact. This recommendation was revised and he was awarded a Silver Cross. He received his award at a ceremony where his father was awarded the OLM (Officer of the Legion of Merit) for his services to the Karoi community. The presentation was by Lieutenant General Sandy McLean. Lieutenant Colonel Pearce and Coast's family attended the ceremony. It was a proud day for the Coasts and the Grey's Scouts.

For Neill Halliday the road to recovery took some time. His wound was serious and the doctors recommended that his lower leg be removed. His horrified father refused to allow it. He eventually had seven operations and seven months of further treatment. Thankfully for Neill, this proved to be the correct decision as today he walks about quite normally. He remains saddened that his horse, a dappled grey named Eagle, was killed in the firefight that day.

Tom Honiball's injuries were all, fortunately, flesh wounds. He was discharged from hospital after four or five days.

At 0645 on Saturday, 3 November, trackers from 4 (Indep) Coy RR located tracks for 20 ZIPRA insurgents in the sand veldt on the Kazungula road in the Victoria Falls National Park area. In heavy rain, c/s 22 of Grey's Scouts under Sergeant D A Brown began to follow up. Brown's force consisted of 16 men of 6 Troop, along with the three trackers. They followed the spoor in a southerly direction travelling between the railway line and the game fence.

Three hours later, near Jafuta Siding, the insurgents were sighted. The c/s immediately split into two viz: call signs 22 and 22A. C/s 22 continued on the tracks while c/s 22A went right flanking. As c/s 22A moved into position they bumped into the enemy point section. They opened fire immediately and killed two insurgents. C/s 22 then also opened fire to enable c/s 22A to advance. Aware now that they had enemy on both flanks the insurgents bombshelled, running to the south west. C/s 22A went in pursuit firing along the way. Several insurgents were seen to be hit. They heard a wounded insurgent shouting nearby. They came across him and ordered him to surrender. When he failed to comply and continued shouting he was shot dead. Corporal J I Du Preez saw an insurgent lying in a prone position. He fired at him. The round struck the man's pack hitting a grenade within which exploded, blowing the man to pieces – several portions of him then festooned the trees all around. Another insurgent was shot. He had, unseen, been pulling the pin off a grenade. As he fell dead he rolled on to the grenade. Corporal J I Du Preez bent down to recover the man's weapon and the grenade, in a delayed detonation, exploded as the body was rolled over. Du Preez received shrapnel wounds to his mouth, left arm and neck. It was a very lucky escape. C/s 22, meanwhile, had swept the initial contact area.

Fireforce, consisting of a Kcar and two Gcars arrived on the scene. 4 Troop, c/s 21, consisting of sixteen members, were deployed as stops along the road parallel to the railway line to the south-west of the initial contact area (see sketch map). The Squadron OC, Captain C Tipping-Woods, recalls that the deployment of 4 Troop was the result of his assessment of the enemy action and previous

21   See also Alexandre Binda, *The Saints*, p305.

November 1979, 1 Troop, 'A' Squadron, during re-training at Inkomo Barracks. (Simon Austin)

November 1979, Wilf Smit and Buck Rogers with their beer steins at 'A' Squadron party during re-training. (Simon Austin)

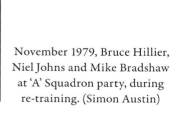

November 1979, Bruce Hillier, Niel Johns and Mike Bradshaw at 'A' Squadron party, during re-training. (Simon Austin)

November 1979, 2 Troop returning from Mozambique at Jersey Tea Estates, after heavy fight with Frelimo. (Simon Austin)

November 1979, unloading horses at Jersey Tea Estates, prior to a cross-border op. SA leads horse down Ramp. (Simon Austin)

November 1979, Trooper mounted in Mozambique. (Simon Austin)

November 1979, SA at St. Lourenço Mission, Manica Province, Mozambique. (Simon Austin)

November 1979, an exploding 122 recoilless shell fired from Espungabera. (Simon Austin)

November 1979, the impact from a 122 recoilless shell. (Simon Austin)

November 1979, Dave Rees hard targeting at the scene of a contact with Frelimo troops in Manica. (Simon Austin)

November 1979, Jose De Abreu, a Portugese in Simon Austin's Section, talking to a European Portugese held temporarily in Manica Province, Mozambique. (Simon Austin)

November 1979, getting a captured Jeep across the border river, Toyota still in Mozambique. (Simon Austin)

November 1979, Jose De Abreu, a Portugese in my section talking to a European Portugese we held temporarily in Manica Province, Mozambique. (Simon Austin)

November 1979, Garry Blauw and Kev Connor wearing Russian and East German helmets after a Successful contact with Frelimo troops in Manica Province. (Simon Austin)

November 1979, Dave Rees acting heavy at the scene of a contact with Frelimo troops in Manica. (Simon Austin)

November 1979, SA
at the Cabbora Bassa
power lines, 35 Ks into
Mozambique, Manica
Province. (Simon Austin)

movements whereby they had to move through the area quickly, from water to water and into a populated area. In the ensuing ground and air action a further nine insurgents were killed and two captured. An insurgent, fatally wounded in the head by c/s 22, ran towards 4 Troop's stop line and dropped dead.

The engagement had lasted just under an hour. The final count revealed that thirteen insurgents had been killed and two captured; four had escaped. Captured enemy weapons were handed in to D/Inspector T Keene at SB Victoria Falls.

The Official Contact Report commented on the troops' general efficiency and excellent shooting. It also noted the enemy's deliberate shooting at the horses and their extensive use of rifle grenades. In addition it recommended that the troops' firepower be augmented with more RPDs.

Under the heading 'Ammunition Expended' Brown detailed:

2 x smoke Grenades
4 x White Phosphorus Grenades
4 x 42z Rifle Grenades
500 x 7.62 rounds of FN ball
500 x 7.62 rounds of RPD ball
3 x M962 Grenades

On Wednesday 5 December, 3 Troop at Victoria Falls had a contact with a group of five ZIPRA and killed three.

Grey's Scouts in Op Thrasher

In April 'A' Squadron's Lieutenant Patrick Ollivier and Don Kenny were ordered to patrol along the Mateke Hills. These hills, in the huge Nuanetsi District, run south-east to north-west on the borders of the Sengwe TTL. The population in the Sengwe TTL and its northern neighbouring Matibi No 2 TTL were very heavily subverted by ZANLA who virtually had things pretty much their own way by this time.

The squadron at this time was under Captain Bosch and based up at Mbizi. Troop Sergeant Ollivier and Kenny had the very competent Dave Blair, and one of their section commanders was the experienced Bobby Hay. For tracker they had Trooper Albert.

They set off at a normal pace. Ollivier likened the dry arid scenery to the French Causses bordering the Lozere. As they approached the entrance to a rocky gorge near a riverbed they were ambushed. The ZANLA insurgents, concealed in deep cover, poured down a furious fusillade. This was accompanied by shouted obscenities. But the troops reacted swiftly despite the surprise. Dave Blair countered with rifle grenades while five of the Scouts did a flanking move along the zigzag course of the dry riverbed. The enemy then bombshelled. The call signs linked up on the kopje for a breather whilst air support was summoned from Buffalo Range. They then began a follow up and came up to the insurgents on another elevated feature. In the ensuing firefight one of the Scouts was wounded and three horses were hit. The Lynx struck the enemy position with frantan (napalm). The strike was fatal. When the troops charged forward all they found were charred bodies. One of the insurgents was captured wounded.

Ollivier attended to the wounded Scout whilst a casevac was requested. He also found himself particularly upset at the sight of the wounded horses, one of which, very badly wounded, was lying on its side in terrible pain. The chopper arrived with a medic and a vet. The vet put the badly wounded horse down but was able to stabilise the other two. Looking on at the injured, innocent and loyal beasts, Ollivier reflected on the cruel futility of war and man's stupidity; *'Il laissa s'attarder sa pensée sur les malheureux chevaux mutilés, innocentes victimes de l'imbécilité humaine.'* [22]

On 21 August Simon Austin turned 32. On that day also he, along with the rest of his section, arrived at Chisumbanje east of Chiredzi to join the rest of the Troop at the 'A' Squadron base on the edge of the Sabi River. Austin had found, on return from R&R, that he had been promoted to full corporal. He comments: ' ... towards the middle of 1979 conscripts were coming straight from Llewellin Barracks and being trained in infantry tactics and taught horsemanship at the same time with, in my opinion, a lowering of standards. We were always short of officers, as those coming out of Officer Training were understandably nervous of commanding horse soldiers, so many of the Troops were run by NCOs. I myself ran 1 Troop for some time as a lowly Corporal!' [23]

On arrival they discovered that one section was coming in from border control operations whilst Lieutenant Lance Smith and the rest of 1 Troop were away on a ten-day external operation in Mozambique.

On 24 August a report was received from Smith that a camp, occupied by a mixed force of 200 ZANLA and Frelimo, had been discovered near São Lourenço Mission. Clive Midlane, a member of Smith's call sign recalls:

We had received some sketchy intelligence that Frelimo had set up a camp near the Mission.

22   See Patrick Ollivier, *Commandos De Brousse*, pp 228–245. Pub. Grasset. 1985.
23   Note that this comment by Austin again confirms the view that, in the words of Richard Wood, the Rhodesian Bush War was in many ways a 'Corporal's war'. Wood writes: ' ... the Corporal had under him, an MAG general purpose machine-gunner and two riflemen, one of whom was trained as a medic. Out in the bush, the corporal had autonomy and responsibilities not found in many armies at that level'. Having said this Chris Pearce adds the following: 'There was a general shortage of officers all around outside of the major units. It was an ongoing issue to try and recruit, train and retain sufficient numbers of them, particularly for 'A' Squadron where we were lucky to get even one national service officer in a year let alone a regular. Kevin 'Canvas' Tennant volunteered for Grey's Scouts and was the unit's first regular army 2nd Lieutenant to join directly from his Officer Cadets' Course. However Simon is correct in that there were some periods where 'A' Squadron had to rely heavily on its senior and junior NCOs. In 'B' Squadron we had some depth with several experienced TA officers and a number of excellent senior NCOs.

This was to aid ZANLA cadres of the Monomotapa Sector to infiltrate into Rhodesia's Op *Thrasher* area.

Late in the afternoon we saw a kraal sited on the edge of a small escarpment. Our farrier, a Shona called Chipinga, was fluent in the Ndau dialect. With great daring he offered to go and visit the kraal to find out what he could. We got into a LUP nearby. Chipinga, with his combat jacket turned inside out revealing only its mottled brown colour, set off for the kraal armed with Dave Rees RPD.

Arriving at the kraal he told the headman that he was a ZANLA cadre who had lost his way and was looking to re-join his comrades. The headman replied that he was in luck as the ZANLA camp was at the bottom of the escarpment not more than three or four kilometres away. He even offered to guide him there. Chipinga declined the offer saying he could find his own way there.

As soon as Chipinga got back and briefed us on this 'windfall' we headed down the escarpment where we located a narrow dirt track. We based up in some thick vegetation and had an 'O' Group where it was decided that Chipinga and Corporal Bruce Hillier would conduct a recce of the enemy camp whilst we remained on stand-by ready to react should the shit hit the fan. Bruce and Chipinga returned after last light with the news that the enemy camp was occupied by a joint ZANLA and Frelimo force of over 200.

This intelligence was relayed back to base where it was decided that Smith and Bruce's sections would move back to the border area (a long night's walk) to RV with the rest of 'A' Squadron and bring them in to attack the camp. My section, meanwhile, was tasked to base up near the kraal and at first light we were to round up all the villagers and move them away.

The rest of 'A' Squadron (HQ & Don Kenny's mortar section) led by the OC, Captain Williams, now deployed for the cross-border operation. Simon Austin's c/s, equipped with an RPG7, embussed and drove 15 kilometres to the border arriving there at dusk. Here they met up with Mike Bradshaw's section who knew the way to the RV with 1 Troop. Unfortunately they lost their way in the dark so halted and based up.

At first light Bradshaw, now aware of his bearings, led them into Mozambique and at 1100 hours they linked up with Smith. The lieutenant briefed them on the situation and a rough attack plan was outlined. An airstrike on the enemy camp was requested for the following day. The squadron, with Austin's section as rearguard, moved on heading towards the Mission walking the horses as the country was very rugged. By evening they were five kilometres from the target area and based up. In the pre-dawn light the squadron saddled up. At 0545 hours HQ and 3 Troop took up their assault positions. Austin's section, accompanied by Smith and armed with the RPG7, crossed a stream and took up a position on the Espungabera[24] Road so as to stop any Frelimo armour coming to the support of the enemy camp. Clive Midlane and his section had rounded up the 20 or so inhabitants of the kraal and moved them away.

The airstrike, two Hunters and a Canberra, went in at a belated 1000 hours with Frantan and were bang on target. 3 Troop then assaulted the camp but found it empty. The troops had obviously been detected earlier and the enemy had bombshelled. A totally frustrating experience for all troops involved. Midlane writes:

It turned out that an early morning Frelimo clearance patrol had picked up our horse spoor and evacuated the base camp immediately. For my section it was even worse as they put a mortar platoon on our spoor. We had been instructed by Lieutenant Tennant to leave the villagers and move to a riverline south of the enemy camp to act as a stop group. As soon as we moved off, Frelimo bombed us with their 82mm mortars. We kept moving all day dodging the mortar fire

---

24 'Wilderness of the Rock Rabbits'.

which was fairly random with Frelimo hoping for a lucky shot.

The Troop watered their horses, lunched on tinned mackerel obtained from a store and moved back to the border. Here they halted at Jersey Tea Estates by the border minefield and the following day the Engineers arrived to guide them through it. Clive Midlane was a member of Smith's call sign. He recalls:

A few kilometres from the border we entered into really difficult terrain. It was a type of flood plain, a huge *vlei* in fact – about a kilometre wide and made up of reeds. It was full of narrow gullies, all over a metre in depth, that couldn't be seen until your horse fell into one. Horse after horse kept falling into these and it was a real struggle to get them out again. Lieutenant Smith's horse fell into one. We first got him out then his horse. During this exhausting work, Smith's canvas map bag that he wore around his neck snapped off unnoticed and fell into the reeds. The bag contained not only his maps but his shackle codes and placard codes. He only noticed the loss when we were miles away.

When they got back to Chisumbanje, Captain Williams debriefed the section leaders and gave them a severe dressing-down on the lack of success caused by the troop presence being compromised by, from what he deduced, their own carelessness. The fact that Lieutenant Smith had also mislaid his map-case containing his maps, shackle codes and top secret codes inside Mozambique added to the embarrassment. Williams was livid. He ordered them back to attempt a 'needle in a haystack' recovery attempt. Austin's diary entry for the day noted ' ... there was a bit of shit flying around at this stage!'

The troop returned to the area on 3 September and two days later, incredibly, Smith's lost maps were found along with his compass, pens and torches, but the case itself had vanished. For this carelessness Lieutenant Lance Smith, a former Milton schoolboy and Nuffield cricketer, was posted out of the unit.

On 8 September Captain Hope detailed 1 Troop to OP duties. Lieutenant Okkie Strumpher, now returned from RR, had taken over from Smith. He ordered Austin's call sign 1.1C to OP Zinvayi Mountain in the Ndowoyo TTL. The c/s left at dusk in a Guard Force Puma (mine-proofed vehicle) and were dropped off after dark. They began the three kilometre walk-in to their OP positions in the pitch black carrying a four-gallon jerrycan of water. It was heavy going as the hill was very steep. They got to the summit at midnight after an exhausting climb. Austin took the northern side with Troopers De Abreu and Smith whilst his 2i/c Tony Wilkinson took the southern end with Troopers White and Groenewald.

The next day they noted what appeared to be a group of about 12 *mujibas* heading east in the direction of call sign 1.1B position. They passed the info on.

The following day, tormented by mopani flies, Austin's call sign had an uneventful time. Not so c/s 1.1! In the late evening a gang of cattle rustlers drove their herd right into their ambush position. The call sign opened up, killing four of the rustlers and capturing one. Fourteen head of cattle were also killed.

At dawn on the 11 September the OP heard what sounded like a contact to their south east. They reported the incident and c/s 1.3C was sent in as reaction stick and discovered an overturned Internal Affairs vehicle which had been ambushed by a group of 10 insurgents. Three of the occupants were injured. The call sign with 1.1B as reinforcements went on follow up but a horse became lame and the pursuit was called off.

All call signs were moved out on 13 September back to Chisumbanje.

On 19 September Captain Hope informed everyone that Lieutenant Loxton and Corporal Kufa Buku had been killed at Victoria Falls. Several other Grey's scouts had been wounded. Everybody was shocked at the news as these were the first Grey's fatalities in over two years. Austin, along with several others returned to Inkomo to attend the funerals on 21 September.

Grey's in Op Repulse:

Very soon after Chris Pearce took over from Mick McKenna in January, 'B' Squadron was deployed to Rutenga under the command of Captain Pip Erasmus. The squadron was placed under command JOC Rutenga where the senior army officer was Lieutenant Colonel Alastair Boyd-Sutherland, CO of 1RDR (Rhodesia Defence Regiment). Squadron HQ was based up at Bob van der Sande's farm near Rutenga Village. A few days after its arrival, Chris Pearce, Mike Wilson and the Grey's Scouts QM, Vince King, travelled down from Salisbury to visit 'B' Squadron. Following discussions, Chris Pearce indicated that he intended to implement a policy of the TA being commanded by the TA, hence Cedric Tipping-Wood would take over as OC 'B' Squadron immediately. The following day Captain Erasmus accompanied the CO and his team back to Salisbury where he took over as Adjutant with the additional responsibility of taking on special projects for the unit.

Cedric Tipping-Woods writes:

Sometime after I assumed command of 'B' Squadron we deployed to Battlefields Ranch which was south west of Nuanetsi. The area was very dense and remote. We were plagued by pepper ticks which affected horses and men. Dipping both solved the problem! Battlefields Ranch had been attacked on several occasions, resulting in the death of a farmer at his gate and the wounding of his brother. *Mujibas* poisoned a borehole with organophosphate dip which caused minor illness to some of my men. The insurgents here were very sure of themselves and aggressive. Our resupply vehicles were ambushed repeatedly on the way to the main Beit Bridge Road. On one occasion, Trooper Harry Barrett, who was driving one of the vehicles, sustained a serious head wound when a gook stepped into the middle of the track and fired at him.[25]

Subsequent activity with a wounded capture from JOC Rutenga resulted in Corporal Du Preez and his stick getting into a contact with a group of insurgents. During the engagement Du Preez called for an airstrike on the enemy camp. The place was stoncked with Alpha Bombs. Du Preez and his stick, despite being within the bombs danger range, then went forward and engaged the insurgents. For his leadership and bravery under fire he was awarded a Bronze Cross.

After the funerals of Willie Loxton and Kufa Buku and a few days R&R 'A' Squadron were mustered and told that they were moving back into the Op *Repulse* area but that their new base would be at Chipinda Pools. The next morning 1 Troop loaded their horses as well as those of 2 Troop – an additional 31 animals. They left in a 13-vehicle convoy heading for Chisumbanje via Fort Victoria and Chiredzi. Lieutenants Taylor and Tennant had already gone ahead to recce a new camp area for the unit at Chipinda Pools.

When the convoy finally got to Chiredzi they discovered there was no water at Chipinda Pools, so they loaded the 104 horses and made for Nuanetsi Ranch arriving there in the evening where 2 Troop joined them. They bedded down on the lawn in front of the ranch house while at the same time ogling two young women in the house.

At about 0500 hours on 2 October, Lieutenant Kevin 'Canvas' Tennant shot himself dead with his pistol. Everyone was shocked at the news. Austin's diary notes for that day reflect: ' … whether by accident or intention no one knows. Great shock to everyone, as a highly respected man and soldier … '. Clive Midlane adds:

---

25   Barrett recovered and was still farming in the Middle Sabi area, post-independence, right up until he was forced off the land. He then moved to the UK.

December 1979, point man, Groenewald, near the Murongwezi River, Manica Province, Mozambique. (Simon Austin)

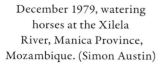

December 1979, getting water out of a hole in a dry riverbed, in the Mossorise River Valley, S of Alguerido, Manica Province, Mozambique. (Simon Austin)

December 1979, watering horses at the Xilela River, Manica Province, Mozambique. (Simon Austin)

December 1979, Jose De Abreu, after walking 140 Ks through Mozambique. A complete patrol, because his horse developed bad saddle sores. (Simon Austin)

Without a doubt one of the finest officers we ever had. Before attending his 12 month officer course Tennant had served as an NCO in the RLI. He would often visit us in the Corporals' Mess to see how we were. He always, also, brought along a crate of beer. A very special officer who we really missed.

The unit finally set up camp at Nuanetsi Airstrip on 3 October. On the next day those not attending Tennant's funeral set up bivvies tents and began digging slit-trenches and sandbagging.

In early October, 'B' Squadron were based up on a farm in the Sengwe TTL area. They received a call from a TA unit operating nearby who had come across enemy spoor. Nigel Ramshaw and David Boardman deployed with two of the unit's hounds. Ramshaw writes:

We were asked if it was possible to follow up with the hounds on leads. It wasn't something we were trained for but we both jumped at the chance.

We got to the call sign's position and set off successfully, running on spoor until one of the accompanying TA guys needed medical attention due to dehydration and heatstroke. This delay caused the follow up to be aborted and Dave and I were uplifted out of the area with the casevac. When we got back to camp Major Tipping-Woods, OC 'B' Squadron, congratulated us. We said we hadn't done anything but he didn't agree, replying that it had been a good follow up as we had covered 15 kilometres. We found that amazing but he had worked the distance out on the map!. We had proved that dogs could be run on spoor on a lead.

On 7 October 1 Troop deployed after lunch on normal border control. Austin was on Bengal, Bruce Hillier's horse, as he couldn't find his own. They reached the Nuanetsi Bridge then split into sections all moving eastwards towards Nuanetsi Ranch where they all based up. At first light they watered the horses at a cattle trough and then followed the main Mbizi road to join Strumpher and c/s 1.1B at the confluence of the Magondi River. After comparing notes c/s 1.1C moved off and rode south to RV with c/s 1.1 at dusk, north of the Chikombedzi road where they based up for the night. They had ridden twenty-eight kilometres that day and everyone was done in. The following day

Austin's call sign took off at 0700 hours heading east for nine kilometres, then cutting south to the Nuanetsi river and then west to check out the dip at Van der Sander's Ironwood ranch where the 180 head of cattle had been slaughtered in January. There was no enemy sign at the dip nor was there any water for the horses. October being the hottest month of the year in Rhodesia meant the call sign had to ride to the Chomusume river and dig for water in the riverbed. They mounted up and by evening reached the ranch's cattle pens and checked the area out. There was no water at the pens either so they rode to the Chomusume again and watered the horses before basing up.

The next day they re-checked the ranch's dip and cattle pen area, then patrolled along the fence line for eight kilometres looking for enemy sign as well as Edenvale homestead. It was very difficult going as the country was dense thorn scrub. Austin lost his sub c/s in the thick jesse but found them an hour later. A stop was made when a water reservoir was found and, a further seven kilometres on, they reached Edenvale homestead on the Nuanetsi. The following day c/s 1.1B left to walk back to camp as one of the horses had rope-burn (caused by poor picket lines or bad tying/hitching). Four other horses had thrown shoes so they were left to be uplifted. Austin, now riding Haggis (Smith's mount), led his c/s south to check out a paddock and a dip marked with a painted number '20' on the map which, intelligence from a captured insurgent stated, had a hidden arms cache nearby. Nothing was found despite a long search. Just to be sure, another dip four kilometres away was checked out with the same result. Everyone was back at camp by mid-day on 12 October.

In camp Lieutenant Patrick Ollivier had taken over 2 Troop.

On the very hot and cloudy morning of 14 October there was a call-out as tracks for twenty-five insurgents had been found on the Nuanetsi. 1 Troop with three Shangaan trackers set off in pouring rain. They tracked spoor for six insurgents and went at a canter until one of the horses went lame. The pursuit was slowed down but by 1600 hours they were five minutes behind the gang which then bombshelled. Tracks were followed until last light when the call signs found good rainwater and based up. Nothing was found the next morning so the call signs were uplifted back to camp. That evening a Land Rover detonated a landmine near the Bubye (pronounced 'booby') River. At first light call signs 1.1C and 1.1A deployed to investigate and follow up. No tracks were found due to very heavy rain. 'Tomorrow', wrote Austin, 'Camp has to be jacked as the CO Major Pearce, 'B' Squadron's 2i/c, and two of the unit's South African benefactors who have helped the unit with equipment are coming for a visit.'

Thursday, 18 October, a clear sunny and very hot day, saw 'Beefy' Heath's section c/s 1.1B take the captured insurgent out with them to find the supposed arms cache near the dip marked with '20'. 'My section', writes Austin, 'was ready at 12.30 to patrol and cross-grain the cut-line north-east from the camp to the Mbizi–Rutenga railway line. It's about twenty-one miles and we took James, one of the Shangaan trackers with us.'

The section worked its way up to the line and based up at 1730 hours, not having found water but it poured down later that evening. The next day having not found any enemy sign they returned to camp where they remained on stand-by for 2 Troop. Later that day 3 Troop arrived.

20 October dawned bright and sultry. At mid-day the siren went. A gang of thirty insurgents had been spotted the previous evening across the river. 1 and 3 Troop saddled up and deployed but failed to locate any tracks and returned to camp where they were told to remain on stand-by for the following day. In the morning while everyone was getting a 'rev' (dressing down) for leaving rifles around, firing was heard emanating about 500 metres to the south. Call signs deployed to the area. Heavy rain had washed away any tracks so they split up. One of the sections then had a contact wounding one insurgent and capturing another. This capture later revealed that the gang consisted of five insurgents and fifteen Cubans!

On 23 October the camp was packed up ending this bush trip.

On 6 November, after ten days of gruelling retraining (see above under 'Regimental and Training'),

1 Troop fell in and was given convoy orders by Lieutenant Strumpher and to make ready to head for Mount Selinda in the Op *Thrasher* area the following day. 3 Troop were detailed to Victoria Falls for operations in the Op *Tangent* area.

1 Troop reached the JOC at Chipinga at 1030 hours on 8 November. Troop officers went to the JOC while the troops found a base site with water not far from the border. Here they watered the horses and set up camp. The next two days were spent erecting tents for an Officers' Mess and Sergeants' Mess as well as establishing a cookhouse, canteen and digging shit pits.

> We were based at Chisumbanje' says Clive Midlane. 'From there we would move in troop strength, i.e., three sticks of eight, plus two Shangaan trackers who were also mounted. These Shangaans trackers were masters of their craft. They had been trained up by Mark Sparrow.[26] In addition, attached to the troop was a farrier. This last was a new concept due to the time spent away.

10 November dawned with a cold drizzling rain. The troop was ordered to collect radios and ration packs for ten days as they were heading for Mozambique the next day. They also drew RPG 7s. Lieutenant Strumpher then gave Wilkinson, Austin and Clive Midlane their orders for the following day. 'Our mission', recalls Midlane, 'was to try and locate temporary ZANLA transit camps and generally harrass Frelimo troops.

> Engineers would breach the minefield at the border near Jersey Tea Estates and we would cross over into Mozambique. Once over the border we would ride about 50 kilometres east towards the power lines, then head north for the next two weeks. The direction was parallel to the border and roughly opposite Chipinga. The total area to be covered would be about 200 kilometres or so. After this we would back-track on our route and re-enter Rhodesia. These trips were so long that in the rainy season our clothes literally rotted on us.

These long bush trips are confirmed by the OC Captain Theo Williams. Williams, also a founder member of the Selous Scouts, says that bush trips of up to six weeks were not uncommon. Midlane continues:

> On these externals we were heavily armed. Each troop had six RPDs – 2 x RPDs per stick with 250 rounds. We had three RPG7s – one per stick with six rockets each – and we also had a 60mm mortar with twelve bombs. There was no base plate but our saddle shop had invented a special leather grip that fitted onto the mortar tube enabling it to be hand-held and fired. The troops were all armed with G3s.

Austin's Operational Notebook entry for the day details the orders as follows:

> **Situation:** CTs infiltrating to resupply internally. Now move in North of Espungabera. Booby-trap tea estate vehicles with limpets and PomZ. Ambush vehicles on main road.

> **Enemy Strength:** Unknown. Carrying old weapons as China has ceased supplying. Some folding-butt AKs. Russians taking over. Additionally there are 1,000 infantry (Frelimo) and 30 Russian tanks and Katushka (Stalin Organ rocket launcher) at Mapai. Large numbers of ZANLA reported at Espungabera.

> **Dress:** Assorted civvie, some female clothing.

---

26   Son of the legendary lowveldt stalwart Ray Sparrow.

Sergeant Rusty Leggitt. (Dick Weidermann)

Locals: Offsides

Friendly Forces: 'D','C' and 'A' companies 4RR, Recce Platoon at Humani Ranch; Anti-Tank Platoon with 81s and 106mm at Zona and Jersey Tea estates. Armed militia.

Mission: Three-fold:
    a.   Recce.
    b.   Disrupt and destroy CT resupply.
    c.   Eliminate all armed forces in the area.

Execution: Move from here by vehicle to Jersey Tea Estates; breach the minefield and cross into the area.

Grouping: RPG with three rockets. C/s 1.1A mortar with twelve bombs. Sparrows attached to outgoing section.

Command and Signals: Radios: 3 x TR48s plus 8 x small means (VHF radios). Schedules: VHF with sputnik at 0900, 1200, 1500hours.
    Call Signs: 5=HQ, 5.1=A,B,C.
    a.   1.8=Juliette 20
    b.   3.8 Juliette 22
    c.   4.8 Juliette 6

VHF Channel – Hotel 81. For c/s1 – Alpha 82
Shackle: IDOQO (Mapai) Unshackle.
1 spare nicad and 1 extra battery.

Admin and Log:
Dress: as usual.
Ammo: 140 rounds, 2 grenades.
Rations: ten days
Vet pack and Medic pack. 1st field dressings.
Dog tags.
Rifle cleaning kit plus 4 cammo cream bottles per section. Water purifying tablets. One day's supply of horse cubes.

Casualty Evacuation: Chopper from Chiredzi. Thirty minute delay at least.'

The three NCOs were also warned that there was to be no skull-bashing intimidation of locals. They had license to stop civilian vehicles and bring them back if possible. Any enemy military vehicles to be destroyed.

After this they went off to brief their sections accordingly. Austin's call sign was:

Austin (smoke grenades)
H. Payne (RPD)
J. De Abreu
Rogers (TR48, Zulus and wire-cutters)
Mangiza (claymore, binoculars and panga)
Judas (Vet pack)
Dakiwa (Medic pack)

They set out in cold and heavy rain the following morning heading for Jersey Tea Estates where the Engineers were waiting to guide them over the border minefield into Mozambique. From here they rode off in troop formation making for São Lourenço Mission. They based up that evening after a meal. It rained in the night.

They moved off at first light and captured an off-duty Frelimo soldier who was questioned by Trooper De Abreu. It turned out he was a tank commander from Mapai![27]

Wilkinson's and Austin's sections rode off to check out the area around the Xinica River while Midlane's section moved to the Mission. All sections based up in the vicinity for the night.

At dawn the troops set off in dry but very hot, humid weather along the Espungabera Road. They crossed the Xinica and came across a store which they looted. Two kilometres further on they stopped for a break at an orchard. A few minutes after they had set off with Wilkinson and Midlane up front one, of the Shangaans, Smungalisa, came trotting back. He was pointing at the very dense tree line and calling 'mortar, mortar'. The troops dismounted and peered into the impenetrable bush straining to see where the enemy mortar was. Before long they discovered that the tracker meant 'motor' as his eagle eye had spotted a 6-cylinder Toyota Landcruiser. On the passenger seat was a sombrero and when they turned the radio on they heard Meat Loaf belting out, 'You took the words right out of my mouth'! Strumpher decided to take the vehicle back to Rhodesia for use by either the SAS or Selous

---

27   This individual proved to be quite useful. The Rhodesians at this time had 'acquired' a few Russian T55 tanks. The engineers of 'E' Squadron 1RHE set the tanks up at Inkomo and the prisoner became a brilliant instructor on their operation.

Scouts. They got the vehicle going and drove it back to their base near the Mission. A few hours later they came under ineffective 122mm mortar fire. They decided to move anyway.

The next day, Wednesday 14 November, Strumpher decided to take some men and go back to the orchard area to tempt Frelimo into attacking the troop. This would be done while the others drove the captured vehicle back to Rhodesia. The troops drove along and emptied two further stores to deny supplies to the enemy. They also found a Willy's Jeep, got it going and, with Trooper Norval as driver, headed for Jersey Tea Estates to cross the minefield. At a river crossing, Bert Chianese who was driving the Toyota with the Frelimo prisoner tied up in the back, hit a rock and the vehicle flipped. Bert was okay as was the Frelimo prisoner who appeared more upset about the muddy state of his trousers! They got both vehicles back into Rhodesia and handed them over to 2 Troop. Later, they were resting in a mango grove when they came under intensive fire from Frelimo at Espungabera using 122mm rockets, RPG7s with air-bursts. The troops returned fire with their 60mm mortars and Frelimo went silent. Apparently a Frelimo section had been shadowing the Grey's and had called down fire on them. The troop then set up night ambush positions.

The next day, fully resupplied, the OC, Captain Williams, sent them back across the border. Everyone was 'switched on' as they expected a heavy stonking from Frelimo after the events of the previous day. They reached the Espungabera Road, and rode for seven kilometres before stopping and basing up in the pouring rain which went on all night. They awoke soaked and miserable and moved off down the Alguerida Road back to São Lourenço Mission. As they were setting up camp, they captured a local Portuguese European civilian who happened along on a motor cycle. He was Mozambique born and and operated a maize mill nearby. He told them Frelimo left him pretty much alone as he was a civilian. He wasn't too happy with Frelimo as they had press-ganged his two sons into the army. Clive Midlane remembers that members of 2 Troop later reported that the miller had been murdered by Frelimo perhaps because they suspected him of collaborating with the Rhodesians. He continues :

> We kept him with us that night. At first light we let him go as we began to move next to a large kraal complex. Sergeant Wilkinson's section saw a group of twenty to thirty Frelimo on the Troop's right flank. They were fully dressed in conventional war gear complete with helmets. Wilkie just said, 'Fred's right', on the A76 . His stick was on higher ground slightly above Lieutenant Strumpher's stick. With Austin's section on the left and slightly ahead Wilkinson and I led our sections into the attack. It had been a simultaneous sighting and a very brisk firefight went on for a few minutes. Austin's section then went left flanking but Frelimo saw them and 'gapped it' into the cover of the huts in the kraal complex.

Wilkinson and Trooper 'Buck' Rodgers dismounted and tethered their horses. Both then began moving across a field towards the huts. They were in the open with no immediate cover nearby when Frelimo began to fire at them from the huts. They could see the enemy scampering around the huts and adopting firing positions. Rodgers launched two RPG rockets at them one of which went right into the doorway of a hut. Unfortunately there were no enemy casualties but the rocket counter-attack startled the enemy into a running withdrawal. (Don Kenny later criticized Rodgers for wasting the rockets but Wilkinson quickly interjected that Rodgers, and not Kenny, had been under heavy fire and that they'd both been in an exposed position. At this Kenny backed off.)

The troops then found various pieces of equipment dropped by Frelimo in their flight including German and Russian helmets. (Later intelligence from locals gave out that they had killed one and wounded three enemy.) After this they decided to head for Jersey Tea Estates and back into Rhodesia. As they did Austin's horse, Gemini, trod on an anti-personnel mine. The blast caused her to bolt and after some trouble she was brought under control. On examination she was found to have sustained some minor shrapnel wounds to the gut and leg. It had been a very lucky escape. Everyone was back by dusk on 19 November.

Clive Midlane also mentions that Trooper Neville 'Star Wars' Croxford's horse Comet, also trod on an AP mine which blew a hole in its gut. The animal survived but Croxford had a long walk!

On Wednesday 21 November, with Sergeant Mike Wilkinson in charge, 2 TCVs made for Fort Victoria to collect hay and camouflage nets ordered from Inkomo. On the way they were fired at by insurgents hidden near the roadside. They drove through the killing ground returning fire as they went. Everyone then rapidly debussed and did a sweep of the area but the enemy had 'gapped it'.

2 Troop, who had taken over in Mozambique from 1 Troop on 19 November, were ambushed by over thirty Frelimo near São Lourenço Mission on Monday 26. Two horses were killed and seven others wounded. Corporal 'Bones' Forde was wounded by shrapnel. Frelimo were using the Mission church tower as an OP from which they had detected the troops. On the next day 1 Troop was deployed to the area to assist in locating the missing animals. Austin's c/s 5.1C crossed the minefield first heading south then east in a circling patrol around the mission. Everyone was very tense as they expected to be ambushed at any moment. At dusk, just before basing up, they saw four uniformed men at a distance. The call sign set up camp on a thickly wooded kopje.

At first light, in pouring rain and thick mist, they set off. They met some locals who told them that Frelimo was in ambush position and waiting for them by the bridge on the Mossurise River. These locals also let out that Frelimo's rivals, Renamo (Mozambique National Resitance army) had given Frelimo a bloody nose near the power lines. Acting on this the troops planned an attack but found nothing at the bridge. Two days later the troops, walking along the power lines and with Trooper De Abreu as interpreter, questioned every local they found concerning the enemy's whereabouts. No information was ascertained. Water was running short and everyone was walking now due to saddle sores from all the recent hard riding. Finally, on the very hot morning of 2 December, they arrived at the border and the Murongwezi river. Austin set up camp just inside Rhodesia near a large pool of water. It had been a frustrating operation. When they reached camp they were told that nine truckloads of Frelimo had arrived at the Mission area shortly after they had left it. Don Kenny the SSM planned to blow up the tower at São Lourenço but Comops quashed the planned operation as Frelimo would use it as international propaganda to show the world that the Rhodesians had attacked and bombed a school. They were also told that Frelimo had captured 2 Troop's missing horses and taken them to Sofala where they had been seen on international television.

On 17 December Captain Williams assembled everyone and briefed them on the cease-fire. He also told them that the incoming insurgents, ZANLA and ZIPRA, would be collected and gathered into Assembly Points throughout the country. At these Assembly Points they would be supervised by the incoming British Commonwealth Monitoring Force. The Rhodesian Security forces would have no direct interface with former enemy at this stage.

On 22 December the unit was confined to camp while the masses of returning ZANLA insurgents began to be collected and placed in their respective Assembly Points.

On Christmas Day the troops were told that operations would cease by 29 December. On Boxing Day the unit sent a few members to Chiredzi to pick up the International Monitoring Troops detailed to the area. These in fact arrived in their own helicopter and consisted of a Captain and a Sergeant from the East Anglian regiment.

Two Troops of 'A' Squadron were now based up on Lone Star Ranch. Williams had sited the camp next to a huge dam. He writes:

This enabled the lads to build a 'foofy slide' for off-duty enjoyment. I believe we all understood that the war was over. With the relaxation of war-tension the mood became one of general light-heartedness. Even the horses sensed it and just about every mare came into season. The consequent amount of equine sex going on was unbelievable. We had recently completed a prolonged bush trip and had planned a party at Salisbury's Monomotapa Hotel only to be told that we were confined to camp. This was to allow the gooks to move to their Assembly Points. It was difficult to keep up morale when we were all so used to a war-time situation. The sudden cessation of patrolling and normal operations was not easy to accept. We were a really special bunch of guys. In fact, the Grey's Scouts were the only truly fully integrated unit of the Rhodesia Army at all levels. My time of departure from the unit was just after Xmas. It was a very sad time for me personally. We had been through so much together with very little R&R. I handed over to Alistair Hope as I was being posted to Kariba as JOC Commander for the Op *Splinter* operational area.

The next few days were spent distributing cease-fire leaflets to the locals. The Rhodesian War was effectively over.

The Grey's in Op Hurricane

In December 1979 the CO asked Lance Corporals Paul Kirk and John Turner to undertake a private security assignment. Their task was to provide a security presence at Bluegrass Farm in the Sipolilo area. Bluegrass was a cattle/tobacco farm. Attacks on isolated farms had escalated over the years. The CO's mother and the farmer's wife were on the farm and he was obviously concerned for their safety. The farmer, Dick Bruford (Pearce's father-in-law), was away on Police Reserve call-up duty in the Zambezi Valley. The task was to be on a leave basis with Bruford paying the two for their trouble.

A day before New Year's Eve, with Bruford back from call up, in the very early hours of the morning, the farm came under attack by a group of insurgents from ZIPRA's Operational Area 1. This was despite the officially declared nationwide Ceasefire. The insurgents were firing from outside the security fence. Kirk and Turner, shocked out of sleep, leapt out of bed. As they did so a RPG rocket hit the top of their bedroom window sending a shower of concrete, glass and metal into the room. A large chunk of metal shrapnel passed through Kirk's left arm and lower back. At the same time enemy small arms fire was chattering away spraying the building, the rounds striking the roof like hailstones.

With the disoriented Kirk in initial pain and confusion Turner, whilst returning fire, got on the *Agri-Alert* radio and called for help. While this was going on, and in the pitch dark, the two ladies had safely got into the purpose built bunker linked to the house. Kirk and Turner then joined them and the ladies rendered first aid to Kirk.

Firing was then heard emanating from the opposite side of the initial enemy position. This was both surprising and puzzling before it was realised that this was caused by a further insurgent gang mistakenly engaging the other. It was subsequently discovered that both groups believed they were engaging security forces. The firing stopped and shortly afterwards the Police Reserve arrived in a Crocodile (mine-proofed vehicle) and Kirk was casevaced to what he initially thought was a medical centre. It was in fact a research centre for Brahman cattle. The vet on duty gave Kirk some methadone after which he examined his injuries. He told Kirk that his tendons had been severed and that he had a broken arm and various flesh wounds. At first light he was casevaced to Salisbury's Andrew Fleming Hospital for surgery.

The wounds took a couple of months to heal and required plenty of physiotherapy before he was able to regain movement to his left arm and hand.

Pearce adds:

Dick subsequently received a message from the offending insurgents apologising for the attack. They added that their intended target had been a neighbouring farm but, having lost their way in the dark, they attacked the wrong farm!

Chapter Epilogue

The second half of 1979 saw the country undergoing ever-increasing operational pressures and looming political change.

The country, now known as Zimbabwe-Rhodesia, had conducted peaceful elections and voted in a majority African government. This radical change, however, proved insufficient for those who supported the liberation movements. The country re-entered a political quagmire in which the fate of its people was to be manipulated again.

These events were dictated by the decisions made at the Commonwealth Heads of Government Meeting (CHOGM) held in Lusaka, Zambia in August. By 10 September the British Government was meeting with the representatives of the various Rhodesian/Zimbabwe camps at Lancaster House in London. Before the year was out we were to have a British Governor ensconced in Salisbury's Government House.

These events had a profound impact on both the war and the people. The armed conflict effectively increased in intensity as both the liberation movements of ZANU and ZAPU attempted to gain a stronger internal foothold in the country as everyone now realised that there would be a new constitution and fresh elections.

For the Grey's Scouts it was business as usual. The increasing tempo of the war created a backdrop of considerable uncertainty as revealed by the extracts from Lieutenant Colonel Pearce's notebook entries for 1979; additionally, his comments and overview below:

Unit Commander's Conference: 9 May 1979. (post April Elections but prior to Muzorewa becoming Prime Minister on 1 June 1979):

1. Intelligence Briefing:

There are 11000-12000 insurgents in the country. Their significant activities are:
- Mushumbi Pools (JOC *Hurricane*). Both ZANLA and ZIPRA are attempting to dominate the Zambezi Valley.
- ZIPRA is trying to extend its influence onto the Op *Hurricane* area from the west.
- ZIPRA are also trying to cut the Plumtree line of rail.
- New enemy equipment – a booby trap was found sited in a tree with a landmine detonating device.
- ZANLA appear to be remobilising the masses in the TTLs following the Muzorewa Election results.
- ZIPRA is still making efforts to establish footholds in predominantly ZANLA areas.
- We face a war of attrition rather than a massive conventional threat.

2. Points from the National JOC:

- The famine situation has lead to increasing stock theft. This presents a real threat to the national herd.
- The army is likely to continue running the SFA (Security Force Auxiliaries)
- The Air Force is to establish an Air Force Regiment for airfield defence at New Sarum in Salisbury, Thornhill in Gwelo and the 10 Forward Airfields (FAFs) spread around the country.

3. Army Commander's Message

May 1979 – Bronze Cross of Rhodesia
In front: 2Lt GC Rae BCR RhACR, Mr and Mrs van Niekerk,
parents of Cpl NJ van Niekerk BCR (Posth) 1 RLI.
Behind them: Cpl NK McLaughlin BCR 1 RLI, L Cpl MR Wilkinson BCR Grey's Scouts, Capt PJ
Cooper DMM 1RLI, Pte CWE McCanlis BCR 1RDR, C Sgt JFA Norman DMM 1RLI, WO2 L Monson
DMM 1 RLI, WO1 DC Bismark-Pettit DMM 1RDR, WO1 NN Amato DMM 1RDR. (Mike Wilkinson)

- A repeat of the pre-election message –we have a hard road ahead etc. etc.
- We are now in a post-election vacuum. This is a survival fight we have to live through. It is a crucial time but we are nearly at the top of the hill.
- The statement by Bishop Muzorewa that the army will be under a Black man doesn't mean a Black General. Rather a minister. As there have already been Black ministers it wont change anything.

Unit Commander's Conference: 28 June 1979.
1. Intelligence Briefing:

Mozambique:
- There has been a logistics build-up by FPLM in support of ZANLA. We can expect an enemy push via the Op *Hurricane* area towards Salisbury. We cannot allow ZANLA to infiltrate into vital areas.
- For every two insurgents infiltrating the country one is eliminated. Surrenders have increased

but hinge on their junior commanders being convinced that theirs is a lost cause.

- There is the possibility of the movement of insurgents from Tanzania to Mozambique by aircraft. This will give ZANLA between 7 500 to 10 000 reinforcements.

Zambia:

- The operation against Joshua Nkomo attacking his house in Lusaka failed. This failure to eliminate ZAPU's leader has, however, had a psychological effect on ZIPRA who have dispersed their command element making for disruption and creating co-ordination difficulties.
- A further raid on ZIPRA's Intelligence HQ has added additional disruption to its chain of command.

Botswana:

- There is now a ZANLA office in Francistown.
- There has been a significant drop in the numbers of refugees and enemy recruits crossing into Botswana.

2. General:

- International efforts are being made to unite the Patriotic front union of ZAPU and ZANU.
- On 18 June Nkomo called for a meeting of his ZIPRA to be members of the proposed ZIPRA/ZANLA Joint High Command. 12 members of each faction were to represent their respective organisations. There was nil attendance. Nkomo called a second meeting at which only 15 ZIPRA turned up to attend. All this indicates that considerable political and military division continues to exist between both enemy organisations.
- There has been a report that there are two ZIPRA radio call-signs operating inside Zimbabwe-Rhodesia.
- On 26 June four Hunters attacked ZIPRA at their Zambian FC Camp and five Cheetahs attacked the ZIPRA Intelligence HQ also in Zambia. The Zambian Air Force took an hour to get airborne. One of its MIG's deployed to Mumbwa at 26 000 and then asked to land. There was no armed contact between Rhodesian and Zambian Air Forces during the incidents.
- G Branch advised that the SFA(Security Forces Auxiliaries) were being overhauled and rationalised. This involves the introduction of a rank structure together with embellishments and badges of rank etc.
- The cost of Air Force operations was tabled. There was concern about the costs where an abortive operation was launched. A recent example occurred on Friday 18 June following the report of the presence of a group of 100–150 insurgents in the lower Gwelo area. Hunters were deployed for an airstrike at a cost of Rh$28 000. It proved abortive and when it turned out that there was no hard/real intelligence to support the initial report.
- The Zimbabwe-Rhodesia Council of Ministers met to discuss the issue of Amnesty for surrendered insurgents. A complete pardon with assistance to return to normal life was the approach agreed.
- An increase in enemy Electronic Warfare (EW) has been noted. Instructions have been issued to increase awareness of this threat and Voice Procedure has been tightened up.

After this conference the Notebook records a flurry of activity regarding Grey's Scouts preparations for external operations by 'A' Squadron. This included pre-deployment training in the Lake Kyle area; progress on lightweight rations; longer-life A76 (VHF) radio batteries; haversacks for heavy barrel FN magazines; one extra set of combat clothing per soldier; increasing 'A' Squadron's Farrier complement to two both of whom had to be able to ride. It ends with a question directed at WO2 Bill Lewis, our Chief Farrier – 'Can we make MAG tripods?' Bill, a Scotsman with a fine curling moustache, was a modern day Hephaestus and could forge anything out of metal ...

Unit Commander's Conference: 16 September 1979
1. Intelligence Briefing:

Mozambique:
- Op *Uric* – Not regarded as a success. This major external operation had been mounted by Rhodesian security forces against Mapai and other major targets in Gaza Province. FPLM Anti Aircraft weapons had been moved to alternate positions. The FPLM also made effective use of its trench system and deception tactics at Mapai. BM21x122mm 'Stalin Organs' were also deployed at Mapai and Malvernia. (Note: an account of this operation was reconstructed by Alex Binda, author of this work, in *The Saints, The Rhodesian Light Infantry* pp 394-421. Pub. 30 Degrees South 2007). The overall lesson for our security forces here is that our ability to conduct cross-border raids with impunity is coming to an end.
- There is rapid enemy AA (Anti Aircraft weapons) deployment along our entire north-east border with Mozambique.
- The situation is also changing in terms of the threat from Surface-to-Air missiles with a range of up to 6 000 kilometres. These could be deployed against South Africa also.
- There is an increase in the use of non-metallic(minimum metal) landmines.

This Intelligence Briefing shows the increasing momentum towards conventional warfare with ZANLA deploying more and more sophisticated weaponry and supporting arms. Unfortunately there is no Intelligence on the ZIPRA fronts of Botswana and Zambia.

2. General:

Rationalisation of the TA (Territorial Army):
    a.   There are 700 RAR troops surplus to establishment.
    b.   There are currently 1 400 AS (African Soldiers) serving alongside white TA troops.
This footnote to the Briefing struck a cord with me. It was ultimately to set in motion the formation of our 'C' Squadron.

The opposing forces involved in the Rhodesian Insurgency had ratcheted-up the war, sucking neighbouring countries into the conflict. But matters came to a head with the meeting of the opposing factions at London's Lancaster House Conference of 10 September 1979. Despite this the war continued with as much ferocity as ever. The last Rhodesian external raid was Operation *Miracle* which took place from 28 September to 1 October 1979.

The Lancaster House Agreement was finally signed on 21 December and a ceasefire came into play.

Following the signing of the Lancaster House Agreement the Prime Minister, Bishop Abel Muzorewa, addressed senior military officers. I recorded the following main points:
- Security forces, the Police and Government Departments would continue to run their own agencies during the two months that the incoming British Governor, Lord Soames, would be in Zimbabwe-Rhodesia. There will be no interference by the Governor. He will act on our advice.
- Sanctions will be lifted by Britain and the United States as soon as the Governor arrives.

- International business has shown great interest in the country
- Three weeks after the elections the new Government will be automatically recognised.
- The Front Line States are committed to the Lusaka Accord (recognition of the government).
- The elections are crucial. The Patriotic Front will participate.
- We cannot afford an irresponsible government. We must ensure the enemy does not come into power. The entire country is relying on the Security Forces.
- The Patriotic Front armies will be confined to Assembly Points (APs). Any found outside these APs are fair game.

As 1979 slipped away, we all wondered what the new year held in store ...

6

Zimbabwe-Rhodesia 1980

On Saturday 5 January Simon Austin recorded in his diary:

> Listening to the news, apparently 18,000 insurgents have come in over the last few days. More than I thought were in Rhodesia. Half of them will be *mujibas* or Frelimo.

On the following day his troop left for Chiredzi as the guys from National Service intake 163 were standing down. At JOC Chiredzi they saw eight captured insurgents who had been brought in, surprisingly, by Security Force Auxiliaries (SFA).

The next few days poured with rain which meant that a disgruntled intake 163 could not leave. Furthermore all the horses bar 30 decided to run off to Chipinda Pools. In any case, everyone was confined to camp as returning insurgents, en route to their Assembly Point, were moving past the Grey's Camp.[1]

By 8 January most of the horses had been recovered. Information from Fort Victoria was that Fireforce had a couple of 'scenes' attempting to get two groups of insurgents to lay down their weapons and come in. Three days later, with most of the horses recovered and loaded on the HCVs, they set off for Chisumbanje but were stopped for a few hours by Commonwealth Monitoring Troops at the BSAP Support Unit camp on the Sabi River Bridge and not allowed to cross for a couple of hours. They finally reached Chisumbanje where 2 Troop was deployed.

On 13 January Austin's call sign with four horses in their HCV set off for Lundi Bridge and the Matibi no. 2 TTL to collect the last horses. At the bridge they were delayed as a vehicle from 1RDR (Rhodesia Defense Regiment) had overturned. While they waited they watched a Hercules dropping supplies to the insurgents at the nearby Assembly Point Golf. On the following day Brigadier Peter Rich arrived to brief everyone on the forthcoming general election.

On 17 January 2 Troop were recovered from deployment. At 1100 hours Bobby Hay's call sign reported capturing two African women sneaking over from Mozambique to Assembly Point Golf. Austin's call sign set off to RV with Clive Midlane's section six kilometres away to bring in a further six civilian prisoners.

At first light on 19 January, reacting to reports that two insurgents had raided a store in the Veneka PV, the troop set off. They decided to walk the last kilometre in case of landmines. At the store they spoke to the SFA who had chased the insurgents off. Austin, now joined by 2 Troop, put his Shangaans on the tracks. The spoor led directly to the No Go Area three kilometres south of the PV. Here 2 Troop, escorted by BSAP Support Unit, were allowed in. At 1000 hours Austin joined them at the Sabi Bridge until the touchy, bad-mannered and jumpy British Commonwealth Monitoring Force HQ at the Assembly Point ordered them to leave the area. Better at the social graces, a few insurgent Patriotic Front officers from the AP then showed up and told the Grey's that, if the culprits

---

1   There were 18 designated Assembly Points spread around the country. They were code-named Alpha to Romeo. APs Alpha to Hotel held ZANLA insurgents (AP India was non-operative). APs Juliet and Kilo held ZANLA and ZIPRA. APs Mike to Romeo housed ZIPRA insurgents. Assembly Point Romeo, which will feature in this narrative, was sited near the Umfuli River in the Hartley-Sinoia district.

January 1980, Cpl. Clive Midlane and section on patrol E of Chisumbanje, near the Moz. Border, while Monitoring Assembly Point Golf. (Simon Austin)

January 1980, Buck Rogers and Bill Thurman (Australian) at dinner camp, whilst patrolling around Assembly Point Golf, near Chisumbanje

January 1980, Patrol crossing the Sabi river near Chisumbanje.

turned up, they would be handed over to the BSAP Support Unit.

The next few days were spent on routine patrolling.

On Sunday, 27 January, the Troop returned to Salisbury. Robert Mugabe had arrived in Rhodesia. Austin commented ' ... met busloads of his supporters as we came into the berg. Nearly started a new war!'

On 30 January Austin was discharged from the Rhodesia Army as his contract had ended.

On Thursday, 7 February, Grey's Scouts Dave Sparkes killed himself playing Russian roulette in the Monomotapa Hotel's Prospectors' Bar. David Rees, a fellow Grey's Scout and friend recalls:

I was not present at the 'Deer Hunter' incident at Prospectors' Bar but if I had been I certainly would have prevented things getting that far. I was asked to identify his body at Andrew Fleming Hospital the next day and was interviewed later by Lieutenant Rod Garnett, Grey's Scouts Adjutant, at the official Board of Inquiry. Dave was an excellent soldier and instructor and his senseless death haunts me to this day. I met his son Daniel at our 30th reunion in November 2010 and it was a very tough reminder of a tragic loss.

Cedric Tipping-Woods says:

I was chuffed to be promoted to major at Victoria Falls. I am proud to have been the only G commissioned TA Officer to achieve this rank in the unit's history.

Just before the final elections, 'B' Squadron was deployed to the Sinoia area where our presence was intended to maintain stability and influence 'hearts and minds'. We were also there to train for action against the Assembly Point at Hoya should the election be hung. We got promises of 155mm artillery and major air support from South Africa which shows you how gullible we were! The district contained Chief Chirau supporters. During this period one insurgent was killed.

Early in the month, 'A' Squadron had been positioned near Assembly Point Romeo which was sited some 50 kilometres south-west of Sinoia (now Chinhoi) in the Magondi TTL. This assembly point had been a late addition to the list of APs agreed at the London Lancaster House final accord. It had been filling up with returning ZIPRA insurgents and now housed over 1,000 of them. (The ZIPRA commander of this AP was Richard Mataure who was the leader of the insurgent gang involved in the contact of 21 October of the previous year in which John Coast won his SCR.) It was a very tense time as ZIPRA's incoming cadres were very touchy and suspicious about the entire AP business. Feelings were mutual as Cedric Tipping-Woods reveals:

Captain Rory Hensman, as our liaison, was in attendance with the British Monitoring Force at Assembly Point Romeo near Sinoia.

We received info that a group of between twelve and fifteen ZIPRA had indicated their willingness to join the AP but were pretty jumpy. The Brits contacted Lieutenant Colonel Pearce about this and he ordered me to deploy with two sections near a village in the area to RV with the group at a specific time. After waiting for several hours well past the RV time schedule, we received notification via locals that the insurgents were ready to come in and parley. But they were seeking safety guarantees and proof that we 'came in peace'.[2]

---

2   Author's note: this comment from Tipping-Woods reveals the fearful respect the insurgents still had for the Rhodesian Security forces, even at this late stage. I had personally encountered this same apprehension and suspicion when visiting an AP in the south-east to conduct Pay Parade! I had arrived earlier, by vehicle, whilst my colleagues with trunkloads of cash flew in by Dakota. When the aircraft came overhead to land there was near-panic amongst the insurgents around me. They obviously believed they were going to be stonked! By the Pay Corps!?

Tipping-Woods elaborates:

As I approached, the sensation of being watched was overpowering. I felt the hair on the back of my neck stand up. An insurgent then showed himself. He was armed with a bayoneted AKS. A few more appeared and I held my breath. Slowly the AKS was lowered and the leader asked my name and how did it feel to lose the war. I holstered my pistol. He then said I could address him by his *nom de guerre* 'Sam the son of a Shithouse'.

This broke the tension and I actually laughed. We then went back to the vehicles where the insurgents were loaded onto the vehicles and we set off for the AP. On the way we stopped at a roadside store as the insurgents wanted to buy food, toiletries and booze. By now my adrenalin level had stabilised and I realised I hadn't sent my sitrep to Base. The CO was very angry ... As we drove along the insurgents began to imbibe some of their drink.

When we arrived at AP Romeo we were greeted by Rory and Richard Mataure, the ZIPRA commander. Mataure proceeded to brief the group we had brought in. He gave them a severe dressing down for delaying us as well as for being drunk and insubordinate. I believe they got confined to a latrine-like pit for several days as punishment.

After the war Richard Mataure remained as battalion commander at Mount Darwin. He subsequently became a member of the Zimbabwe Diplomatic Corps in Kenya, and ended up as a highly respected Traditional Healer (*Nganga)* in Harare.

'A' Squadron was based about ten kilometres from the AP and well away from its five kilometre buffer 'no go zone'. They were tasked with routine patrolling and generally seeing that all was alright in the area. Corporal Neil Johns and his section had laid up for the night in ambush positions not too far from the buffer zone. At first light they discovered tracks for about six insurgents on a nearby path. The tracks led away from the AP. This was against the official ceasefire agreement which stipulated that the returning insurgents, once in the AP, were not to leave it for any reason. Johns set up an ambush on the path and that evening captured two insurgents, now dressed in civilian clothes, who were in the process of returning to the AP. The captures were reported to HQ the following morning. In camp was Corporal Mike 'Brady' Bradshaw whose section was in reserve as a reaction force. Bradshaw remembers:

We were detailed to go and collect the captures. The eight-man section – Bruce Hillier, myself, Trooper Earl Wakeford and one other took the lead vehicle while Colin Welensky and three others followed in the second. They were both armour-plated trucks (MAPs). It was standard procedure to take two vehicles in case one broke down or to support each other in case of attack.

We had the usual short briefing. I reminded my guys that we would be driving fairly close to the AP buffer zone to RV with Johnsie (Johns). I didn't envisage any problems as the ceasefire was well in place. In any case we were not driving to the AP itself.

Bruce had the wheel and I sat alongside. The two troopers were riding in the back. Colin was driving his truck with his three guys in the back. We kept dust distance between us, about 100 metres. As we went along I consulted my map from time to time to ensure we were on course. The road was terrible and we crawled along at just over 20 kmh.

At the point where the road was closest to the AP we suddenly came under a barrage of small arms fire. Bruce, reacting instantly, accelerated to get us through the killing ground. The firing was very intense and absolutely deafening. They were also using RPG7s and the flash and whoosh of the rockets as they went past was unmistakable. Thankfully most missed. Colin's vehicle was hit in the rear but the strike angle deflected the rocket and it glanced off. His front right-hand tyre had been shot-up making control very difficult. In the lead vehicle we returned fire while I shouted to Bruce to keep going. About 200 metres ahead we were stopped by a fallen tree lying right across the road with no way around. We leapt off the vehicle and adopted all round defensive positions. They had us where they wanted us and we were all pretty convinced they would take us out. Colin's truck joined us moments later and we all waited. There was no question we were outnumbered.

I did a quick assessment. We needed to change the tyre on Colin's vehicle before we could go anywhere. I got on the set to Johnsie and told him what had happened. He said they had heard the firing and were on their way to join us.

A few minutes later a MAP with about eight policemen aboard came down the road. I stopped them and told them what had happened. They said that they had been attending a political meeting with the locals and were on their way back to base. After what had just happened to us, I let them know that I didn't think it would be a good idea for them to drive that way. They simply replied that there was no other way and continued on. They hadn't got more than 150 metres down the road when they were ambushed and their vehicle came to an abrupt halt. The insurgents had obviously stuck around.

Even though the odds were against us we knew we had to do something. We got into a sweep line and headed towards them. When we got there we found that the enemy was withdrawing. We let off a few long-range shots at each other and secured the area. Then we turned our attention to the police vehicle and found it to be unoccupied. They had 'gapped it' (fled) leaving three rifles and some webbing behind. We jumped into their vehicle and drove back to our trucks. Johnsie and his guys had now come up. We got busy changing the tyre and I gave HQ a sitrep. We were ordered back to camp.

We split our guys between the three vehicles. We also split the captures. We made one lie face down in the lead vehicle and the other in the same posture in the tail vehicle with the police truck between us.

We said farewell to Johnsie and I took the wheel. Bruce was on the seat beside me while Wakefield was in the back with the capture at his feet.

Less than two kilometres down the road there was a flash of an RPG7 just before my small armoured windshield as the insurgents initiated another ambush. This was immediately accompanied by the roar and chatter of small arms fire. I saw very quickly that the enemy, now obviously reinforced, had a longer ambush line this time. The killing ground was over 200 metres. And they also now had armour-piercing weapons (the PKM – this has a longer round than the AK and has tungsten armour-piercing heads). These were now coming at us and through the vehicle's armour plating. I'd left my fold-down window open. Stupid really but here this oversight saved me. A round came through my side of the vehicle and its shrapnel was blocked by the steel flap which was hanging down. Another penetrated just above the open window and was deflected downwards, hitting Bruce in the neck and back. Fortunately these were flesh wounds and not serious. In the back Wakeford had been shot in the arm rendering him pretty much out of action. The insurgents were aiming at us drivers so as to immobilise the vehicles – that much I knew. I put my head and foot down and continued through the killing ground for what seemed like eternity. Once through I glanced quickly about to make sure the police vehicle was still with me. I then sped on for the air strip. Once we got there I realised with dismay that Colin Welensky's vehicle wasn't with us. He had taken a hammering and again his front tyre had been shot up making steering extremely difficult. Like me he had left his fold-down window open and, like me, this also saved him. The steel flap was hit and flew up violently and with great force hitting him on the elbow. The Shangaan tracker, Ngungu, took some shrapnel but nothing major. At the air strip Bruce and Wakeford were casevaced while, suitably reinforced, I headed back for Colin. Halfway there his vehicle burst out of the bush, its front tyre billowing smoke

L/Cpl Charles Tiddy on Cavalier. (Charles Tiddy)

and nearly afire with the friction being caused by the rim. As we drew up alongside, three heads popped up and the relief on their faces – and ours! – must have been pretty obvious. There were a few minor wounds but nothing serious. Johnsie's section had again heard the firing and come sweeping along the road to support us but found that the insurgents had gone.

The day's events were a sensitive affair, what with the ceasefire and all. Captain Richard Passaportis BCR, the Fireforce commander based at Sinoia, flew in to debrief us. Bruce Hillier and Earl Wakeford were airlifted to Sinoia Hospital.

The author agrees here with Bradshaw's conviction that this was the last armed encounter/contact between Rhodesian security forces and insurgents of the Rhodesian Bush War.

The national newspaper, *The Rhodesia Herald*, reported the incident. It quoted Brigadier Vic Walker, Deputy Commander JOC Hurricane, saying that the ambushes were 'blatant ceasefire violations'. They also mentioned that the complaint had been forwarded to the British Monitoring Force; this last was totally superfluous as that organisation, as everyone well knew, was as effective as a chocolate teapot.

On Thursday 14 February, in the evening, a bomb was detonated outside Salisbury's Monomotapa Hotel. Simon Austin found the building still completely sealed off the following morning. He decided to visit Umtali where he booked into the Cecil Hotel: ' ... I appear to be the only guy out of uniform today. The whole country has been called up for the elections. The call-up starts today.'

On 27 February voting began in the General Election. Austin recorded: ' ... a million people are supposed to have voted today. Mugabe has gapped it back to Mozambique ... '

Two days later about 90% of voters had turned out, either voluntarily or through intimidation.

In February Paul Kirk rejoined Training Troop having recovered from the wounds he sustained during the ZIPRA attack on Bluegrass Farm. He writes:

Just prior to the election results, at the beginning of March, 'A' and 'B' squadrons deployed to Assembly Point Foxtrot at Dzapasi in the Buhera district in the Op Repulse area. We were to be part of the Operation Quartz. The operation was to be a coup if Mugabe won the election. We all waited but nothing materialised. We all also realised that things had come to an end and we were merely going through the motions.

On 1 March, Grey's Scouts John McNeilage and Dan Brandt were featured on TV at a ZIPRA Assembly Point where they were training Joshua Nkomo's troops for integration into the future National Army.

On 4 March Austin's diary entry reports: 'A major disaster for Rhodesia! Mugabe won the election hands down, collected 57 seats, Nkomo 20, so between them the Patriotic Front has 77 seats out of 80.'

Two days later Austin booked an air ticket to the Greek Isles.

Cedric Tipping-Woods concludes:

The final chapter of the Grey's Scouts history was closed by 'B' Squadron. In typical fashion, after many 'tinoits' of strong alcohol at the Orange Grove Motel in Sinoia, we, led by Sergeant Bruno Rabie and WOII Charlie Davies, with great pomp and ceremony, buried 'Cockie Robin' for the final time.

A Final Regimental Parade followed by a Dining Out dinner in May 1980 saw the end of the unit as the men of 'B' Squadron knew it. It had been a great service; everyone was proud to have served in it but felt no need to talk of it later.

The Grey's had ridden out of history for their country. Having done all and everything that had been asked of them they now, quietly, almost ghost-like, rode back into the past and vanished.

⊹⊱────⊰⊹

Not all members left the unit at independence. Paul Kirk, stayed on. In April he attended a battle camp in Mazoe with Intake 167. The SAS were carrying out an escape and evasion exercise in the area at the same time. They asked the Grey's to try and track down some of the SAS guys on the exercise. It was all very interesting and included a Lynx attack on the SAS base camp using flour bags for bombs. A number of the SAS tents took direct hits.

Intake 167 passed out at the end of May. The Passing Out Parade was very well attended by family and friends. Kirk recalls:

I remember that the unit called in both 'A' and 'B' Squadrons for a final regimental photo. It was the last time the complete regiment was together.

With the war over and Rhodesia now Zimbabwe, most of the newly qualified members of Intake 167, including Kirk and Turner, were posted to 'C' Squadron which would now absorb Intake 168 which were still in training. 'C' Squadron composed of:

OC Major Bill Morrison, an American.

2i/c Lieutenant Patrick Ollivier.

Troop Commanders: Lieutenants Vermaak, Hank Verdain, John Hopkins, and Nick de la Casa.[3]

---

3   De la Casa and his wife were murdered by Islamic Kurds in Kurdistan in 1991 when serving as BBC freelance reporters. Their bodies were recovered by Royal Marines.

In September/October 1980, Kirk was serving with 'C' Squadron in an anti-poaching operation in Ngezi. After this, most of the officers and men began to put in for early release as they realised which way the country was now going politically. Kirk was discharged in December 1980 after which he moved to South Africa and, in January 1981, he joined the South African 5 Reconnaissance Commando in Phalaborwa.

I am indebted to Lieutenant Colonel Chris Pearce for the following very informative conclusion.

Chapter Epilogue

The political situation dominated 1980. It was a year of change on a massive scale. At the end of the day, stability within the country was provided by the professionalism of the Rhodesian military forces. They played a key role in the transition from war to peace.

On Friday 4 January, the Commander COMOPS, General Peter Walls, briefed what was possibly the largest gathering of Rhodesian Army and Air Force officers ever assembled. He laid out the reasons for the forthcoming elections. He also explained the key strategic reasons why the Lancaster House talks had ended in agreement. He went on to stress that no one wanted a Marxist government in power. This included the British and South African governments. The war-weary frontline states of Mozambique and Zambia, who had borne the brunt of Rhodesian external operations, supported the agreement.

ZANLA and ZIPRA forces with their Commonwealth Monitors, said the general, were making their way into the various designated Assembly Points They had been given 5 January as a 'Buffer Day' after which, the implication was, any found outside the designated area would be arrested – 'if necessary with a bullet between the eyes'.

Walls said that whilst he and his planners did not envisage a sweeping election victory for Bishop Muzorewa's UANC, they did see the opportunity for a coalition. This would exclude ZANU but would include the white bloc, UANC and Nkomo's ZAPU. He then spoke of contingency plans: 'By whatever means are necessary we are not going to let the Patriotic Front win'.

At this time Walls was optimistic. Like him no one anticipated the massive vote that Mugabe's ZANU PF would take. This was to exorcise the UANC as a political force.

A day before Mugabe's return from exile, a further briefing was held at COMOPS on Saturday 26 January. This briefing was attended by a small group of commanding officers of 1RLI, 1SAS, Selous Scouts, and Grey's Scouts amongst others. Chris Pearce writes:

General Walls addressed us with the following:
There was to be a contingency plan to neutralise all the Assembly Points in the event of an unacceptable election result or a hung election. This plan, which was not firm, was code-named Operation Melba.[4]
My notes contain an outline of the plan. The key points were:
Assembly Point PAPA. Top Priority. This contained over 2,000 insurgents dug in and with heavy weapons and AA guns.
Assembly Point BRAVO. Top Priority. This contained 600/700 insurgents.
Assembly Point ALPHA. Second Priority. This contained over 1,300 insurgents.
Assembly Point CHARLIE. Priority 3. (No numbers given)
I can't recall why these four APs were mentioned in isolation since the briefing went on to lay out the various priorities for attacking the remaining APs (Delta/Foxtrot/Golf/Hotel/Juliet).
I can't recall why these four APs were mentioned in isolation since the briefing went on to

---

4   Author's note: There may be some latter-day confusion about the title of this operation. Many post- Rhodesia analysts of the Bush War have designated this contingency plan as Operation Quartz. Quartz, a sub-operation within Operation Melba was in fact mostly concerned with the elimination of Robert Mugabe.

lay out the various priorities for attacking the remaining APs. Also you will note that some APs would only be subject to air strikes only. No ground forces.

I recorded the following and, after all these decades, offer apologies for any omissions or mis-read notes;

Assembly Point	Priority	Remarks	Troops to Tasks
Alpha	2	+/- 1 300 CTs	2 x Sqns Grey's Scouts
Bravo	1	+/- 6/700 CTs	1 RR
Charlie	3	No number recorded in notes	Nil
Delta	1	+/- 2 500 – 3 000	6 RR, RhACR, Sp Unit (BSAP) **
Echo	3	No number recorded in notes	Nil
Foxtrot	1	+/- 5 000	2 RAR, 4 RR plus 2 x Fire Forces, 2 x Indep Coys ex-Op Thrasher, RhACR, Arty Bty 88mm, 3 x BSAP Sp Unit Coys plus 1 x BSAP Sp Unit Tp
Golf	2	No number recorded in notes	9 RR plus A Coy BSAP Sp Unit and 1 x local BSAP Sp Unit Tp
Hotel	1	No number recorded in notes	Fire Force X-Ray, 4 Bde Def Pl, 1 x BSAP Sp Unit Tp plus 81 mm Mortar Pl
Juliet	1	+/- 1 600	Fire Force Yankee and Zulu plus 1 x BSAP Sp Unit Tp
Kilo	3	No number recorded in notes	Nil, but will be alternate target for Fire Force Zulu if not engaged at AP Juliet
Lima	2	No number recorded in notes	2 RR. 1 Bde Def Pl, 1 x Bty 88mm, plus local BSAP Sp Unit Tp
Mike	1	+/- 1 500	1 RAR, Fire Force, 1 x Bty 88mm, RhACR Sqn, 4 Indep Coy, BSAP Sp Unit Tp
Papa	1	+/- 2 000	1 RLI, 5 RR, 8 RR plus Fire Force, 1 x Arty Bty 88mm, 6 x 140mm Reciless Rifles
Romeo	1	+/- 700	10RR and Sinf Dem Coy, Fire Firce, BSAP Sp Unit Mounted Tp
PF HQ	1	No number recorded in notes	1 SAS plus 1 x Tank Sqn
Reserves			DRR x 150. Balance to 1 Bde DRAR x 150. Balnce to 4 Bde Sinf x 100 Gwelo RLI x 200 Recruits (Week 5) to 2Bde Selous Scouts 63 to 3 Bde 1/2/3 Indep Coys remain under command their respective brigades Guard Force to be deployed as commanders see fit

With the exception of APs Alpha, Charlie and Echo which were to be second phase attacks, there were to be simultaneous air attacks. This air effort would be supplemented by South African Air Force (SAAF) aircraft consisting of six Mirage F1s, three Canberra bombers and eight Impalas. Fireforces X-Ray, Yankee and Zulu were to be allocated to JOCs Repulse and Tangent. On receipt of a given code-word which would be the Warning Order for the operation,

January 1980, Paul Kirk recovering from shrapnel wound received in terr
attack on Bluegrass Farm, New Year's Eve 1979. (Paul Kirk)

units were to abandon their election deployments and move to Assembly Areas in preparation
for the attacks. Best case scenario would be a 96-hour warning. From this time frame there
would be seven code-words issued to cancel each phase if necessary.

Troop deployments, in conjunction with requests for AP layout plans, included RHACR
(Rhodesian Armoured Car Regiment), RHA (Rhodesian Artillery) and the British South
Africa Police Support Unit.

Only air photos would be possible. There was to be no ground recce.

As far as Grey's Scouts were concerned, our role was to deal with Assembly Point Alpha: to
hold the escarpment but not attack the camp itself. (This changed later and air support and a
TA unit under command was allocated see below.) 1RLI were allocated AP Papa with TA units,
artillery and Fireforce support. 1 and 2RAR were allocated leading roles. My notes record that
every single unit in the army would have been deployed under this plan though nowhere was
there mention of a Selous Scouts role. 1SAS were allocated a tank squadron in support and their
target was the Patriotic Front's HQ. At this stage the operation was codenamed 'Melba' and four
initial activation code-words were allocated: CARRIER – meaning engage both ZANLA and
ZIPRA APs; CANOPY – only engage ZANLA APs; JARGON – only engage ZIPRA APs;
FALLACY – cancel the operation.

With the insurgents moving into their respective Assembly Points the Rhodesian forces,
mobilised in strength, were in their designated operational areas under command of the
various Brigade HQs. Grey's Scouts were detached as an entire unit under command HQ 2
Brigade for the election period. Our allocated operational area encompassed the town of Sinoia
(now Chinhoyi) and its surrounding area. We were now part of Sub-JOC Sinoia which was
subordinate to JOC Hurricane. Our Area of Responsibility was wide and included the key

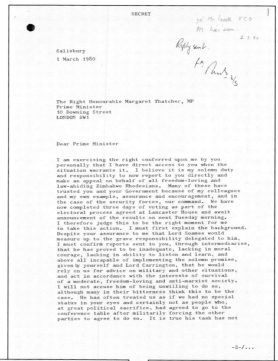

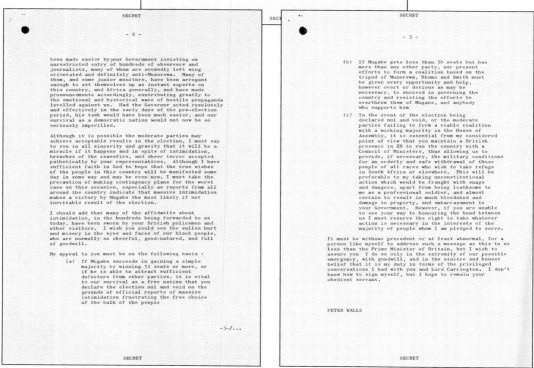

Letter to Mrs Thatcher of 1 March 1980. (Paul Kirk)

location of ZIPRA Assembly Point Romeo, some 30 kilometres from Sinoia. All Grey's Scouts

Umfangazie National Park, 'C' Squadron loading up for anti-poaching ops, July 1980. (Paul Kirk)

operational sub-units were, for the first time, deployed as an entity; Regimental HQ, 'A' Sqn and 'B' Sqn with supporting elements. Under command for operations were two companies of RDU (Rhodesia Defense Unit) as well as elements of the BSAP.

We deployed to Sinoia and set up our Regimental HQ on a farm near the town. From there we proceeded to mount patrols aimed at ensuring the insurgents were contained within the APs' five-kilometre buffer radius. Two contacts resulted as a result of these patrols, one of which has already been described in this chapter. After this, things settled down somewhat.

Shortly afterwards, as part of the 'reconciliation' process, I was ordered to link up with a British Lieutenant Colonel from the Commonwealth Monitoring Force and accompany him to Assembly Point Romeo. Here there was to be enacted a Peace Ceremony led by Joshua Nkomo himself. I was ordered to travel unarmed. I complied and met the Lieutenant Colonel who was travelling in a short wheelbase Land Rover. As I sat in the back, I was flung about for some 40 minutes by the breakneck speed with which the Brit corporal driver went. I suspect they were both having a joke at my expense; pretty shallow sense of humour.

On arrival we were met by a young British major in charge of the British troops in the AP. I was also introduced to Richard Mataure who, readers might recall, was the commander of the ZIPRA group which had engaged 'B' Squadron at Victoria Falls on 21 October 1979 when John Coast won his SCR. Mataure was now a brigadier in the British Army – or appeared to be as he was wearing the appropriate insignia! He was certainly introduced as Brigadier Mataure. I found it surreal engaging with an enemy we had been very recently trying our hardest to kill. This sense of surrealism continued when, later in the afternoon, a British Gazelle helicopter landed in the AP and Joshua Nkomo alighted. Having lost a very good friend in the second Viscount tragedy this was a difficult occasion for me.

Nevertheless, we had tea and apples and spoke about the conflict ending and people engaging once more in a more mundane and safer life. General Sandy Maclean, Commander of the Rhodesian Army, and Major General Bert Barnard, Chief of Staff at COMOPS, then arrived along with a BSAP representative. The ceremony was held near the British HQ tent on open ground which doubled as both parade ground and football pitch. Nkomo spoke strongly, emphasising that the war was over and he expected his ZIPRA forces to accept that. After he left I strolled about engaging various cadres in conversation. Some were truculent but most greeted me civilly enough.

Not long after this we were instructed by COMOPS to position a liaison officer in the AP. I asked Rory Hensman, 2i/c of 'B' Squadron, if he would take on the role. Rory, a level headed, dutiful and practical man, was a successful farmer from the Sinoia area and a fluent Shona speaker. It was an inspired choice. Using all his attributes, he established a sound working relationship with Mataure which was essential in those tense days leading up to the elections which ran from 27 February to 1 March. Here I must also give Richard Mataure and his commanders due credit in ensuring that peace was held, and there were no clashes between any ZIPRA rogue elements and the security forces. It was a difficult time for us all.

Very shortly after this we were ordered to take over from the British forces at AP Romeo.

Keeping some 700 armed men disciplined without a legal framework presented a challenge. ZIPRA's disciplinary measures were harsh. One, a standard form of punishment, was called simply 'The Pit'. For a serious transgression the culprit would be stripped, whipped and thrown into a pit filled with water up to his neck where he was left to reflect on the error of his ways. It was callous and crude but, unsurprisingly, it worked and serious incidents of indiscipline were minimal. Captain Rod Garnett, our Adjutant, who took over from Rory at the AP, reported that one of the ZIPRA commanders had scars on his back consistent with a savage whipping. Someone then let slip to Rod that this particular individual, against orders, had shot down one of the Viscounts. We will never know if this was true or not as the man literally disappeared overnight. This led to speculation that his presence might have caused a confrontation between the Grey's and ZIPRA in the AP. A second form of punishment was more terminal. A somewhat shaken Rod took me aside during one of my visits to the AP and told me about the result of a ZIPRA 'court martial'. The defendant was charged with the second offence of raping a local woman. He was sentenced to death. Rod was asked to be witness to the execution of the sentence which was carried out by the accused being summarily shot through the head with an AK. The scene left Rod understandably stunned. I reported the event to the Sinoia Police who basically agreed that nothing could be done in the prevailing climate.

In the meantime plans for Operation Melba were changed and updated. It was replaced with Operation Rodent. Assembly Point Alpha, the Grey's target, was upgraded to Priority 1 and the AP was given the code-name Labrador.

We began planning in earnest. Colour Sergeant John McNeilage who was ex-SAS and one other were tasked with conducting an approach route reconnaissance to AP Alpha. They carried out the task successfully and reported back that the AP was teeming with insurgents. At this stage Grey's Scouts could field 120 mounted infantry (Sabres) and some 80 personnel as conventional infantry. The limitation was the number of horses available. We were also given five 60mm mortars.

At AP Alpha we could expect to encounter bunkers, trenches and heavy weapons positions (especially AA). We asked for an Air LO to help coordinate our air support but got no response although our air support had been upgraded. Meantime the TA support battalion allocated to Grey's Scouts was changed to a different one which comprised four rifle companies with a support company. Additionally they had an 81mm mortar platoon, a 106mm recoilless rifle platoon, an assault pioneer platoon and a recce platoon.

I flew to the location where the TA battalion was based to coordinate details. Imagine my surprise when the battalion commander told me that he flatly refused to take part in such an operation, and was not going to order his men to do so. This was a set-back. But regardless as to whether or not he changed his mind, the Grey's Scouts continued preparations to be ready to react should the order be issued. I was thankful that our people, National Service, Regular Army and TA, would do what was needed. We would need every bit of kit and ammunition we could get our hands on. If we attacked the AP, we would need to inflict as many enemy casualties as possible because we knew the surviving insurgents would scatter and then regroup to re-ignite the war.

Back at Umgusa Barracks the rear party had collected additional First Line Ammunition stocks. We had also drawn extra bunker-bombs as we needed to do some training with these crude but very effective blast grenades.

For us, the tense run-up to the elections passed without incident following the ambush on Corporal Bradshaw's vehicle narrated above. Polling commenced on the 28th of this leap year month of February 1980. Outwardly it appeared to go peacefully enough. No signals came through to activate Operation Rodent, despite the SB team at JOC Sinoia advising us that there was a massive voter swing to ZANU underway. On day two of the elections, 29 February, Mike Wilson and I knew it was all over. There was still no signal. Would it come? As time ticked by it began to seem more and more unlikely. In the end nothing happened – we didn't even receive the code-word 'Fallacy' signal cancelling the operation.

On 3 March we attended yet another briefing at COMOPS. They were all aware of the huge voter swing towards Mugabe's ZANU PF party, but were still hoping it would not be of sufficient magnitude to prevent the formation of a coalition against it. Alternatively they were also looking to the elections being anulled due to the widespread intimidation of voters by ZANU PF. There

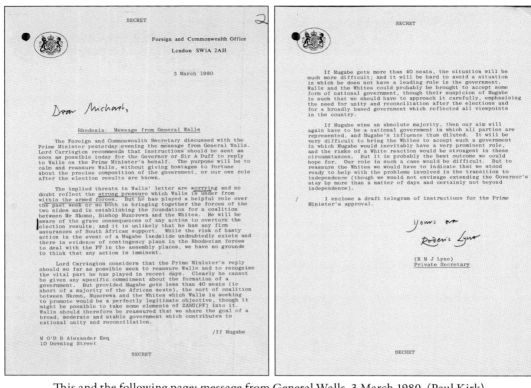

This and the following page: message from General Walls, 3 March 1980. (Paul Kirk)

was also the final hope that the British Prime Minister, Mrs. Margaret Thatcher, would respond positively to a message from General Walls which laid out the following three main points:

1. The Rhodesian security forces do not accept the way Lord Soames is governing. He should be removed because he is weak and indecisive and has given the Patriotic Front too much leeway.

2. The Rhodesian security forces do not want to be put in a position where they have to take illegal action. Despite what observers say, there have been high levels of intimidation and the election should be declared null and void.

3. The British should continue to maintain a presence until the political mess has been sorted out.

There was no reply to this message. Margaret Thatcher had reneged on her promise.

Muzorewa's UANC gained three parliamentary seats; Joshua Nkomo's ZAPU PF gained 20 seats and the remaining 67 seats went to Robert Mugabe's ZANU PF. On this outcome there could be no coalition. These results were announced on the morning of Tuesday 4 March 1980.

I addressed our officers, warrant officers and senior NCOs and let them know that, on the basis of the election results, there was simply no leeway. We would need a very steady hand at AP Romeo where our small detachment was based with Mataure's ZIPRA. Mike Wilson went to check on the situation with a view to implementing an emergency escape plan if necessary. Mike still recalls the utter disbelief by everyone in the AP. Rory Hensman was shaking his head in uncomprehending astonishment at the result. Richard Mataure himself was unable to understand how all the work he had put into dominating the Sinoia area by browbeating the locals into voting for ZAPU PF had failed. Mike says it would have been comical were it not so serious. A couple of days later, at Umgusa, we received a sitrep from our team at the AP: 'All back

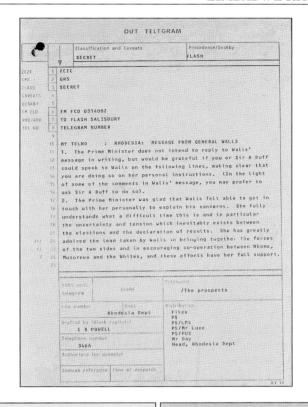

OUT TELEGRAM

Classification and Caveats	Precedence/Deskby
SECRET	FLASH

ZCZC   1 ZCZC
GRS   2 GRS
CLASS   3 SECRET
CAVEATS 4
DESKBY 5
FM FCO 6 FM FCO 031400Z
PRE/ADD 7 TO FLASH SALISBURY
TEL NO 8 TELEGRAM NUMBER
        9
       10 MY TELNO   : RHODESIA: MESSAGE FROM GENERAL WALLS
       11 1. The Prime Minister does not intend to reply to Walls'
       12 message in writing, but would be grateful if you or Sir A Duff
       13 could speak to Walls on the following lines, making clear that
       14 you are doing so on her personal instructions. (In the light
       15 of some of the comments in Walls' message, you may prefer to
       16 ask Sir A Duff to do so).
       17 2. The Prime Minister was glad that Walls felt able to get in
       18 touch with her personally to explain his concerns. She fully
       19 understands what a difficult time this is and in particular
       20 the uncertainty and tension which inevitably exists between
       21 the elections and the declaration of results. She has greatly
       22 admired the lead taken by Walls in bringing together the forces
       23 of the two sides and in encouraging co-operation between Nkomo,
       24 Muzorewa and the Whites, and these efforts have her full support.
       25

NNNN ends telegram	BLANK	Catchword /The prospects
File number	Dept Rhodesia Dept	Distribution Files
Drafted by (Block capitals) C D POWELL		PS PS/LPS PS/Mr Luce PS/PUS
Telephone number 3466		Mr Day Head, Rhodesia Dept
Authorised for despatch		
Comcen reference	Time of despatch	

X.Y 48

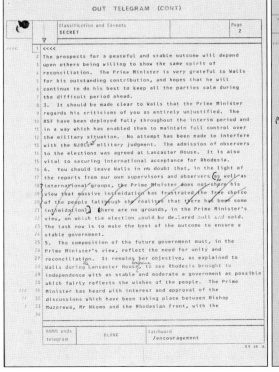

OUT TELEGRAM (CONT)

Classification and Caveats		Page
SECRET		2

<<<<
1 <<<<
2 The prospects for a peaceful and stable outcome will depend
3 upon others being willing to show the same spirit of
4 reconciliation. The Prime Minister is very grateful to Walls
5 for his outstanding contribution, and hopes that he will
6 continue to do his best to keep all the parties calm during
7 the difficult period ahead.
8 3. It should be made clear to Walls that the Prime Minister
9 regards his criticisms of you as entirely unjustified. The
10 RSF have been deployed fully throughout the interim period and
11 in a way which has enabled them to maintain full control over
12 the military situation. No attempt has been made to interfere
13 with the NJOC's military judgment. The admission of results
14 to the elections was agreed at Lancaster House. It is also
15 vital to securing international acceptance for Rhodesia.
16 4. You should leave Walls in no doubt that, in the light of
17 the reports from our own supervisors and observers (as well as
18 international groups, the Prime Minister does not share his
19 view that massive intimidation has frustrated the free choice
20 of the people (although she realises that there has been some
21 intimidation). There are no grounds, in the Prime Minister's
22 view, on which the election could be declared null and void.
23 The task now is to make the best of the outcome to ensure a
24 stable government.
25 5. The composition of the future government must, in the
26 Prime Minister's view, reflect the need for unity and
27 reconciliation. It remains her objective, as explained to
28 Walls during Lancaster House, to see Rhodesia brought to
29 independence with as stable and moderate a government as possible
30 which fairly reflects the wishes of the people. The Prime
31 Minister has heard with interest and approval of the
32 discussions which have been taking place between Bishop
33 Muzorewa, Mr Nkomo and the Rhodesian Front, with the
34

NNNN ends telegram	BLANK	Catchword /encouragement

X.Y 48 A

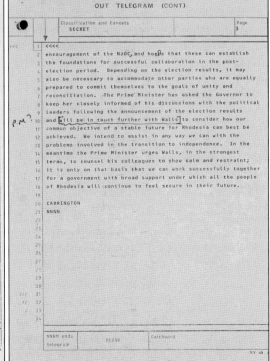

OUT TELEGRAM (CONT)

Classification and Caveats		Page
SECRET		3

1 <<<<
2 encouragement of the NJOC, and hopes that these can establish
3 the foundations for successful collaboration in the post-
4 election period. Depending on the election results, it may
5 also be necessary to accommodate other parties who are equally
6 prepared to commit themselves to the goals of unity and
7 reconciliation. The Prime Minister has asked the Governor to
8 keep her closely informed of his discussions with the political
9 leaders following the announcement of the election results
10 and will be in touch further with Walls to consider how our
11 common objective of a stable future for Rhodesia can best be
12 achieved. We intend to assist in any way we can with the
13 problems involved in the transition to independence. In the
14 meantime the Prime Minister urges Walls, in the strongest
15 terms, to counsel his colleagues to show calm and restraint;
16 it is only on that basis that we can work successfully together
17 for a government with broad support under which all the people
18 of Rhodesia will continue to feel secure in their future.
19
20 CARRINGTON
21 NNNN

NNNN ends telegram	BLANK	Catchword

X.Y 48 A

The Guard of Honour at Lt Geoff Armand's Wedding
Captain J. Thornton (RLI), Captain M. Walters (RLI), Captain G. Lawley (RAR), Captain C. Bosh (Rhodesia Regiment), Captain A. Hope (Greys Scouts), 22 March 1980 Gwelo. (Geoff Armand)

to normal in AP Romeo. The present situation has in fact created unity.'

There was a lot more to it all. There were more conferences as everyone settled down to face the emerging situation. There was talk of a mass exodus of whites and even talk by some who still felt a military solution was possible. At Grey's we simply awaited orders on what would be required from us. I was acutely aware that we had conscripts with us whose call-up was due to expire soon. Our 'B' Squadron personnel needed to resume their civilian lives and occupations. A number of signals to HQ 2 Brigade produced no response. Faced with this I made the unilateral decision to stand down the Grey's Scouts and its attached units, return to Umgusa Barracks and begin picking up the pieces.

The war was over.

With my notes still before me I can offer these final snapshots:

1. I sent 'A' Squadron off to Madziwa to join 1RLI who had been banished from Salisbury while the post-election issues were being sorted out. The entire national army was to be re-oriented to a very different future.

2. Two Peugeot carloads of senior Government Ministers – Enos Nkala, Nathan Shamuyarira, Eddison Zvobgo and Herbert Ushewkunzwe and others – descended on us one day. They were astounded to discover that the Grey's Scouts had always been a fully racially integrated unit as regards living and messing facilities at our barracks. Perhaps this kept the unit from subsequently being disbanded in-toto.

3. Once we knew we were not on the disbandment list, we made the decision to protect our AS (African Soldiers) by creating 'C' Squadron as soon as possible. As a first step we integrated almost all the POU (Psychological Operations Unit) AS who volunteered to join Grey's, as

Captain Roy Elderkin with Colour Sergeant John Strouts and Grey's Scouts at
the final parade, Umgusa Barracks, May 1980. (Neville Croxford)

well as many of the RAR badged AS serving with TA battalions in Harare and with some volunteers from Mutare. This was then followed by the planned integration, selection and training of former ZANLA and ZIPRA cadres.

4.   We managed to rid ourselves of an obnoxious and racist ZANLA 'Green Board' (officer-designate) who spent his whole time delivering after-hours political harangues to our AS in their barrack rooms instead of learning soldiering.

5.   We were able to maintain our people's morale by keeping them informed

6.   In late May we held a Passing Out Parade for Intake 167. It was the first time we had had a formal parade complete with the Corps of Signals' band. The day coincided with the standing down of 'B' Squadron. A regimental photo was taken as a memento of the occasion. In the evening the officers attended a formal Dining Out night in the Monomotapa Hotel (known affectionately by those who served as 'The Claymore', given that the shape of the building is identical to the directional landmine of the same name!).

For the Rhodesian Grey's Scouts the second call to arms in the defence of the country was over. Like their forebears, they had answered the call and had done their duty when called upon.

Afterword

As the last Commanding Officer, I am privileged to have the opportunity to add a few words to this history of Rhodesia's Mounted Infantry regiment, the Grey's Scouts. Before I continue, however, I must add my thanks to those made by Mike Wilson in the foreword to those former members of the unit who contributed to this history. In particular, all our thanks must go to Albert (Dick) Weidemann who did so much to spread the word and encourage former members of the regiment to contribute their stories

The history has been written against the backdrop of the latter part of the 15 years in which the Rhodesian armed forces conducted counter-insurgency operations, both externally and within their own country. The conflict was, in fact, probably closer to a civil war than an insurgency. It engulfed not only the white population but also the other racial and ethnic groups making up the nation. For example, over 40,000 Black Rhodesians fought alongside their white compatriots, many with distinction. Some of these men served in the Grey's Scouts.

The Grey's Scouts made their mark in Rhodesian Military History for a relatively short period of time, and readers of this history will realise how much effort went into making the unit a cohesive fighting force. It was a struggle, yet there was always a sense of energy and determination to progress. This thread is evident from the early days of the experimental Animal Transport Unit (ATU) to the creation of the Mounted Infantry Unit (MIU) as a fledgling unit fighting for recognition, and finally gaining that recognition and a place in the Rhodesian Army Order of Battle as the Grey's Scouts. Losing its first CO, Tony Stephens, to illness at a critical time caused a loss of traction and focus for a while, but that was firmly restored by the team of McKenna and Wilson who, together, pulled the unit back on course. By the latter part of 1978, a metamorphosis had taken place and the Grey's Scouts were again fully engaged in the war. A steady period of consolidation and growth followed and, reading the stories of the young men who fought in what was often referred to as a "Corporal's War", one senses their growing confidence in themselves and their capacity to take the fight to the enemy and win the fight – sometimes facing overwhelming odds.

The Grey's were mounted infantry. They were not cavalry. For mounted infantry the horse was the means of transport and not a fighting platform unless the circumstances were exceptional. The characteristics of the horse added to the capability, and hence military value, of the mounted soldier. The advantages of mounted infantry have been discussed in the book and some key aspects bear emphasis. Among these was "Shock Action" where the enemy was overcome by the sheer power and speed of the mounted soldier pursuing him, to the point that he often broke contact and fled. Other key advantages included the cross-country capability of the horse, and the ability of a small Grey's Scouts sub-unit, to cover large areas and long distances which the ordinary infantry soldier could not possibly match. Also, the inherent ability of the horse to cross differing and difficult terrain, to live off the veldt if necessary, naturally shortening the line of forward communications; to work effectively at night if needed; to provide early warning visible to the rider through physical indicators, such as the ears going forward to indicate interest in something ahead, and others which need not be repeated here. Perhaps the most significant characteristic of mounted infantry was flexibility and, in a war where helicopter support was always at a premium, the Grey's could offer this advantage to a commander.

If I were to sum up what made the Grey's Scouts what it was I would, without any hesitation, say it was the men and women who served in the unit. That has come across so clearly in this book. It has been written based largely on the recollections and the memories of those who served in the regiment. There are very few surviving records, unfortunately, but that has made the stories come alive. Much African history is oral in nature and that tradition has been continued in this book, albeit by default rather than design! That there are other interesting stories to tell is undoubtedly the case and only a small number of the over 600 personnel on the regiment's Nominal Roll have contributed here. Yet those contributions have encapsulated the ethos of the Grey's, revealing the spirit of the unit and calibre of its people.

In addition to telling the story of the Grey's Scouts, we who served must continue to remember with pride and respect those who made the ultimate sacrifice and who were killed in action. We must also remember those who died in other circumstances, for they were also victims of war. They too played their part and did their duty.

Just a short while ago I attended the funeral of an ex-member of the Grey's Scouts who was in the unit during my time. It reminded me that those who served Rhodesia are now a diminishing resource. Hence I am glad that this story has been told and I commend its legacy to you.

Lt. Col. C. J. Pearce, BCR
Former Commanding Officer
Grey's Scouts

Photographic appendix

The images on this and the following pages come from a number of private collections. They depict the Grey's Scouts in barracks and on operations. Invariably taken by amateurs and with limited capability cameras, this collection captures the essence of the Rhodesian conflict as never before. Frozen forever on film and in time, this *is* the Grey's Scouts ...

(Mike Wilkinson)

(Mike Wilkinson)

(Neville Croxford)

(Clive Midlane)

(Paul Kirk)

(Tony Butler)

(Tony Butler)

(Tony Butler)

(Tony Butler)

(Tony Butler)

(Tony Butler)

(Tony Butler)

(Tony Butler)

(Tony Butler)

General Hickman and Roy Elderkin. (Dick Weidemann)

(Tony Butler)

Appendix I

Grey's Scouts Roll of Honour

The ROH detailed below is an extension of Neville Croxford's original listing with further additions by the author. Additionally, since 8 August 2012, many former members of the unit have, very helpfully, come forward with further details and additions.

ADDED 08/04/14 – Mark Ellement known to many as "Ellos" passed away Sunday 6th April 2014 in Harare.

Corporal Kufa Buku. 2 Troop, 'A' Squadron. KIA at Chamabonda Vlei in the Victoria Falls National Park area (Op Tangent) on 18 March 1979

Trooper David A. Carshalton. KIA in the Gona-re-Zhou National Park area (Op Repulse) on 27 August 1976

Trooper Simon Clark. KIA

Trooper Charles F. Johnson. 2 Troop 'B' squadron. KIA in the Nyajena TTL (Op Repulse) on 28 March 1977

Trooper Mark Anthony Harris. 2 Troop, 'A' Squadron. KIA at Borehole No2, Chamabonda Vlei in the Victoria Falls National Park area (Op Tangent) on 11 October 1977

Recruit J Khabo. KOAS 22 October 1979. Khabo was murdered by terrorists whilst on leave at his ancestral kraal.

Lieutenant William Leslie Loxton. 2 Troop, 'A' Squadron. KIA at Chamabonda Vlei in the Victoria Falls National Park area (Op Tangent) on18 September 1979

Trooper Carl Meyer. 1 Troop, 'A' Squadron. KIA in the Gona-re-Zhou National Park, (Op Repulse) on 9 June 1977.

Corporal Phanuel Ndokanga (aka Cpl Fanwell). KIA in the Kotwa area (Op *Hurricane*) on 15 February 1977

2nd Lieutenant Kevin Hugh Tennant. Died on active service in the Nuanetsi area (Op Repulse) on 2 October 1979.

Captain (Veterinary Surgeon) Luis Vieira. KIA in vehicle ambush on the Panda-ma-Tenga road in the Wankie/ Victoria Falls area (Op Tangent) July 1978.

In Memorium:
Corporal Mark Beckley. Killed in aircraft accident, Tzaneen (South Africa) 29 June 2007.

Corporal Gary Blauw. Killed in a road traffic accident in Botswana. Date unknown.

Trooper Dan E Brandt. 'A' Sqn.Passed away after prolonged illness bravely borne on 18 October 2013.

Trooper Robert 'Rabies' Brown. 3 Troop, 'A' Squadron. Killed in a road traffic accident 1981.

Trooper CT Clayton. KIA when serving with his parent unit RHE (Rhodesian Engineers on 10 March 1978.

Lieutenant Nick de la Casa, 'C' Sqn. Murdered by Islamic Kurds in 1991 when he and his wife were serving in Kurdistan as freelance reporters for the BBC.

Captain Fitzgerald. Formerly Grey's Scouts Training Troop. Appointed CO after Independence. Died of illness (diabetes).

Lance Corporal Liam 'Bones' Ford. Died of natural causes on 27 January 2013

Terry Ford. Murdered by Robert Mugabe's 'war veterans' in an incident televised worldwide. Many viewers of this incident were particularly moved by the loyalty of his Jack Russell terrier Squeak who refused to leave his body which lay covered in a white sheet.

This letter came from his family:

Our older brother, Terry, was a member of one of the Grey's Scouts. They went into remote, difficult to access areas on horseback. He would take his own horses with him. He was not one to talk about his experiences in the war, but we remember one time in particular when his team were out on patrol and were ambushed. His horse was shot and killed underneath him. He made it back home that time unscathed physically – it was a close call. Like many others, a vehicle he was in hit a land mine and he lost the function of one of his kidneys

We have no idea what non-physical scars he sustained – we don't believe the things he saw or went through left him unscathed mentally and emotionally, and yet he still had infectious laugh. He loved his country whole heartedly and right up to the day he died, he was optimistic that things would get better. He did not consider the sacrifices he made to be too big.

Looking back, perhaps the sacrifices were too big. The whole war seems to have been in vain. The farm was not worth our brother's life. But that's just our opinion. Terry was visited by Sabina Mugabe who wanted the farm. He told her to get lost, it cost him his life. His badly battered body, with a bullet in his head, was found by his cook on 18 March 2002. His faithful dog Squeak guarded his master. Our family have never been the same. Dad has passed on now, Mum is frail, but her heart still aches.

RIP Terry, Shamwari, we miss you. Yvonne, Su, Lorna, Paul and Mum.

Major Alexander 'Beaver' Fraser-Kirk. Passed away peacefully at Garden Village in Bulawayo, Zimbabwe on 21 February 2014 after a long illness accelerated by the death of his wife in June 2012. A true professional soldier and imaginative individual. Fraser-Kirk was initially a member of the Rhodesia Army Services Corps. He was responsible for conceiving and forming the Animal Transport Unit (ATU) in 1974 later renamed Mounted Infantry Unit (MIU) which led directly to the re-formation and re-birth of the Grey's Scouts Regiment in 1976.

Trooper Mark Hunt. Died of long term illness. July 2006.

WOII Don Kenny. 28 November 2011

Trooper Simon Maberly. Killed in a road traffic accident on the Karoi-Kariba road. Date unknown.

Lieutenant Roderick MacDonald. Killed in a shooting accident 3 days after being demobilised. Date unknown.

Trooper Martin Olds. Murdered by Robert Mugabe's 'war veterans' on 19 July 2000 in a 'land grab' incident televised worldwide as Terry Ford's above.

Trooper Graham Richards. Killed in a road traffic accident 1983.

Trooper Morris Solomon Sher. Death by suicide on 27 July 1978.

Sergeant Dave Sparkes. Shot himself in a senseless 'Deer Hunter' incident of Russian Roulette in the Prospectors Bar in Salisbury's Monomotapa Hotel on 7 February 1980.

Trooper Tony Wilkinson. Killed in a road traffic accident on 14 November 2002.

Lance Corporal Steve Ziegler. KIA in a vehicle ambush on 16 January 1978 when operating with the French troops of the very short-lived 7 (Indep) Company, The Rhodesia Regiment. He formerly served as a Grey's Scout in 1977 and was Corporal Ndokanga's 2i/c in the contact of 15 February 1977 when the latter was KIA (see above). He subsequently transferred out of Grey's Scouts.

Horses that were killed or wounded in action
504 Sitrep, 517 Drumbeat, 631 Tom Thumb, 616 Max, 635 Gazu, 507 Minstrel, 513 Tommy Tucker, 541 Blue Boy, 628 Tau, 656 Douglas, 666 Sabre, 696 Jarome, 749 Harry, 634 Buttens, 825 Knight, 852 Kirk, 761 Samantha, 815 Blanco, 861 Snowy, 565 Lord Nelson, 521 Duke, 964 Grimeko, 539 Nugget, 540 Run On, 542 Star, 727 Renown, 512 Rommel, 509 Jester, 508 Whisper, 505 Scamp, 605 Calcheek, 659 Quebec, 652 Matchless, 618 Ngazi, 717 Pacific, 759 Mac, 800 Van, 635 Hennessey, 623 Sergeant, 502 Sandhurst, 569 Cheraka, 531 Spock, 831 Roman, 709 Octavius, 633 Betsy, 756 Simon, 780 Timmy, 713 Victory, 094 Houchou, 052 Hercules, 978 Geneva, 123 Honkie, 851 Gemini, Jim Boy, Eagle, Count Yorga, Fencer.

Stop press
Major Anthony P. Stephens, first Officer Commanding Grey's Scouts, passed away on 25 August 2015 in the Orange Free State, South Africa, after a long illness. He had previously served in the Federal Army and in the Rhodesian Light Infantry.

Appendix II

Honours and Awards

Silver Cross of Rhodesia (SCR)
Corporal John Coast

Bronze Cross of Rhodesia (BCR)
Corporal Johannes Jacobus Du Preez
Lance Corporal Michael Rory Wilkinson

Military Forces Commendation (Operational) (MFC)
Temporary Sergeant David Walker Scott

Defence Medal for Meritorious Service (DMM)
Lieutenant Stanley Vincent King

Citations to Awards

Silver Cross of Rhodesia (SCR):

1. Trooper John Medland Coast
For conspicuous gallantry in action. Trooper John Medland Coast is a Territorial Army member of Grey's Scouts.

On 21 October 1979, 4 Troop, 'B' Squadron, Grey's Scouts, of which Trooper Coast was Acting Section Commander, located and followed up a group of 70 terrorists who had infiltrated into Zimbabwe-Rhodesia.

At 1500 hours that afternoon, the Troop were ambushed by the enemy. In the initial stages of the action Trooper Coast was wounded in the head and body by shrapnel from an enemy grenade which exploded two metres from his position.

Despite his wounds Trooper Coast retained control of his section and conducted a skirmishing action against the enemy. During this assault he continuously directed fire and indicated enemy positions to his troop commander who, in turn, directed supporting aircraft onto the target.

Notwithstanding the aggressive action taken against them, the enemy held their positions and continued to direct heavy and accurate fire against the attacking troops and aircraft.

During the contact, which lasted for over three hours, Trooper Coast's section was engaged at a range of some 35 metres by an enemy group. In the ensuing firefight, two members of the section were badly wounded and immobilized in the enemy killing ground. With total disregard for his own safety, Trooper Coast deliberately exposed himself to draw enemy fire away from the wounded men. In so doing he was able to locate and neutralize the enemy position. He then continued to put down effective covering fire whilst supervising the evacuation of the wounded.

By last light the engagement was virtually over, although a few small enemy groups continued to resist. Trooper Coast nevertheless refused to be evacuated and remained with his section in an

John Coast, April 1980 receiving his award of the Silver Cross of Rhodesia from General Sandy McLean. Lieutenant Colonel Chris Pearce (partially obscured in centre) looks on. (John Coast)

ambush position throughout the night.

Throughout the entire contact in which 35 terrorists were accounted for, Trooper Coast's gallantry and leadership were outstanding. His conduct was an inspiration to his fellow soldiers and his clear thinking in extremely dangerous circumstances contributed significantly to the success of the engagement.

Date of award: April 1980.

Bronze Cross of Rhodesia (BCR):

1. Corporal Johannes Jacobus Du Preez

For gallantry and leadership in action. Corporal Johannes Jacobus Du Preez is a Territorial Army member of Grey's Scouts and has been engaged in operations since January 1976.

During the past two years he has distinguished himself in numerous contacts with terrorists as an aggressive and determined Section Commander.

During the period 29 January to 10 March 1979, whilst on operations in the South East of Rhodesia, Corporal Du Preez' section was responsible for the elimination of five trained terrorists and ten terrorist recruits.

In one action during that period, Corporal Du Preez' quick thinking and leadership accounted for the elimination of two terrorists.

Several days later Corporal du Preez' section located an enemy base camp containing fifteen terrorists. The camp was situated in very broken and densely vegetated terrain which severely hampered observation. Corporal Du Preez was forced to penetrate the perimeter of the base with two members of his section in order to physically observe the terrorists.

They remained in this position for over an hour while he attempted to call the Fireforce on to the target. However, due to the unfavourable weather conditions, the Fireforce was grounded and unable to provide support. Realizing that the terrorists were about to leave the base, Corporal Du Preez and the other two men assaulted the position. In the ensuing firefight Corporal Du Preez' group killed three terrorists and four terrorist recruits. Corporal Du Preez personally accounted for two terrorists, one of whom he wounded and then followed for some distance, at times crawling through thick vegetation, before locating and killing him.

Some days later Corporal Du Preez reconnoitered the same base camp which was found to be occupied. In the assault six terrorist recruits were killed.

Throughout his period of service with Grey's Scouts, Corporal Du Preez has gained the reputation of being a determined and exceptionally aggressive soldier. His leadership and disregard for his own personal safety under dangerous conditions has earned him the respect and admiration of his fellow soldiers.

2. Lance Corporal Michael Rory Wilkinson

For gallantry and leadership in action. On 13 March 1979 Lance Corporal Michael Rory Wilkinson was in command of a six-man mounted patrol in the operational area.

At approximately 0700 hours the patrol was moving through an area of dense riverine vegetation when they were halted by the lead scout who indicated movement ahead. Corporal Wilkinson immediately moved forward to assess the situation and saw a terrorist. Realizing the patrol had not been seen, Corporal Wilkinson ordered his men to dismount. He quickly deployed three members of the patrol to a flank to act as a stop-group, whilst he and the two remaining soldiers moved into an assault position.

As Corporal Wilkinson's assault group was moving into position they were observed by fifteen terrorists who opened fire with automatic weapons and rockets. A savage firefight ensued, forcing the assault group to take cover. Despite being under a heavy volume of fire Corporal Wilkinson Ordered his men, who could not physically observe the terrorists, to continue firing into likely positions of cover. So successful was his fire control that the terrorists commenced breaking contact.

Realizing the enemy might escape, Corporal Wilkinson immediately assaulted their position. In the ensuing engagement he personally killed four terrorists, whilst two others were killed by members of his patrol. Blood spoor was also located later, indicating at least one other terrorist had been wounded.

After this action Corporal Wilkinson's section was joined by the remainder of his Troop who followed-up those terrorists who had escaped. As Corporal Wilkinson's section was short of ammunition they were ordered to remain with the terrorist bodies and captured equipment to await a helicopter.

At approximately 1515 hours that afternoon a group of thirty terrorists approached Corporal Wilkinson's position. The terrorists assaulted the section, laying down heavy automatic and rocket fire. The section returned fire but, as they were short of ammunition and outnumbered, it was apparent that the terrorists would gain the upper hand.

Realizing that the lives of his men were seriously endangered, Corporal Wilkinson collected the terrorist weapons captured in the previous action and, whilst still under heavy fire, coolly moved around his section distributing them. Using these weapons the section regained control of the situation and Corporal Wilkinson, with three other men, was able to assault the terrorists causing them to flee the area.

Throughout the two actions Corporal Wilkinson's leadership was outstanding. Despite being heavily outnumbered, this young non-commissioned officer acted aggressively and his calm manner under dangerous and trying conditions was an inspiration to his men.

Military forces Commendation (Operational)

Temporary Sergeant David Walker Scott

For leadership and determination in action. On 27 August 1976 Sergeant Scott was in command of a small group of horsemen from the Grey's Scouts, operating in the South Eastern operational area of Rhodesia. His group located tracks of a large party of terrorists and recruits which they followed for a considerable distance with determination, speed, efficiency and skill, eventually concluding in a most successful contact. The command and control exhibited by Sergeant Scott during this follow up was exceptional for an NCO of his limited experience and background and was an example of determination and natural ability which was admired by all in circumstances and conditions which demanded considerable speed of action and acceptance of consequent risks.

The Defence Medal for Meritorious Service (DMM)

Lieutenant Stanley Vincent King.

Lieutenant Stanley Vincent King was appointed Quartermaster of Grey's Scouts on 2 August 1976.

At the time he took up his post the unit was still in its infancy, having just completed the transition from an experimental unit to an accepted unit of the Rhodesian Army. There were no buildings at Grey's Scouts except for those constructed on a self-help basis, neither were there any trained or qualified personnel in the Quartermaster's department.

Despite the poor working conditions and lack of facilities and staff, Lieutenant King immediately set about laying the foundations of the efficient system which presently exists. His work often entailed long hours and frequent visits to sub-units on operations. On occasions, due to lack of officers, he has carried out tasks which are more in keeping with the duties of a General Duties Officer than those of a Quartermaster.

Charged with the responsibility of expanding the stores, accommodation and many other aspects so vital to the day-to-day efficiency of the unit, Lieutenant King approached his numerous duties with dedication and enthusiasm. Through his sheer hard work, constant enthusiasm and example he earned both respect and affection from his subordinates.

Since January 1978 great changes have taken place within Grey's Scouts. The unit has increased in size and has expanded considerably in terms of stores, accommodation and equipment. In addition to coping efficiently with these increases, Lieutenant King has also been responsible for the daily maintenance of over three hundred horses. This aspect alone takes considerable work and control of funds by Lieutenant King.

Lieutenant King has proved himself to be an outstanding Quartermaster. Despite extremely adverse working conditions in the formation stage of Grey's Scouts, and the ever-increasing workload of the present, Lieutenant King's loyalty, dedication and perseverance have been of the highest order and are worthy of recognition.

Appendix III

Grey's Scouts Nominal Roll

No known Roll exists. Records are taken verbatum from numerous sources to compile here.

Surname	Initial	Rank	Number	Awards	Remarks
Abrams	RB	Cpl	730224		
Abrey	R	Tpr			1 Troop 77
Addison	DR	Tpr	730371		AB
Addison	PW	Tpr			
Alexander	MG	Tpr	83913		MIU
Alford	SCE	Tpr	121902 / 730148		
Allan	KD	Tpr	94011		
Allen	PW	Lt	781116		ADJT
Anderson	DR	Tpr	730371		
Anderson	F	Pte	727989		
Anderson	J	Tpr	103708		MIU
Anderson	P	Tpr	728079		
Araujo	ACO	Tpr	111946		MIU
Armand	GEN	Lt	781290		1 Troop 77
Atkinson	JW	Tpr	728875		Para Course Bloem 7808
Atkinson	MG	Sgt	727544		
Austin	G	Cpl	724559		
Austin	SF	Cpl	729909		
Baker	RGB	Cpl			
Bakker	GL	Tpr	724567		
Bales-Smith	HI	Tpr	730095		
Ball	P	Tpr	727979		
Bancroft	NF	Tpr			B Sqn
Banda	MK	L Cpl			
Banks	PA	Sgt	36648		MIU
Barclay	PM	Tpr	728100		
Barker	C	Tpr			
Barnet	CR	Tpr	728310		
Barr	KJ	Cpl	728158		RHAMC
Barrable	ME	Cpl	94196		MIU
Barrable	ND	Tpr			

Surname	Initial	Rank	Number	Awards	Remarks
Barratt	HS	Tpr	46178		MIU
Beckinsale	D	Tpr	728829		
Beckley	MD	Tpr	727848		1 Troop 77
Bekker	GL	S Sgt			
Bell	L	Tpr	728575		1 Troop
Benade	JR	Tpr			
Bennet	WAB	C Sgt			
Bernhard	CBO	Cpl	726722		
Bezuidenhout	RP	Tpr	26840		MIU
Bezvero	G	Tpr			
Bishop	CJ	Tpr	108069		MIU
Bishop	JL	Tpr	727084		
Blackett	AE	Tpr			
Blair	DJ	Sgt	728521		1 Troop 77
Blamire	R	Tpr			
Blane	JD	Tpr	78736		
Blauw	G	Cpl	730431		Zim Comm Bravery
Blignaut	PJ	Capt			B Sqn
Bluff	JE	Tpr	728683		AB
Bosch	JC	Capt	781229		
Bosworth	NVJ/NG	Sgt	111972		MIU
Botes	RE	Tpr			
Botha	CE	Cpl	728185		
Botha	RA	Sgt			
Boulton	RC	Tpr	85331		MIU
Bowyer	RD	Cpl	730223		
Bradfield	SG	L Cpl	728727		
Bradshaw	MJ	Sgt	728806		
Braham	MF/MJ	Tpr			
Brandt	DE	L Cpl	728660		
Brassington	MA	Tpr	730613		
Braunstein	K	Tpr			
Bright	GS	Cpl	730424		
Bristow	JD	Tpr	78736		B Sqn
Brits	LL	Tpr			
Britz	AR	Tpr	730411		
Broers	RMA	Cpl	730422		
Brooks	AFV	C Sgt	37561		
Brown	DA	Sgt			B Sqn
Brown	DGJ	Cpl	728430		

Surname	Initial	Rank	Number	Awards	Remarks
Brown	JJ	Tpr			
Brown	NE	Tpr			
Brown	RW	Tpr			
Brown	W	L Cpl	727875		
Buckingham	PL	Cpl	724913		
Buff	JE	Tpr	728683		
Buku	K	Cpl	648330		KIA 15.09.79
Bulaimu	R	Tpr			
Burden	AA	Tpr	728649		
Burnett	G	Cpl	728839		
Burrows	M	Tpr	728911		
Butler	AEO	Cpl	126855		A Sqn
Butler	DV	Tpr			
Byford	AR	Sgt	10145		MIU - B Sqn
Caillet	PJ	Tpr	728281		
Campbell	GA	Lt			B Sqn
Campbell	K	Tpr	728545		
Campbell	LR	Sgt			B Sqn
Campbell	R	Cpl	728906		
Carey	JD	Tpr	728164		
Carshalton	DA	Tpr	PR66139		KIA 27.08.76
Chadwick	PJ	L Cpl	730133		
Chamanga	D	Smn			
Chamutinya	N	Tpr			
Chandler	RD	Sgt	18872		MIU
Chatima	M	Tpr			
Chianese	LGA	Tpr	730135		
Chibaro	R	Tpr	662416		
Chimombe	C	Tpr			
Chipinga	M	Cpl			
Chirata	JL	Tpr			
Chirmunza	J	Tpr			CM
Chirundu	M	Tpr			
Chiutsi	JC	Tpr			
Chiutsu	CJ	Tpr			
Chiwande	RD	L Cpl			
Chiyangwa	GD	Tpr			
Chizirika	I	Tpr			
Christian	L	Tpr	121125		
Clark	CB	Cpl	99691		MIU

Surname	Initial	Rank	Number	Awards	Remarks
Clark	S	Rct	728864		
Clarke	BJ	Pte	770480		RWS
Clarke	DE	Tpr	730372		
Clarke	FD	Tpr			
Clarridge	PA	Tpr	727952		
Clayton	CT	Tpr	727780		KIA RHE 10.03.78
Clayton	KR	Sgt	14567		
Coast	JW	Cpl	113816	SCR	
Cock	EV	Lt	3228		MIU - Medical Directorate - Officer
Coelho	VMC	Tpr	109503		
Colborne	NE	Tpr			
Coleman	ES	Tpr	730114		
Coles	SW	Cpl	730107		
Collier	A	Tpr	124834		
Condy	JB	Capt	3181		MIU
Connear	MP	Tpr	730426		
Corbet	AJ	Pte	770609		RWS
Cormack	AJ	Tpr			
Cormack	RJ	Tpr			
Costello	IAN	Tpr	730425		
Coutts	WC	C Sgt			B Sqn
Cowell	AL	Tpr			CM
Cramer	FW	Tpr			
Creighton	AM	Tpr	728712		
Crowley	NR	Tpr			
Croxford	N	Tpr	121860		
Cunliffe	GK	L Cpl	701903		
Daniels	EG	Tpr	9978		MIU - RHAF
Danks	BC	Lt	3342		MIU - Medical Directorate - Officer
Dardagan	BA	Sgt	69686		MIU - B Sqn
Davidson	NC	Tpr			
Davies	CJR	Wo2	725857		SSM B Sqn
Davis	JP	Tpr			
Davison	JG	Tpr	50704		MIU - RHAF
De Beer	G	Pte	726550		
De Gatellier	A	Tpr	729538		
De Tappie	HMJF	Tpr	727934		

Surname	Initial	Rank	Number	Awards	Remarks
Dekusazbra-Dabrwoski	HAV	Tpr	62088		
Dela Rosa	R	Tpr	123398		Wounded FF
Des Tombe	PA	Tpr			
Devenish	AS	Sgt	725898		
Dodd	DH	Tpr	111652		MIU
Dodd	GJ	L Cpl	112081		MIU
Doliveux	PJ	Tpr	728280		
Dormer	RH	Pte	770165		RWS
Du Plooy		Tpr	32452		MIU
Du Preez	JJ	Cpl	103671	BCR	
Du Rand	LA	Tpr			B Sqn
Du Toit	J	Tpr	727630		
Ducasse	CV	Tpr	730559		
Duffield	D	Tpr			A Sqn.FB DAVE
Dunn	P	Tpr	728167		1 Troop 77
Dzoma	R	Tpr			
Dzonzi	I	Tpr	663141		
Eagar	O	Sgt			
Eatwell	HA	Tpr	727384		
Edwards	CD	Tpr	60405		MIU
Edwards	DR	Tpr			B Sqn
Eksteen	WJ	Tpr	111375		MIU
Elderkin	R	C Sgt	727132		
Eldridge	PB	Lt	781264		
Ellement	MH	Tpr	729703		
Elliot	PJ	Tpr	122174		
Ellison	R	Cpl	728104		1 Troop 77
England	JF	Sgt	41636		MIU
England	RA	Tpr	52730		MIU
Erasmus	PC	Capt	781266		
Esterhuizen	AR	Tpr			
Esterhuizen	CJ	Sgt			B Sqn
Evans	T	Tpr	728889		
Fairey	IC	Tpr			
Farnden	DJ	Wo2	724169		
Fayrer-Hosken	RA	Tpr	85043		MIU
Feneysey	G	L Cpl			AB
Feneysey	M	Sgt	117627 / 727937		MIU
Feneysey	RCG	Cpl	728572		

Surname	Initial	Rank	Number	Awards	Remarks
Finniss	CD	Tpr			
Fitzgerald	GP	Maj	780581		OC HQ Sqn. SAS Malaya
Fitzgerald	KJ	Tpr			
Flanagan	HO	Maj			
Ford	BB	Sgt	77570		
Ford	TS	Cpl			
Forde	LA	Cpl	729953		
Forrest	GJ	Tpr	729723		
Fournier	CMJ	Lt	781140		
Francis	CJ	Tpr	31383		MIU - Intaf VDT
Frankleyne	NW	Tpr	729702		
Fraser	CP	Tpr			B Sqn
Fraser	A	Tpr	728766		
Fraser-Kirk	AW	Maj	780763		
Funnekotter	PC	Tpr			
Garnett	RG	Lt	728050 / 781321		
Gertenbach	AJ	Cpl	105273		
Gibb	L	Tpr	728747		
Gobbett	CB	L Cpl	730126		
Godfrey	BK	Tpr	22380		
Goodwin	A	Tpr			1 Troop 77
Gordon	K	Rct	728730		
Graham	CI	2 Lt	114537		
Grant	D	Tpr	93874		MIU
Greeff	BFG	L Cpl	99756		
Greeff	JN	L Cpl			B Sqn
Green	G	C Sgt	727859		
Greyling	B	C Sgt	726652		1 Troop 77
Greyling	CP	Sgt	726239		1 Troop 77
Grimwood	CA	Tpr			
Grobler	DJ	Tpr	725504		
Grove	BL	Cpl	730247		
Gwenzi	G	L Cpl	661080		
Hales	N	Tpr			A B
Hamilton	G	Tpr			FB Charlie? A Sqn
Hancock	SR	Tpr			
Hanekom	W	Tpr	729584		
Harcourt	LM	Tpr	728736		
Harding	BB	Wo2	730257		
Harpur	DG	Cpl			B Sqn

Surname	Initial	Rank	Number	Awards	Remarks
Harrington	MG	Tpr			
Harris	MA	Tpr	728601		KIA 11.10.77
Harrison	DM	Tpr	728800		
Harwood	S	Tpr	730100		
Hatting	C	Sgt			B Sqn
Hawke	AE	Tpr	725436		
Hawnt	ICF	Capt	V3410		Padre
Hay	CC	Cpl	729704		
Hay	JA	Cpl	728184		
Hayden	JTM	Tpr	725022		
Hayden-Payne	CC	Sgt			
Hayden-Payne	HJK	Sgt	730433		
Hayman	DR	Tpr	106690		MIU
Hellam	B	Cpl	1927		MIU
Hencil	NC/NL	Sgt	730164		
Henderson	IR	Sgt	770457		RWS
Henderson	TA	Rct	729854		
Hensman	GB	Lt			
Hensman	RM	Capt			2IC B Sqn
Herbst	SA	C Sgt	722835		
Herselman	D	Tpr	730502		
Heslin	GH	Tpr	730400		
Heuer	CL	Tpr	730451		
Hewitson	RW	Tpr	104339		MIU
High	T	Rct	728327		
Hill	FWC	Capt	781015		
Hill	LJ	Tpr	728383		
Hill	RJ	Sgt			
Hilliard	W	Sgt	727229		
Hillier	BM	Cpl	729716		
Hodkin	DJ	Tpr	106291		MIU
Hogg	K	Tpr	728305		
Holman	ANG	Tpr	76724		MIU
Honiball	TP	Tpr			B Sqn
Hope	AR	Capt	781107		ADJT
Hopper	H	Sgt			B Sqn
Hosking	AF	Wo2	723836		SSM
Huck	IR	Tpr			
Hugo	BD	Tpr			CM
Hunt	M	Tpr			

Surname	Initial	Rank	Number	Awards	Remarks
Hutchinson	CH	Cpl	728019		
Hyman	RJ	Tpr			
Inglis	B	Tpr	728522		
Jacobsen	CGI	Pte	770631		
Jacobsz	DA	Cpl	729939		
Jago	GA	Tpr	730407		
Jamieson	JA	Wo2	722767		SSM
Jansen	SJ	Rct	729604		
Jarvie	AC	Tpr	730458		
Johns	NV	L Cpl	728807		
Johnson	A	Tpr			
Johnson	BA	Cpl	728229		1 Troop 77
Johnson	CF	Tpr	PR67593		KIA 28.03.77
Johnstone	W	C Sgt			B Sqn
Jones	A	Cpl	770040		RWS
Jones	WR	Tpr	728458		
Kabesa	M	Tpr			
Kagwere	C	Tpr			
Kamonde	T	Tpr			
Kane	JG	C Sgt	42359		
Keightly	D	Tpr			1 Troop 77
Kelly-Edwards	A	C Sgt	33771		MIU
Kenny	DP	C Sgt	724576		SAS
Ker	AI	Tpr	727238		
Kettmann	R	Tpr	730350		
Kew	HH	Cpl			
Khabo	J	Rct	527649		KOAS 22.10.79
King	G	Sgt			
King	SV	Capt	780616	DMM	QM
Kirk	PS	L Cpl	730410		
Kirsten	C	Rct	729586		
Kirton	E	Tpr	726947		
Kloppers	JC	Tpr			
Kohler	C	Pte	728663		
Kok	AI	Tpr	91277		MIU
Kok	DJ	L Cpl	728006		
Korb	AC	Wo1	720363		
Kotze	AHJ	Tpr	730378		
Kriedemann	D	Sgt	728399		1 Troop 77
Kruger	LH	L Cpl	730134		

Surname	Initial	Rank	Number	Awards	Remarks
Kruger	MS	Sgt	730385		
Lambert	C/J	Rct	727971		CM
Lambert	N	Pte	770414		RWS
Landsberg	GD	Tpr			
Lane	S	Tpr			
Langridge	PW	Tpr	730487		
Langworthy	IM	Rct	729721		
Lawrence	JA	Capt	3105		MIU - Medical Directorate - Officer
Lawton	GD	Cpl	108224		B Sqn
Lay	GE	Capt	3190		MIU
Le Roux	JJ	Tpr			CM
Lees	JC	Tpr	730423		
Leggatt	DJ	Cpl	724819		
Lennox	CM	Lt	68939		
Lennox	Q	Cpl			
Lewis	A	Sgt			
Lewis	JFM	Sgt	724813		
Lewis	NO	C Sgt	723134		
Lewis	WWW	Wo2	727125		
Liebenberg	CJJ	Capt	780974		ADM OFF. RIC
Lourens	AS	Cpl			
Lourens	PJ	Cpl	725161		
Loxton	BC	Lt	126880		
Loxton	WL	Lt	781385		KIA 18.09.79
Lucas	BG	Tpr			
Maberly	SA	Tpr	120313		B Sqn
Macdonald	RI	2Lt	V3152		Died hunting accident
Macgregor	SJ	L Cpl			B Sqn
Machado	AJ	Tpr	102422		MIU
Macilwaine	RL	Lt	67611		B Sqn - 4 RR
Macilwaine	TJ	Lt	727455		
Macleod	TE	Tpr	728405		
Madzima	D	Cpl	661266		
Magee	GW	Tpr	729724		
Maio	JEF	Sgt			
Majoko	O	Tpr			
Malden	RC	Cpl	93338		
Malin	M	Cpl	728799		
Mallett	NA	L Cpl	97146		MIU

Surname	Initial	Rank	Number	Awards	Remarks
Mangiza	D	Tpr			
Manhanga	KK	Tpr			
Markun	H	Sgt	727724		
Mashonga	M	Tpr			
Masiya	D	Tpr			
Mason	BKJ	Sgt	96374		MIU
Masvosva	SC	Tpr			
Mathe	D	L Cpl			
Matthews	RM	L Cpl	701806		B Sqn
Mc Ateer	WC	Cpl	728392		
Mc Farlane	AR	Sgt			
Mc Gillivray	DH	Cpl	108854 / 728546		MIU
Mc Girr	WE	Maj			
Mc Ilwaine	EGH	Tpr			B Sqn
Mc Kenna	MF	Lt Col	780524		CO
Mc Lean	DW	Tpr			B Sqn
Mc Lean	MG	Cpl	89626		MIU
Mc Leod	TE	Tpr			
Mc Mahon	KJ	Tpr			
Mc Neilage	JR	C Sgt	726577		RLI
Mc Nish	NS	Sgt	723487		
Mc Robert-Smith	ES	Tpr	117709		MIU
Meda	JD	Tpr			
Meeser	BR	Tpr	728529		
Meikle	AD	Tpr	123599		
Mellett	GMN	Sgt	725023		RLI
Mellett	JS	Cpl	724857		RHAF PJI
Melville	KC	Tpr			
Meyer	KC	Tpr	728010		KIA RLI
Mhalabeni	G	Tpr	662347		
Mhanda	AN	L Cpl			
Midlane	CS	Tpr	729714		
Mills	GA	Sgt			B Sqn
Minnaar	PC	Tpr	124810		
Minter	NP	Sgt			B Sqn
Mitrovich	WG	Tpr	728700		
Mitsou	D	Tpr	101031		MIU
Mlambo	T	Tpr			
Moore	AH	Lt			B Sqn
Moore	BR	Sgt			

Surname	Initial	Rank	Number	Awards	Remarks
Moore	IS	Tpr	82203		MIU
Moore	JR	Lt	781269		
Moorecroft	C	Rct	728618		
Morpuss	P	Tpr	728492		
Morrisby	EJ	Tpr			
Morrison	WH	Maj	781089		
Mosley	CA	Cpl	727752		FB
Mostert	AC	C Sgt	725020		RHASC
Mostert	JD	Tpr	109022		MIU
Moul	EL	Tpr	730155		
Moyo	CP	Smn			
Mpofu	B	Tpr			
Mpukuta	S	Tpr			
Msanje	S	Tpr			
Mtombeni	CK	Tpr			
Mudheredhe	O	Tpr			
Mudzingati	E	L Cpl	660938		
Muench	EG	Tpr	120139		MIU
Mugocha	R	Tpr			
Muir	D	Tpr	728586		
Muir	M	Tpr	727713		1 Troop 77
Muncaster	P	Tpr			
Musange	C	Tpr			
Museve	T	Tpr			
Mutanda	RS	Wo2			
Mutizwa	P	Tpr	660987		
Myles	J	Sgt	727983		
Nathan	G	Tpr	728796		
Naylor	L	Spr	728286		
Ndimanda	D	Tpr			
Ndokanga	P	Cpl	645603		KIA 15.02.77
Ndlovu	P	Tpr			
Nel	BH	Sgt	728454		
Newbold	R	Tpr	34726		MIU
Newett	SDE	2 Lt	781457		
Nhari	SD	Cpl			
Nielsen	O	Sgt	46771		MIU
Nieuwenhuizen	HJ	Tpr			B Sqn
Nkomo	R	L Cpl			
Nkomo	T	Tpr			

Surname	Initial	Rank	Number	Awards	Remarks
Norvall	CM	Tpr	730432		
Novais	R	Cpl	727560		
Nsamba	E	Tpr			
Nyandoro	I	Tpr			
Nyaungwa	GJ	Tpr			
Nydam	I	Cpl	63280		
O'connell	K	Cpl			1 Troop
O Conner	AN	Sgt	96627		MIU
O' Toole	KE	Sgt	770615		
Olds	DC	Cpl	104831		
Olds	M	Tpr	97407		B Sqn
Olds	OE	Tpr			
Ollivier	PJF	Lt	727837		1 Troop 77
Ormowe	J	Tpr	108516		
Palmer	GR	Sgt			B Sqn
Palmer	TH	Cpl	92654		MIU
Parker	EF	Lt			
Parry	AD	Tpr	84420		MIU
Patterson	PD	Sgt	99416		
Patterson	R	Tpr	100872		MIU
Paver	CH	Tpr			
Pearce	CJ	Lt Col	780637	BCR	CO
Pearce	DR	Tpr	728165		
Penford	JS	Lt	781069		
Pereira	WD	Tpr	730222		
Perrett	FA	Tpr			B Sqn
Perryman		Tpr			
Pettigrew	DA	Cpl			B Sqn
Pickles	C	Cpl	728045		
Pienaar	C	Tpr			
Pieterse	GC	Tpr	730193		
Pile	EA	Tpr	730318		
Pile	KM	Tpr	730429		
Pollard	KPA	Wo2	723204		RHASC
Posthumus	D	Tpr	728677		
Powell	CR	Tpr			
Prendergast	FP	L Cpl	728162		
Purchase	RB	Tpr	117227		MIU
Quin	GD	Tpr	727999		
Quinlan	LE	L Cpl	728681		

Surname	Initial	Rank	Number	Awards	Remarks
Rabie	BdeW	C Sgt			B Sqn
Raft	AG	Cpl	108177		
Ramshaw	NF	Tpr	728778		
Randall	I	Tpr			
Ratcliff	EJ	Cpl	724255		
Reed	RA	C Sgt	730085		Selous Scouts
Rees	DS	Tpr	728848		
Reid	K	Tpr			
Reid	SB	Tpr	117484		
Reid-Rowland	EJ	Maj	3102		MIU
Rendall	GF	Cpl			B Sqn
Retief	PM	Cpl	725952		
Rex	AE	Tpr	730430		
Reynolds	TP	Tpr			B Sqn
Ricardo	RR	Sgt	724414		
Richards	GN	Tpr	728737		
Richardson	GC	Sgt			
Rider	RJ	Tpr	106878 / 728155		MIU
Riley	BK	Tpr	730449		
Robertson	J	Tpr	84423		MIU
Robertson	S	Tpr	727609		
Robinson	B	Tpr	727840		
Rocha	AJR	S Sgt	727637		
Rodgers	BG	Tpr			B Sqn
Rodrigues	JP	Cpl	729903		
Rogers	PE	Tpr	67262		MIU
Rogers	BRO	Tpr	730149		
Rogers (Dawson)	HM	Sgt	770243		RWS
Rondell	B	Cpl			
Roy	AD	Tpr	728205		
Rugonye	PC	Cpl	645182		
Sadie	FA	Tpr			
Salles	JL	Tpr	728042		
Samson	TF	Sgt	727825		
San Giorgio	M	Tpr			
Sansbury	DM	Tpr	730286		
Santowski	JM	Tpr	730160		
Saul	RD	Tpr	114956		B Sqn
Schaap	P	Tpr	730147		
Scharff	B	Tpr	724795		

Surname	Initial	Rank	Number	Awards	Remarks
Schlachter	KG	Lt	728151		
Schonken	AJ	Tpr	730191		
Scott	DW	Sgt	40175	MFC (OPS)	
Scudieri	L	Tpr	728528		
Shadreck	H	Cpl			
Shaw	DJ	Tpr	730334		
Shearer	A	Tpr	119637		
Shepherd	C	Lcpl	113696		
Sheppard	NJ	L Cpl	728811		
Sher	D	Tpr	110647		
Sher	MS	Tpr	4318		DOAS 25.07.78
Shipley	IK	Sgt	728401		1 Troop 77
Shipster	FA	Cpl	729572		1 Troop 77
Shiridziwodya	H	Tpr			
Shulman	KP	Capt			Vet
Silbersiepe	HF	Tpr	728121		
Silva	C	Tpr	728536		
Silva	NA	Tpr	728913		
Simbamba	F	Tpr	662418		
Size	JR	Tpr			
Skinner	CT	Capt			
Slater	WJF	Lt	76000		
Sletcher	CM	Cpl			
Smit	JG	Tpr	107985		MIU
Smith	A	Rct	729581		
Smith	CA	Tpr	730146		
Smith	N	C Sgt	727595		
Somba	M	Tpr			
Somerville	IR	Cpl	92725		B Sqn
Spalding	K	Tpr			
Sparkes	DF	C Sgt	727903		DOAS 07.02.80
Spies	MA	Sgt	728248		
Stacey	TG	L Cpl	728548		
Stafford	HC	Rct	730265		
Steele	MD	Tpr	93674		MIU
Stephens	AP	Maj	780375		CO
Stevens	M	Tpr			
Stewart	AC	Tpr			
Stewart	RA	C Sgt	728818		

Surname	Initial	Rank	Number	Awards	Remarks
Steyn	CJ	Cpl	730614		
Steyn	TFJ	C Sgt	44450		MIU
Stone	MA	C Sgt			
Strouts	JM	Sgt	730035		
Strumpher	OC	Lt	781380		
Sutton	KS	Tpr	92414		B Sqn
Taonezyi	C	Tpr			
Taylor	SN	Cpl	727120		
Temple	SC	Rct	730251		
Tennent	KH	2 Lt	781340		DOAS 02.10.79
Terblanche	NJ	Tpr	86118		MIU
Teubes	CR	Tpr	109283		MIU
Theron	JW	Tpr	57760		MIU
Thomas	G	Tpr	728861		
Thompson	GC	L Cpl	728016		
Thurman	WE	L Cpl	729971		
Thurtell	A	Tpr	103005		MIU
Tiddy	CE	Tpr			
Tilley	CB	Tpr			
Tipping-Woods	CJ	Maj	V2909		OC B Sqn
Towers	N	Tpr	105913		MIU
Turner	J	L Cpl	730409		
Tweede	J	Tpr			1 Troop 77
Ukama	S	Tpr			
Van Blerk	S	Lt	723333 / 781283		
Van Breda	AJ	Sgt	108178		MIU
Van Breda	PJ	L Cpl	108475		MIU
Van Den Bergh	NJK	Wo2	726340		RLI
Van Der Heever	LAM	L Cpl	729778		
Van Der Merwe	FL	Tpr	729828		
Van Der Merwe	IJ	Cpl			CM
Van Der Riet	LM	Cpl	724434		
Van Geems	C	Tpr	728657		
Van Heerden	NB	Wo2			
Van Houten	W	Tpr	45848		MIU
Van Niekerk	J	Cpl	725182		
Van Reenen	HM	Tpr	38099		MIU
Van Schalkwyk	GE	Sgt			
Van Schalkwyk	J	Tpr			
Van Schalkwyk	PR	Cpl			B Sqn

Surname	Initial	Rank	Number	Awards	Remarks
Van Vuuren	PH	Tpr	114107		
Van Zyl	J	Tpr			
Vant	CP	Tpr	110670		B Sqn
Varkevisser	GS	Tpr	730294		
Veldsman	IR	Cpl	91323		
Venter	W	Sgt	727248		
Vermaak	C	2 Lt	781469		
Vermeulen	BP	L Cpl	728520		1 Troop 77
Vieira	LFBG	Capt	729677 / 781277		KIA 20.07.78
Viljoen	DM	L Cpl	728332		
Viljoen	WP	Sgt			B Sqn
Von Memerty	SP	Tpr	729701		
Voster	CD	Tpr			
Waddell	CJC	Cpl	728007		
Wairaven	RJB	Tpr	114106		MIU
Wakeford	EL	Tpr	730450		
Walker	DG	Tpr	36259		MIU
Walker	KW	Cpl	729680		
Walraven	R	Tpr			
Walsh	AK	Tpr	106847		
Walters	KJE	Tpr			
Wandel	EL	Tpr	728444		
Ward	DPJ	C Sgt	728776		
Ward	NC	Tpr	728511		
Warth	GT	Tpr	101091		
Washaya	L	Tpr			
Watkins	L	Tpr			FB Lyall
Watson	M	Tpr			FB
Watson	R	Wo1			QM
Watt-Pringle	JD	Cpl			B Sqn
Webb	A	Sgt	770409		RWS
Weidemann	AJ	L Cpl	728673		
Welensky	CB	Tpr	728366		1 Troop 77
Wheeler	C	Tpr			FB
Wheeler	TG	Tpr	728659		
Whittaker	W	Tpr			FB
Whitehead	RN	Sgt			
Wiggel	RE	Tpr	726571		
Wiggill	IJ	C Sgt	724832		RLI
Wilkinson	A	Tpr			

Surname	Initial	Rank	Number	Awards	Remarks
Wilkinson	D	Tpr	728472		
Wilkinson	MR	Sgt	728271	BCR	
Williams	AJ	L Cpl	728584		
Williams	LH	Maj	781076		
Williams	TF	Capt	780843		OC A Sqn
Williamson	MR	Tpr	116905		MIU
Wilmot	J	Tpr	55241		
Wilson	IB	Tpr			
Wilson	MGH	Maj	780795	MFC (OPS)	2IC
Wilson	MP	Sgt	727877		SAS
Wolmarans	JJ	Tpr	730311		
Woodworth	FR	Tpr			
Wright	AB	C Sgt			
Wright	RB	Tpr	729715		
Yeomans	D	Tpr			
Young	D	Pte	770410		RWS
Ziegler	SOB	L Cpl	728011		KIA 16.01.78
Ziemann	RG	Sgt	48898		B Sqn
Zinyoro	AM	Wo2	644088		
Zulu	G	Tpr			
Zvokuomba	AE	Tpr			
Queries					
Thelwell's Dragons					Who is Thelwell?
Cradock		Sgt			Dog Section. FB
Davel	Danie				FB
De Abreu	Jose	Tpr			
Della Casa	NGC	Lt	730404		
Gill	Bruce				FB
Hopkins	John	Lt			JP OR JW?
Potgieter	Ken				FB
Terbanche	Gerhardt				
Warren	Vince				
Waugh	Graham				

Key

AB = Alex Binda
CM=Chas Mosley
FB = Face Book
MIU = Mounted Infantry Unit

Appendix IV

Grey's Scouts Songs

1. The Regimental Song: The Grey's Scouts Ride Again

Far, far away there's a bugle blowing,
Saddle your horse for war.
Farewell my love for I must be going,
Our grandfathers did it before
Soon I'll be there with them bullets flying
Ride with a gun in your hand
Brave men and cowards will both be dying
We are the best at defending the land.

CHORUS
Now the Grey's Scouts ride again
Out of history they came
And the new ones are the same
Mounted men of fighting fame

Check on your girth and stirrup leather
Saddle your horses for war
Mount with your rifle and ride together
Our grandfathers have done it before
Open your eyes while the horse is walking
Ride with a gun in your hand
And let your rifle do the talking
We are best at defending the land

CHORUS
Now the Grey's Scouts ride again
Out of history they came
And the new ones are the same
Mounted men of fighting fame

Trouble a-brewing on the border
Saddle your horse for war
Ride out to meet it in battle order
Our grandfathers have done it before
Search for them Terrs, until you catch 'em
Ride with a gun in your hand
Then shoot to kill and so despatch 'em
We are best at defending our land

CHORUS
Now the Grey's Scouts ride again.
Out of history they came
And the new ones are the same
Mounted men of fighting fame.

We are the men on a higher level
Saddle your horses for war
We'll ride to hell just to fight the devil
Our grandfathers have done it before
We are the men who patrol on horses
Ride with a gun in your hand
The very Elite of the fighting forces
We are best at defending our land.

CHORUS
Now the Grey Scouts ride again
Out of history they came
And the new ones are the same
Mounted men of fighting fame

In 1979, the Grey's Scouts Commanding Officer, Lieutenant Colonel Chris Pearce, BCR, asked Major Frank Hayes, the Rhodesia Army's Director of Music to put the song into a suitable regimental march format which he did.

Grey's Scouts Troop Song
1.They gave him his colours,
At the Grey's Scouts Barracks,
Saying Son you're a Grey's Scout now,
You're one of the best,
You've been put to the test,
Get out there and show them all how.

2.They went riding on out,
With no fear of danger
And crossed into Mozambique
With their heads held high,
They were willing to die
To seek out the terrorist clique.

3. He was only nineteen,
But a grown man already,
And he had been through many firefights,
He had strength in his eye,
He had seen many men die,
On hot days and lonely cold nights.

4. He turned round and said,
To his grizzly old sergeant,
It's going to be a long hard day,
But this little horse is tough,
Though he's had it fairly rough,
I'll put my life on this little dark bay.

5. They rode into the valley,
With guns at the ready,
And with no sense of fear,
When the mortars fell round,
They were in the killing ground,
And completely cut off to the rear.

6. They charged through the guns,
And the mortar positions,
And silenced the RPGs,
When the little bay fell,
He'd been hit by a shell,
And slowly he sank to his knees.

7. The terrs were running and,
Many were dying,
And the young man took his share,
He shot Comrade Nyoni,
Who had killed his pony,
And left many more dying there.

8. As they rode back home,
As they took it in turn to ride,
The Grey's Scouts are the best,
You can keep all the rest,
When you mention them say it with pride.

McCleland Saddle

McCleland Saddle that carried me into war
Lies in a corner, gathering dust on the floor
What once was my pride, is of no use to me anymore
For the fighting is done and the war has been won
And my rifle is locked up in armoury store

CHORUS
Raise your glasses
And drink to the days gone by
When mounted men rode out to fight or to die
They paid with their lives for
Wearing the Grey's beret
Many's the day we rode over mountain and dale
In battle formation, riding by night and by day
Nothing would stop us and often the army say
If the goings too rough and the task is too tough
Just get on the radio and call the Grey's
CHORUS
Many's the night I lay with the stars overhead
My saddle a pillow the hard stony ground for a bed
My horse chewed away at a handful of grass
He's been fed and tied to a tree
So he wouldn't fall on me, in case the night
Should erupt in a trading of lead.
CHORUS
Where are the horses and where are the men
Gone with the wind and we won't see them again
The horses reduced to riding school hacks in the end
While the men of the Grey's have drifted away
Because there is nothing left for them to defend
CHORUS
No statue will rise to immortalize those that died
No roll of honour will carry their names with pride
The hero's now are all on the other side
But those of us that remain
Will remember the slain
In our desperate attempt to hold back the tide
CHORUS
Now as I live in this foreign far away land
I dream of the time I rode with a gun in my hand
If you were not there
You simply would not understand
What it means when I say
I ONCE WAS A GREY
And I rode with a hard fighting band.

Rhodaf* Song

Rho-daf, Rho-daf, rolling down the strip
Grey's Scouts riders gonna take a trip
Head-em-up, mount-em-up, ride-em to the door
Ride-em all out on the count of four
Grey's Scout, Grey's Scout where you bin
In Salisbury drinking gin
What do you do when you get back
You sweat it out on the asshole track
Lo-rye, lo-rye ye
Lor-rye-ey, lo-rye-ey
Two old ladies lying in bed
One turned to the other and said
I want to be a Grey's Scout rider
Live a life of sex and danger
I want to go to Mozambique
I want to kill those Frelimo freaks
I want to go to Zambia
I want to kill old Doc Kaunda
Drop that Frantan from the sky
We all like our floppies fried
Lo-rye. Lo-rye-ye
Lor-rye-ey, lo-rye-ey
Hold your head up, hold it high
Grey's Scouts riders are passing by.

Chapter sources and bibliography

Chapter 1

Becker, Dr Peter. *"Path of Blood". Rise of the Matabele Nation*. Pub Longman's 2nd impression 1962.

Bulpin, TV. *To the Banks of the Zambezi*. Thomas Nelson. 1965.

Bulpin, T V. *Trail of the Copper King*. Pub. Howard Timmins. Cape Town 1959.

Bulpin, T V. *The White Whirlwind*. Pub. Howard Timmins. Cape Town 1961.

Bulpin, T V. *Discovering Southern Africa*. Fifth edition 1992. Pub. Muizenberg, SA.

Hole, Hugh Marshal. *The Passing of the Black Kings*. London, Philip Allan 1932.

McDonald, J G. *Rhodes – A Life*. Books of Rhodesia 1971. Facsimile of the 1927 edition. Pub. Philip Allen & Co. London .

Mhlagazanhlansi. *My Friend Kumalo*. Books of Rhodesia 1972. Extremely informative work on the Matabele sourced from the Rev. Mtompe Kumalo who was born in the Matabele royal kraal. .

Ransford, Oliver. *The Rulers of Rhodesia*. Pub. John Murray. London 1968.

Selous, F C. *Sunshine & Storm in Rhodesia*. Rhodesiana Reprint Library 1968 (Facsimile of the 2nd Edition of 1896 by Rowland Ward, London). A primary source book on the Matabele Rebellion of 1896 by an informed eye-witness and iconic Rhodesian figure. .

Storry, J G. *The Shattered Nation*. Pub. Howard Timmins. Cape Town 1974. Well researched account of the Matabele downfall of 1893.

Sykes, Frank W. *With Plumer in Matabeleland*. Books of Rhodesia 1972. Facsimile of the 1897 edition by Archibald Constable & Co, London. Excellent eye-witness account by Trooper Sykes' of Plumer's Matabeleland Relief Force.

Vollaire, John. *The First Victoria Cross*. Lion & Tusk Vol 3, No3, March 1992. Also telecon Binda – Vollaire of 1 April 2012.

Vollaire, John. *The Second Victoria Cross*. *Lion & Tusk* Vol 4, No 1, July 1992.

Zeederberg, Harry. *Veld Express*. Pub. Howard Timmins. Cape Town 1971. .

The '96 Rebellions. Rhodesiana Reprint Library 1975. Facsimile of the original report published in March 1898 – good record of the incidents and, along with Selous and Sykes, the best source work on the Matabele Rebellion of 1896 (but not full revealing of all circumstances surrounding the cause of the Rebellion. Understandably so as Earl Grey was a personal friend of Rhodes).

The Lion & Tusk. Magazine of the Rhodesian Army Association. Vol.16, No.2 pp28-30.

Chapter 2

Allan, Keith. Ten page personal monograph of his early days with Grey's Scouts. Provided by Neville Croxford on 7 September 2012.

Austin, Lance Corporal Simon. Personal correspondence to author of May 2012.

Binda, Alexandre. *Masodja,* History of the Rhodesian African Rifles. 2007, pp291-293.

Binda, Alexandre. *The Saints,* The Rhodesian Light Infantry, 2007.

Elderkin, Captain Roy. Four emailed items of 19, 22, 23, 24 and 25 May 2012.

Martin, David & Johnson, Phyllis. *The Struggle for Zimbabwe*. Pub. Faber p/back 1981. .

Rhodesia Army official contact report of 27 August 1976. *Op Repulse*.

Rhodesia Army official contact report of 30 September 1976. *Op Repulse*.

Rooken-Smith, Major Bruce. Email of 24 May 2012.

Wymer, Trooper Adrian. Emails of 24 and 26 June 2012.

Chapter 3
Atkinson, Martin. Email of 13 August 2012.
Cary, Robert and Diana Mitchell. *Who's Who* African Nationalist Leaders in Rhodesia. Pub. Books of Rhodesia. Bulawayo. 1977.
Cilliers, J K. *Counter-Insurgency in Rhodesia*.Croom Helm, USA. 1985.
Elderkin, Roy. Email of 24 May 2012.
Johns, Corporal Neil. Email of 12 October 2012.
MacBruce, James. *When the Going was Rough*. Pub 1983. Femina.SA.
McGillivray, Sergeant Dave. Emails of 13 June and 9 August 2012.
Ollivier, Patrick. *Commandos de Brousse*, Pub 1985. Grasset. Paris.
Parkin, Jim. *Assignment Selous Scouts*, Pub 2006. Galago. SA. .
Petter-Bowyer, Group Captain P J H. Email of 29 June 2012.
Scully, Pat. *Exit Rhodesia*. Pub 1984. Cottswold Press, South Africa.
Tipping-Woods, Major Cedric. Emails of 25 of September and 3 October 2012. .
Van Heerden, Nick. Emails of 2,4,11 and 29 July 2012.

Chapter 4
Austin, Corporal Simon. Pocket diary for 1978.
Erasmus, Captain Peter 'Pip'. Emails of 23 June 2012.
Henderson, Sergeant Rusti: Email of 2 November 2012.
Kriedemann, Sergeant Douglas. Emails of 12 November and 11 December 2012.
MacBruce, James. *When the Going was Rough*. Pub. Femina 1983. SA.
Price, Major Don. Emails of 16 and 17 November 2012.
Ramshaw, Corporal Nigel. Email of 30 January 2013 .
Rees, David. Email of 29 November 2012.
Stiff, Peter. *The Silent War*. Pub. Galago. SA.
Tipping-Woods, Major Cedric. Email of 25 September 2012.
Williams, Captain Theo. Email of 5 and 13 September 2012.
Wilson, Major Mike. Email of 11 June 2012.

Chapter 5
Austin, Corporal Simon. Pocket diary for 1979.
Ballinger, Lieutenant Tony. Email of 4 July 2012.
Coast SCR, Corporal John: Email of 9 July 2012.
Croxford, Neville. Email of 9 August 2012.
Erasmus, Captain Peter Carl. Email of 13 May 2012.
Griffiths, Brian. Email of 8 August 2012.
Hales, Neill. Email of 8 August 2012.
Kirk, Lance Corporal Paul: Email of 31 October 2012.
Kriedemann, Sergeant Douglas. Email of 12 November 2012.
Longstaff, Graham: *'Where Flamelilies Grow'*. PublishAmerica, Baltimore. 2005.
Longstaff, Graham: Emails of 8 and 10 December 2012.
Midlane, Corporal Clive: Email of 15 July and 23 July 2012.
Ollivier, Lieutenant Patrick: *'Commandos De Brousse'*. Pub. Grasset, Paris. 1985.
PearceBCR, Lieutenant Colonel Chris: emails of 3 December and 29 December 2012.
Rhodesia Army Official Contact Report for 21 October 1979 (Op *Tangent*) provided by Major Cedric

Tipping-Woods, OC 'B' Squadron, Grey's Scouts.

Rhodesia Army Official Contact Report for 3 November 1979 (Op *Tangent*) provided by Major Cedric Tipping-Woods, OC 'B' Squadron, Grey's Scouts.

Tipping-Woods, Captain Cedric. Emails of 19 & 20 August 2012 and 25 September 2012.

Wilkinson BCR, Sergeant Mike: Emails of 15 July and 23 July 2012.

Williams, Captain Theo. Emails of 6 July and 29 August 2012 .

Mahachi (Shona: Horse): Grey's newsletter of July 1979 provided by Mike Wilkinson BCR.

Chapter 6

Austin, Corporal Simon. Pocket diary for 1980.

Bradshaw, Corporal Mike. Emails of 23 July and 6 August 2012.

Kirk, Lance Corporal Paul: Email of 31 October 2012.

Pearce, BCR Lieutenant Colonel Email of 29 December 2012.

Tipping-Woods, Major Cedric. Emails of 25 September and 20 November 2012.

Index of people